Didactic Novels and British Women's Writing, 1790–1820

Tracing the rise of conduct literature and the didactic novel over the course of the eighteenth century, this book explores how British women used the didactic novel genre to engage in political debate during and immediately after the French Revolution and the Napoleonic Wars. Although didactic novels were frequently conventional in structure, they provided a venue for women to uphold, to undermine, to interrogate, but most importantly, to write about acceptable social codes and values. The essays discuss the multifaceted ways in which didacticism and women's writing were connected and demonstrate the reforming potential of this feminine and ostensibly constricting genre. Focusing on works by novelists from Jane West to Susan Ferrier, the collection argues that didactic novels within these decades were particularly feminine; that they were among the few acceptable ways by which women could participate in public political debate; and that they often blurred political and ideological boundaries. The first part addresses both conservative and radical texts of the 1790s to show their shared focus on institutional reform and indebtedness to Mary Wollstonecraft, despite their large ideological range. In the second part, the ideas of Hannah More influence the ways authors after the French Revolution often linked the didactic with domestic improvement and national unity. The essays demonstrate the means by which the didactic genre works as a corrective not just on a personal and individual level, but at the political level through its focus on issues such as inheritance, slavery, the roles of women and children, the limits of the novel, and English and Scottish nationalism. This book offers a comprehensive and wide-ranging picture of how women with various ideological and educational foundations were involved in British political discourse during a time of radical partisanship and social change.

Hilary Havens is an Assistant Professor of English at the University of Tennessee. She has written articles on Frances Burney, Charlotte Lennox, Nahum Tate, and digital approaches to paleography.

Gender and Genre

For a full list of titles in this series, please visit www.routledge.com

Series Editor: Ann Heilmann
Editorial Board: Audrey Bilger
Mark Llewellyn
Laura Rattray
Johanna M. Smith
Jane Spencer
Margaret Stetz

6 **Art and Womanhood in Fin-de-Siècle Writing**
The Fiction of Lucas Malet, 1880–1931
Catherine Delyfer

7 **'The Celebrated Hannah Cowley'**
Experiments in Dramatic Genre, 1776–1794
Angela Escott

8 **Dying to Be English**
Suicide Narratives and National Identity, 1721–1814
Kelly McGuire

9 **Jane Austen's Civilized Women**
Morality, Gender and the Civilizing Process
Enit Karafili Steiner

10 **Winifred Holtby's Social Vision**
'Members One of Another'
Lisa Regan

11 **Ann Yearsley and Hannah More, Patronage and Poetry**
The Story of a Literary Relationship
Kerri Andrews

12 **The Lesbian Muse and Poetic Identity, 1889–1930**
Sarah Parker

13 **Domestic Fiction in Colonial Australia and New Zealand**
Edited by Tamara S. Wagner

14 **The New Man, Masculinity and Marriage in the Victorian Novel**
Tara MacDonald

15 **Didactic Novels and British Women's Writing, 1790–1820**
Edited by Hilary Havens

Didactic Novels and British Women's Writing, 1790–1820

Edited by Hilary Havens

LONDON AND NEW YORK

First published 2017 by Routledge

2 Park Square, Milton Park, Abingdon, Oxfordshire OX14 4RN
52 Vanderbilt Avenue, New York, NY 10017

Routledge is an imprint of the Taylor & Francis Group, an informa business

First issued in paperback 2018

Copyright © 2017 Taylor & Francis

The right of the editor to be identified as the author of the editorial material, and of the authors for their individual chapters, has been asserted in accordance with sections 77 and 78 of the Copyright, Designs and Patents Act 1988.

All rights reserved. No part of this book may be reprinted or reproduced or utilised in any form or by any electronic, mechanical, or other means, now known or hereafter invented, including photocopying and recording, or in any information storage or retrieval system, without permission in writing from the publishers.

Notice:
Product or corporate names may be trademarks or
registered trademarks, and are used only for identification and explanation without intent to infringe.

Library of Congress Cataloging-in-Publication Data
CIP data has been applied for.

ISBN: 978-1-138-64413-7 (hbk)
ISBN: 978-0-367-17568-9 (pbk)

Typeset in Sabon
by codeMantra

Contents

List of Figures	vii
Acknowledgements	ix
Introduction HILARY HAVENS	1
1 Charlotte Smith and the Persistence of the Past MORGAN ROONEY	21
2 'Vehicles for Words of Sound Doctrine': Jane West's Didactic Fiction MEGAN WOODWORTH	38
3 Epistolary Exposés: The Marriage Market, the Slave Trade and the 'Cruel Business' of War in Mary Robinson's *Angelina* SHARON M. SETZER	56
4 Moral and Generic Corruption in Eliza Fenwick's *Secresy* JONATHAN SADOW	74
5 Mary Hays and the Didactic Novel in the 1790s ADA SHARPE AND ELEANOR TY	90
6 Lessons of Courtship: Hannah More's *Cœlebs in Search of a Wife* PATRICIA DEMERS	106
7 Maria Edgeworth's *Moral Tales* and the Problem of Youth Rebellion in a Revolutionary Age ANDREW O'MALLEY	123
8 Maria Edgeworth's Revisions to Nationalism and Didacticism in *Patronage* HILARY HAVENS	142

vi *Contents*

9 Didacticism after Hannah More: Elizabeth Hamilton's
The Cottagers of Glenburnie   160
CLAIRE GROGAN

10 A National *Bildungsroman*: Didacticism and National
Identity in Mary Brunton's *Discipline* and Susan
Edmonstone Ferrier's *Marriage*   179
TERI DOERKSEN

Afterword: Lessons Learned   196
SHELLEY KING

List of Contributors   205
Index   209

List of Figures

7.1 Isaac Cruikshank, 'A Republican Belle' (1794).
   From the Library of Congress, Washington, DC.   127

Acknowledgements

This collection owes its existence to Mark Pollard, who suggested that our 'Didactic Novels by Women in the Late Eighteenth Century' panel at the 2012 American Society for Eighteenth-Century Studies conference in San Antonio, Texas, would form an intriguing basis for an essay collection. Mark provided significant early backing for the project at Pickering and Chatto. Ann Heilmann, the 'Gender and Genre' series editor first at Pickering and Chatto and now at Routledge, has been instrumental in her support of the book. I am very grateful for her advice and patience throughout every stage of the project. I am also grateful for the assistance and guidance of Elizabeth Levine, Christina Kowalski, and Nicole Eno at Routledge and Sofia Buono at codeMantra, who helped see the project to completion. Thanks also are due to Bucknell University Press for allowing us to reprint Morgan Rooney's 'The Crumbling (E)state', which forms part of Chapter 1 and originally appeared in Morgan's monograph, *The French Revolution Debate and the British Novel* (2013).

Sarah Skoronski played an important role in the early development of the project: she wrote the first version of the book proposal, helped recruit a number of the contributors, and reviewed initial drafts of some of the essays. I am also grateful for helpful remarks on various portions of the project from the two anonymous readers, Peter Sabor, Shelley King, and my colleagues from the University of Tennessee's 'Transatlantic Enlightenment' seminar, including Misty Anderson, Katy Chiles, Sarah Eldridge, and Mary McAlpin. Finally, I would like to thank my husband, André Marcotte, for his untiring support during the gestation of this project.

Introduction

Hilary Havens

The period from 1790 to 1820 was marked by intense social and political upheaval in Britain and continental Europe. Despite increasing opportunities and expanding suffrage open to men, particularly those of the upper ranks, by the close of the century Englishwomen could not vote, and they were barred from most professions and from voicing their opinions in nearly all public arenas. Women did, however, have one available means to engage in political debate in the public sphere: writing. For women, the most attractive and acceptable of the literary genres was the novel, despite ongoing debate about the genre's potential corrupting influence. While women had been active participants in the literary marketplace since the Restoration, female novelists outperformed their male counterparts in the decades between 1790 and 1820 and predominantly published novels in the didactic genre, a genre that mandates 'instruction as a primary element or tendency'.[1] The aim of this collection is to discuss the multifaceted ways in which didacticism and women's writing were connected during the revolutionary period. The collection can be divided into two parts, which are influenced, respectively, by Mary Wollstonecraft and Hannah More. The early essays encapsulate the mix of radicalism and conservatism in the 1790s, though they share a Wollstonecraftian emphasis on institutional reform. The latter group of essays exhibit a largely conservative turn that epitomizes post-revolutionary British culture in the wake of More's *Cœlebs in Search of a Wife* (1808); they link the didactic with domestic improvement and national unity.

As the didactic novel became popularized and valorised, women were elevated into educational authorities within the eighteenth-century household.[2] Just as it was a mother's duty to educate her children, female didactic writers were able to employ 'the authority inherent in educational discourse' to educate their readers. Rebecca Davies contends that women writers 'were authorised to speak as subjects in this discourse *because* they were women', thus challenging its 'patriarchal domination'.[3] As with More and Wollstonecraft, women were able to use their position as maternal educational authorities to become ideal educational writers. Thus, the late eighteenth-century didactic novel can be seen as a feminine genre, and though the form required certain basic features,[4] it could nevertheless accommodate a spectrum of ideologies – from radical to conservative – which allowed women to blur

2 Hilary Havens

or question political distinctions. Although didactic novels were frequently conventional, they provided a venue for women to uphold, to undermine, to interrogate, but most importantly, to *write* about acceptable social codes and values. According to Eve Tavor Bannet, the didactic novel was thus 'an instrument of real power' that could be used to 'bring about material changes in the conduct of women's social and domestic lives'.[5] This collection brings together new critical analyses of a large range of women's didactic novels published between 1790 and 1820 to demonstrate the reforming potential of this feminine and ostensibly constricting genre, which enabled women to engage with concurrent ideologies despite their invisibility in more public forums. The introduction will trace the evolution of the didactic novel – which emerged in the mid-eighteenth century as a combination of the conduct book and the novel genres – through its literary, political, and critical contexts.

The Rise of the Conduct Book

In the sixteenth century and in the early decades of the seventeenth, conduct books for women comprised only a small percentage of the general advice literature published during the period.[6] During the later decades of the seventeenth century, the focus of conduct books began to shift to gender, supporting the theory that a woman's mind could be formed by reading.[7] In *The Lady's New-Year's-Gift* (1688), George Savile, 1st Marquess of Halifax, addresses his daughter Elizabeth and early on upholds the idea of literary training:

> A great part of what is said in the following *Discourse* may be above the present growth of your Understanding; but that becoming every day taller, will in a little time reach up to it, so as to make it easie to you. I am willing to begin with you before your *Mind* is quite form'd, that being the time in which it is most capable of receiving a *Colour* that will last when it is mix'd with it. Few things are well learnt, but by early *Precepts*: Those well infus'd, make them *Natural*; and we are never sure of retaining what is valuable, till by a continued *Habit* we have made it a Piece of us.[8]

Halifax's prefatory remarks indicate that conduct books were made to be read and re-read until their concepts were inculcated and reinforced. He also introduces the paradoxical idea that what is 'Natural' must be acquired, in this case through reading, and offers concrete evidence for Nancy Armstrong's claim that 'The idea that literacy offered the most efficient means for shaping individuals was the *raison d'etre* of conduct books'.[9]

During the eighteenth century, the rise in conduct books and conduct materials began to influence other literary genres,[10] such as the periodical, in the case of *The Tatler* (1709–11) and *The Spectator* (1711–14) and their female counterparts, *The Female Tatler* (1709–10) and *The Female Spectator* (1744–46). Conduct material was addressed to both women and men, but began to be more specifically directed towards women, especially after the 1740s, 'in keeping with the increased emphasis on domestic education and the growing number of middle-class women readers'.[11] Many of the popular conduct manuals of the mid-century were authored by men, such as James Fordyce's *Sermons to Young Women* (1765) and John Gregory's *A Father's Legacy to His Daughters* (1774). Their popularity endured, even though the limitations of male authorship were acknowledged, for example by Gregory, 'You must expect that the advices which I shall give you will be very imperfect, as there are many nameless delicacies, in female manners, of which none but a woman can judge'.[12]

Conduct books written in the middle decades of the eighteenth century came to fulfil not only the role of an instructor, but that of a parent. Gregory wrote his *Father's Legacy* in 1761, shortly after the death of his wife, and when his work was published posthumously by his son James, James's added preface explicitly casts the work as a substitute for an absent paternal figure: 'His own precarious state of health inspired him with the most tender solicitude for their future welfare ... his anxiety for their orphan condition suggested to him this method of continuing to them those advantages'.[13] Similarly, Lady Sarah Pennington used *An Unfortunate Mother's Advice to her Absent Daughters* (1761) as a means of communication with her daughters. Her coquettish behaviour had led to a formal separation from her husband, Sir Joseph Pennington, and a prohibition from seeing her daughters. In her *Unfortunate Mother's Advice*, Pennington exploits the possibilities of prose and invokes her position as a mother in order to create a literary surrogate: 'The Public is no way concerned in Family Affairs ... but my Circumstances are such, as lay me under a Necessity of either communicating my Sentiments to the World, or concealing them from you'.[14] While Pennington's book is similar in content to contemporary conduct manuals, its tone is markedly different because it is a cautionary text.

Pennington's *Unfortunate Mother's Advice* was only one of many conduct books published during the eighteenth century that were authored by women, for women. Conduct books written by women, for women, 'played a significant role in the expansion of print culture'.[15] A large reason, perhaps, for this expansion was that conduct writing was one of the first genres that was widely acceptable for women.[16] Some of these early didactic female authors reacted against the narrow range of opportunities for women, which many believed were compounded by the poor state of women's education. As early as the late seventeenth century, Mary Astell addresses the disadvantages faced by women in *A Serious Proposal to the Ladies* (1694):

> Women are from their very Infancy debar'd those Advantages, with the want of which, they are afterwards reproached, and nursed up in those Vices which will hereafter be upbraided to them. So partial

4   *Hilary Havens*

> are Men as to expect Brick where they afford no straw; and so abundantly civil as to take care we shou'd make good that obliging Epithet of *Ignorant*, which out of an excess of good Manners, they are pleas'd to bestow on us![17]

Though Astell argues that women's assumed inferiority stems from the 'Advantages' or education that is withheld from them from early youth, she places the blame firmly on the shoulders of men. Subsequent works, such as the polemic *Woman Not Inferior to Man* (1739), are far more critical of masculine behaviour and even assert proto-feminist doctrine and equal women's rights.

Criticisms of the poor state of women's education persisted in conduct books even towards the end of the eighteenth century, though men were not always direct targets of censure. Mary Wollstonecraft, in her *Thoughts on the Education of Daughters* (1787), argues that inadequately-educated women pass on their faulty education to their children, in a cycle of failed motherhood that perpetuates over a series of generations: 'Can they [women] improve a child's understanding, when they are scarcely out of the state of childhood themselves?'[18] Even conduct books by conservative female authors argue for the improvement of women's education. In her *Strictures on the Modern System of Female Education* (1799), Hannah More condemns the artificial nature of female education, which focused on public presentation and not on moral improvement: 'Do we not educate them for a crowd, forgetting that they are to live at home? for the world, and not for themselves? for show, and not for use? for time, and not for eternity?'[19] More believes that women must be able 'to regulate [their] own mind[s], and to be useful to others', without 'having display for their object'.[20] Elizabeth Hamilton, in her *Letters on the Elementary Principles of Education* (1801), also focuses on improving female education, though she ties its stagnancy to the prevailing belief in the correspondence between physical and mental capacity: 'the associations of contempt, which the inferiority, with regard to physical strength, had originally generated, continue to operate, and debar females from those opportunities of improvement which gradually open on the other sex'.[21]

The treatment of female education in conduct books was bound up with questions concerning the acceptability of the novel genre.[22] Advice authors were often divided: some recommended novels with an instructive purpose, while others urged readers to avoid the genre altogether.[23] Pennington prohibited her daughter from reading novels, though she admitted that novels occasionally make a few, rare useful observations:

> Novels and Romances never give yourself the Trouble of reading; though many of them contain some few good Morals, they are not worth picking out of the Rubbish intermixed; 'tis like searching for a few small Diamonds amongst Mountains of Dirt and Trash.[24]

Thomas Gisborne, in *An Enquiry into the Duties of the Female Sex* (1797), recommends reading any 'book that is not a novel' as a means of instilling good domestic habits in women.[25] Hamilton cautions against the dangers of an overbearing imagination, the natural result of novel reading – 'Where the attention has been early engaged in fiction, it will not, without great difficulty, be turned to realities'[26] – though she had published a novel herself, *Memoirs of Modern Philosophers* (1800), within the past year. More's attitude towards the novel was more ambiguous: she recommended 'invigorating reading' for women, which did not necessarily preclude the novel genre.[27] Wollstonecraft, too, proposed 'Judicious books [to] enlarge the mind and improve the heart', though not without a warning that 'some, by them, "are made coxcombs whom nature meant for fools"'.[28] Fordyce and Gregory, unsurprisingly, advocated novels which were didactic in tone. The latter highlights the instructive possibilities of such works: 'Such books as improve your understanding, enlarge your knowledge, and cultivate your taste, may be considered in a higher point of view than mere amusements'.[29] The former similarly argues that instructional novels are especially appealing to the female mind: 'As to works of imagination, it is allowed on all hands, that the female mind is disposed to be peculiarly fond of them; and surely when blended with instruction ... they have a particular claim to your attention'.[30] Fordyce's and Gregory's decisive approval of novels written for an instructional purpose not only heralds the rapid proliferation of the didactic genre, but also reveals the small distance between conduct books and the creative engagement with conduct that emerged in didactic fiction. While didactic novels were allowed imaginative elements, instruction had to remain the primary focus; yet this still left space for intervention by female authors on a number of topics – including politics, class, and gender – that otherwise would not have been acceptable.

The Rise of the Didactic Novel

Although the didactic genre flourished, particularly in late eighteenth-century novels, fiction written before the eighteenth century had long included didactic themes. The most famous of these, and arguably the first novel written, is Miguel de Cervantes's *Don Quixote* (1605, 1615), which ironically warns against the dangers of reading. Many early eighteenth-century British novels, such as Aphra Behn's *Oroonoko* (1688) and Daniel Defoe's *Robinson Crusoe* (1719), contain didactic elements. The early fiction writer Penelope Aubin is the best representative of the early eighteenth-century didactic novel, in which the didactic is focalized through the religious. Aubin rose to popularity in the 1720s by combining the amatory and travel genres that were popular in the early eighteenth century, but the sole didactic aim of her fictions is piety: her exemplary characters are always rewarded by Providence and her wicked ones are invariably punished.

More than any other novelist of the eighteenth century, Eliza Haywood emblematizes the rise of didactic fiction within her long and varied career, which is itself a didactic story of reform. Her early fictions are racy, and her protagonists often violate social and moral codes. Haywood's heroines are often sexual, liberated women, who nonetheless are eventually forced to conform to social norms. Her well-known *Fantomina* (1725) is a gleeful story about a woman who seduces her lover in various disguises so that he will not grow tired of her; it inevitably ends with her pregnancy and banishment to a nunnery in Wales. Neither constrained by rules of decorum nor even comfortable normalcy, Haywood's 'The History of Clara and Ferdinand', from her collection of tales, *The Fruitless Enquiry* (1727), relates the relationship of Clara and her cousin Ferdinand. Clara, raped by Ferdinand, hears that he has been spreading the story of her dishonour, and in an act of vengeance, she castrates him, which leads to his death and her predictable exile to a nunnery. Haywood's fictions underwent a radical change as her incredible productivity of the 1720s began to slacken, and in the following decades, she explored opportunities in translation and in the theatre. She founded the periodical, *The Female Spectator*, which, like its predecessors, dispensed conduct advice to young people. With the publication of *The History of Miss Betsy Thoughtless* (1751), one of the first female *Bildungsroman* which concentrates on the heroine's self-development and search for a suitable marriage partner, Haywood completed her shift to the didactic genre. The commercial success of her foray into the didactic genre is evident: *Betsy Thoughtless* was quickly followed by the similarly moralistic *The History of Jemmy and Jenny Jessamy* (1753). *Betsy Thoughtless* signalled a new direction in fiction, hinting at the popularity of instructional and cautionary tales.[31]

Haywood's transition from the amatory to the didactic may have been prompted by the publication of Samuel Richardson's *Pamela* in 1740, which occurred in the middle of Haywood's less productive period of writing. *Pamela* was the first blockbuster novel of the eighteenth century, and on its original title page, Richardson makes his instructional purpose explicit: 'Published In order to cultivate the Principles of VIRTUE and RELIGION in the Minds of the YOUTH of BOTH SEXES'.[32] Richardson's other two novels were similarly didactic, and all three novels can be seen as revisions of one another: *Clarissa* (1747–48) is a corrective to *Pamela* against the dangers of marrying a rake; and *Sir Charles Grandison* (1753–54) is a lesson to readers seduced by *Clarissa*'s Lovelace, affirming the existence of truly good men in the world. Richardson's didactic purpose was confirmed with his publication of *A Collection of the Moral and Instructive Sentiments, Maxims, Cautions, and Reflections, Contained in the Histories of Pamela, Clarissa, and Sir Charles Grandison* (1755), a distillation of the most important moral principles from his three novels. In the preface to his *Collection*, Richardson explicitly reveals the dichotomy between plot and principle and privileges the latter:

> But as the *narrative* part of those Letters was only meant as a vehicle for the *instructive*, no wonder that many readers, who are desirous of fixing in their minds those maxims which deserve notice distinct from

the story that first introduced them, should have often wished and pressed to see them separate from that chain of engaging incidents that will sometimes steal the most fixed attention from its pursuit of serious truth.[33]

The ease with which Richardson is able to separate his didactic principles from his fictional elements in the *Collection* demonstrates the close kinship between the conduct manual and the didactic novel; for Richardson, didactic novels are merely conduct manuals dressed up by a 'chain of engaging incidents'.

With the ascent of Richardson, instructive fictions began to dominate the literary marketplace. Even Richardson's contemporary Henry Fielding, whose fictions are marked by the earthy and the picaresque, was influenced by the shift. Fielding's first two novels – *Joseph Andrews* (1742), a parody of Richardson's *Pamela*, and *Tom Jones* (1749), his masterpiece – starkly contrast with his didactic final novel, *Amelia* (1751). At the same time, a large number of women writers entered the literary marketplace and were able to employ their femininity as a justification for their work within didactic genres.[34] In his remarks on instructional fiction, Fordyce observes,

> I should not on this occasion do justice to your sex, if I did not say, that such books as those last mentioned [eighteenth-century fictions that are both realistic and didactic] are, in a particular degree, proportioned to the scope of your capacities. Of this I am certain, that amongst women of sense I have discovered an uncommon penetration in what relates to characters, an uncommon dexterity in hitting them off through their several specific distinctions, and even nicer discriminations, together with a race of fancy, and a fund of what may be strictly termed Sentiment, or a pathetic manner of thinking, which I have not so frequently met with in men.[35]

Fordyce argues that 'the scope of [women's] capacities' is linked to instructional material and is shaped by their natural susceptibility to the cult of sensibility. Thus, women were particularly suited to be authors and readers of didactic fiction. According to Nancy Armstrong, towards the end of the century 'conduct books had settled on one kind of fiction as truly safe for young women to read'. Didactic fiction, which 'had the virtue of dramatizing the same principles sketched out in the conduct books', became 'So well established ... that it eventually supplanted everything the novel had formerly been'.[36] Most of the prominent women writers in the latter half of the eighteenth century used instructional themes in their fiction. Sarah Scott's *Millenium Hall* (1762) and Sarah Fielding's *The Adventures of David Simple* (1744) and *The History of Ophelia* (1761), which centre on the education and development of young women (and men), were exemplars of the mid-eighteenth-century didactic novel. Fielding's *The Governess; Or,*

8   *Hilary Havens*

the Little Female Academy (1749), often considered as the first children's novel, has clear didactic aims: the novel attempts to '*inculcate*' good female conduct '*by those Methods of Fable and Moral, which have been recommended by the wisest Writers, as the most effectual means of conveying useful Instruction*'.[37] Charlotte Lennox, like Eliza Haywood, had shifted from the indelicate and the satirical to the instructional with her *Sophia* (1762) and *Eliza* (1767). Other female novelists used the didactic genre to criticize constricting conceptions of virtuous women; Frances Sheridan's *The Memoirs of Miss Sidney Bidulph* (1761) and Frances Brooke's *The History of Lady Julia Mandeville* (1763) are two such novels. Frances Burney, perhaps the most important novelist in the final decades of the eighteenth century, incorporated didactic themes into all of her novels, particularly her first two, *Evelina* (1778) and *Cecilia* (1782). Early in *Evelina*, the eponymous heroine voices her need for a conduct book explaining the fashionable world: 'But, really, I think there ought to be a book, of the laws and customs *á-la-mode*, presented to all young people, upon their first introduction into public company'.[38] Little does Evelina anticipate that her own story will become such a book, albeit a book disqualified from inclusion in the burgeoning didactic convention because of its pervasive satire.

Despite the avenues to literary success available for women writers such as Lennox, Sheridan, and Burney, many obstacles existed. The didactic genre was not an ostensibly empowering one for women: as Mary Poovey claims, it 'called attention primarily to women's weaknesses and helped to drive further underground the aggressive, perhaps sexual, energies that men feared in women'.[39] Didactic literature also perpetuated strict social codes, including traditional notions of femininity, the very norms which women violated by entering the public sphere through the act of publication.[40] The subject matter of didactic fiction was limited: while exemplary heroines were standard, flawed protagonists could be acceptable, provided that they were chaste and would eventually reform.[41] Yet many women writers, most notably Mary Wollstonecraft and Hannah More, were nevertheless able to enter and even dominate the literary marketplace. By capitalizing on their newfound roles as educational authorities, women were able to appropriate the didactic genre to their own advantage,[42] often undermining or correcting assumptions regarding women's capacities and weaknesses.

While a large amount of publication in the eighteenth century was anonymous and the gender of many of these authors has never been identified, it nonetheless appears that women published increasing numbers of novels towards the end of the eighteenth century. James Raven, in his introduction to volume 1 of *The English Novel, 1770–1829*, provides a detailed table dividing the publications of novels in the 1770s, 1780s, and 1790s among male, female, and anonymous authors.[43] Prior to the 1770s, women had a meagre presence in the literary marketplace: 'Only 14 per cent of all new novel titles published between 1750 and 1769 can be identified as by women writers'.[44] In the 1770s, 94 new novels (30 per cent) were published by men, 45 (14.4 per cent) were published by women, and 174 (55.6 per cent) were anonymous; in the 1780s, 99 novels (24.9 per cent) were published by men, 118 (29.7 per cent) were published by women, and 180 (45.3 per cent) were anonymous. The 1790s continued the trend of an increased number of identifiable women authors. In fact, this was the decade in which women substantially surpassed men: 215 novels (31.6 per cent) were published by men, 260 (38.2 per cent) were published by women, and 205 (30.1 per cent) were anonymous. Even though it is impossible to determine the gender identities of the 205 anonymously published novels in the 1790s, it was undeniable 'that female authorship was being deliberately promoted, and it was exactly at this time ... that an unprecedented number of otherwise anonymous title-pages also bore the attribution to "a Lady"',[45] signalling the increasing popularity of novels written by women at the close of the century.[46]

Revolution and Response

The increase in women's writing towards the end of the eighteenth century was set against the political turmoil caused by the French Revolution, which had a significant impact on British life in the 1790s and in the early decades of the nineteenth century. The literary response to the Revolution, most notably Edmund Burke's *Reflections on the Revolution in France* (1790), inspired intense political debate, especially from 'British reformers of all shades of opinion [who] were galvanized into action'.[47] Evolving political rhetoric on both sides laid the groundwork for loyalist and reformist agendas.[48] The British government reacted to the perceived radical threat from the continent by banning seditious writing in 1792 and suspending habeas corpus in 1794. Even ordinarily quotidian spaces and topics – such as the coffee house, the cottage, and the act of hairdressing – became invested with political conflict.[49] Though the British were able to quell a domestic revolution, there were troubles in Ireland and war with the French, which did not end until the Battle of Waterloo in 1815. During this turbulent period, British writers, including women, produced a large quantity of texts, responding to or arising out of the conflict. Several of these works began to question assumptions about gender that earlier conduct book writers wholly acknowledged or only mildly challenged. Conservative gender models were indebted to the writings of Jean-Jacques Rousseau and Edmund Burke. Rousseau's *Émile, or on Education* (1762) links gender differences to physical capacity: 'One ought to be active and strong, the other passive and weak. One must necessarily will and be able; it suffices that the other put up little resistance.... it follows that woman is made specially to please man'.[50] Rousseau's notion of gender is prelapsarian: sentimental, but deeply misogynistic. Burke, in his *Reflections on the Revolution in France*, holds conservative political views that are most apparent in his nostalgia for 'the age of chivalry' that upheld 'that generous loyalty to rank and sex', in which

10   Hilary Havens

distinctions between the classes and the sexes are not only preserved, but emphasized.[51]

Numerous advocates for individual rights emerged alongside and counter to Rousseau's and Burke's publications, expanding notions of women's rights and abilities and, in some cases, advocating women's right to vote.[52] One of the very first was Olympe de Gouges, a French playwright and political activist who was best known for her 'Declaration of the Rights of Woman and the Female Citizen' (1791). Her progressive views are encapsulated in Article 1 of her work, 'Woman is born free and lives equal to man in her rights', which is complemented by a rousing postscript:

> unite yourselves beneath the standards of philosophy; deploy all the energy of your character, and you will soon see these haughty men, not groveling at your feet as servile adorers, but proud to share with you the treasures of the Supreme Being.[53]

De Gouges militates for women's equal rights and even includes a social contract between men and women in her work. Her well-known British counterpart, who responds directly to Rousseau, Burke, and well-known conduct book writers, is Mary Wollstonecraft. Wollstonecraft's *A Vindication of the Rights of Woman* (1792) goes immediately on the offensive against 'writers who have written on the subject of female education and manners, from Rousseau to Dr Gregory', and who 'have contributed to render women more artificial, weak characters, than they would otherwise have been; and, consequently, more useless members of society'.[54] Wollstonecraft's arguments here, as with her *Thoughts on the Education of Daughters*, centre on improved access to education for women, but in this case, she advocates for female empowerment. Wollstonecraft criticizes Rousseau's refusal to 'Educate women like men ... [because] the more they resemble our sex the less power will they have over us', countering that 'This is the very point I aim at. I do not wish them to have power over men; but over themselves'.[55]

These interventions concerning issues of gender were closely linked to discourses concerning nationality and patriotism. Nationalist debates contained within didactic novels were another means by which women could push the boundaries of acceptability in their forays into the public sphere.[56] Proliferating works of national devotion were used by the British as weapons in their literary war against France.[57] The threat of French immorality and a war with France was linked to a large increase in conduct books during the period, in order to save 'the mainstream ideology that was perceived as being under threat'.[58] William St Clair finds a direct correspondence between the demand for conduct literature and the perceived threat of French invasion; demand was highest in the decades from 1790 to 1820,[59] which is the period of inquiry for this collection. These thirty years of political turmoil correspondingly inspired a large number of didactic novels, which were as urgent as the political tracts and as variegated as the conduct books.

As Kevin Gilmartin suggests, the narrow, novelistic form was 'a kind of theater within which radical principles could be safely activated and played out, so that their consequences could be explored and [in the case of the anti-Jacobin[60] novelists] discredited'.[61] Women's role as mothers played an essential part in countering the Jacobin threat: 'maternal domesticity' was valorised 'following the French Revolution in 1789, as part of the cultural de-politicisation of women in horrified response to the Terror'.[62] The gradual shift that occurred in these texts is mirrored in the division of this collection. The most radical texts fall early in the collection; their authors, like Mary Wollstonecraft, had been galvanized by the French Revolution. The later novels, including Hannah More's popular *Cœlebs in Search of a Wife*, support the rise of 'maternal domesticity', as the focus of the didactic genre turns to domestic and national improvement.

Didactic fiction was thus 'an important locus for ideological debate' for both radical and conservative writers;[63] it enabled reformist, if not radical, expression, despite its seemingly conservative generic form.[64] The novel was often used to engage in political and moral debate, and though women were barred from most kinds of participation in the public sphere, they were permitted and even encouraged to use the novel form, especially that of the didactic novel, to express their views. This collection builds on the work of several influential studies that discuss women writers in the revolutionary decades. Chief among these are Gary Kelly's *Women, Writing, and Revolution: 1790–1827*, Eleanor Ty's two monographs, *Unsex'd Revolutionaries: Five Women Novelists of the 1790s* and *Empowering the Feminine: The Narratives of Mary Robinson, Jane West, and Amelia Opie, 1796–1812*, M. O. Grenby's *The Anti-Jacobin Novel: British Conservatism and the French Revolution*, and Lisa Wood's *Modes of Discipline: Women, Conservatism, and the Novel after the French Revolution*.

In his study, Gary Kelly argues that an increase, followed by a decrease in publication by women writers occurred from 1790 to 1827. The initial rise in women's publication was linked to debate regarding the figure of the 'domestic woman', which was not restricted to a single social class, 'a fact which may explain the rapid dissemination of the figure as part of the new culture of "respectability" during the nineteenth century'.[65] Print was a means by which women could participate in public discourse without violating social norms. The domestic woman thus became a 'professionalized custodian of the "national" conscience, culture, and destiny', resulting in a 'feminization of culture'.[66] Kelly argues that the decline in women's writing was hastened by the revolutionary aftermath, when women 'became even more reluctant to assume a professional public identity, undertake professional literary work such as editing and journalism, or attempt the learned discourses and noble genres'.[67] At the same time, he identifies a counter-movement, what he calls a 'remasculinization' of literary forms, especially the reclamation of poetry by figures like Wordsworth, Coleridge, and Southey. In the late 1820s, Kelly argues that women had been again relegated to the

12 Hilary Havens

margins, as men resumed 'writers authority in the domains of subjectivity, domesticity, and extended domesticity that women writers had exploited for half a century or more'.[68] While occasionally perceptive, Kelly's is a narrow view of post-revolutionary print culture that centres on the masculine rise of poetry in the High Romantic period and does not recognize the continued presence of women writers throughout the nineteenth century.

An alternate view of women writers during this period is provided in Eleanor Ty's two books, which are largely informed by feminist methodologies. Ty is one of the few critics to survey a large swath of women writers on both sides of the political spectrum, contending in both cases that writing was a means for women to participate in political discourse while still conforming to gender conventions. Ty's first, *Unsex'd Revolutionaries*, surveys the fiction of Mary Wollstonecraft, Mary Hays, Helen Maria Williams, Elizabeth Inchbald, and Charlotte Smith, focusing on their contributions to female education, conduct, and sexuality. According to Ty, these writers responded to the revolutionary climate of the 1790s and 'developed narrative techniques and methods of representation which enabled them to explore highly charged political topics without censure'.[69] Women writers embedded their political concerns in the didactic novel, which enabled them to subtly and unthreateningly assess or even question sources of power. In her second monograph, *Empowering the Feminine*, Ty continues her examination into 'the various ways women could empower themselves and be empowered without necessarily breaking with cultural definitions of the feminine' in the novels of Jane West, Amelia Opie, and Mary Robinson.[70] *Empowering the Feminine* focuses on the response of these authors to masculine constructions of the feminine. Both of Ty's studies are astute and focus on women from both ends of the ideological spectrum; this collection also incorporates feminist methodologies, and it discusses the limitations placed on women while emphasizing additional historical and cultural contexts.

M. O. Grenby's and Lisa Wood's books are a departure from those of Kelly and Ty in their exclusive focus on conservative novels of the revolutionary period. While Grenby's study is not entirely centred on didactic or female-authored novels, it surveys an impressive selection of anti-Jacobin novels to support its thesis, that these novels represent contemporary conservative contexts, 'which entitles them to be thought of as a vital key to the understanding of British society in an age of crisis and as perhaps the most historically meaningful literary response to the French Revolution and its aftermath'.[71] Wood, on the other hand, argues that didactic novels were primarily the domain of women writers, especially during the period from 1793 to 1815, and the genre 'provided the means for women to conceive of themselves as writers, the rationale for the act of writing, and the basic form of the text produced'.[72] Even though she views the genre as primarily conservative, Wood concedes that conservative women writers were in fact following in the footsteps of their radical contemporaries: 'Yet West and her conservative contemporaries agree that the "vehicles" that convey the "poison" of radical philosophy also provide the best method for countering revolutionary theory'.[73] Wood also discusses the flaws of the didactic genre, including its lack of subtlety and multivalence, acknowledging that these texts are rarely read. It is undeniable that the single-minded didacticism of these works can, at times, be grating on modern ears; while the primary purpose of this collection is not an aesthetic defence of these novels, the recuperative work done by many of the essays emphasizes the ideological *and* literary contributions women made during this period.

Didactic Novels and British Women's Writing, 1790–1820 builds on these previous studies, especially Wood's and Ty's work on women's contributions to the didactic genre, by covering a broad spectrum of writers and political beliefs in order to explore the particularly feminine nature of the didactic novel. These novelists gain authority from their positions as wives, mothers, but above all, educators. Many of the novels in this collection are non-canonical, simply because few didactic novels are as celebrated as their sentimental, Gothic, or domestic counterparts. Yet all of the authors are well-known literary figures from the revolutionary period, and their works were chosen for their resonances with the views of Wollstonecraft and More, the two focal points of this collection. We argue that the didactic novel genre was the property of both conservative and radical authors, who, despite their differing political beliefs, used the genre to further their reformist aims. To varying degrees, these women interrogated traditionally patriarchal aspects of society, not only reclaiming the didactic novel genre as their own, but also using the genre to question the limits of institutionalism and nationalism, while pushing the generic boundaries of the didactic novel itself. Our didactic women novelists were thus able to examine and unravel fictional, societal, cultural, and national structures in exciting and unprecedented ways during this important historical moment in the steady development of women's political voice.

* * *

The women writers whose works are analysed in *Didactic Novels and British Women's Writing, 1790–1820* span three decades, from Charlotte Smith to Susan Ferrier, and the structure of the collection is roughly chronological. It can be divided into two parts: the first half, which is largely influenced by the spectre of Mary Wollstonecraft, addresses both conservative and radical texts of the 1790s to show their similar focus on institutional reform. Hannah More similarly has an effect on many of the essays from the second half of the collection, which reveal how authors after the French Revolution often linked the didactic with domestic improvement and national unity. All of the essays demonstrate the ways in which the didactic genre works as a corrective not just on a personal and individual level, but for larger issues as well, such as inheritance, slavery, the roles of women and children, the limits of the novel, and English and Scottish nationalism.

14   *Hilary Havens*

Chapter 1 by Morgan Rooney focuses on Charlotte Smith's three most radical novels, *Desmond* (1792), *The Old Manor House* (1793), and *The Young Philosopher* (1798). According to Rooney, a prominent recurring target in Smith's fiction is a Burkean adherence to history-as-inheritance, though Smith's responses evolve within her novels. While initially hopeful about the rising generation in *Desmond*, Smith becomes progressively cynical in *The Young Philosopher*, in which her heroes choose exile in America, a land capable of being re-formed because it, unlike Britain, is free from history's inheritances. In Chapter 2, Megan Woodworth discusses two of Jane West's early novels, *The Advantages of Education* (1793) and *A Tale of the Times* (1799), and argues for West's similarly reformist intentions. Woodworth questions the straightforward interpretation of West as an anti-Jacobin because West's novels are heavily didactic and do not feature revolutionary heroines. By reconciling West's pro-revolution poetry with her conservative conduct literature, Woodworth demonstrates that West's novels advocate for social change through Christian and didactic principles, which she contrasts with the self-indulgent standards of the French Revolution.

Mary Wollstonecraft appears as an important presence in the three subsequent essays. In Sharon M. Setzer's essay, Chapter 3 of the collection, she argues that Mary Robinson's third novel *Angelina* (1796) not only overturns notions of parental absolutism, but also contains critiques of slavery and the unpopular war with France. The novel is embedded in Jacobin debate: just as characters within the novel appropriate arguments from Mary Wollstonecraft's *A Vindication of the Rights of Woman* (1792), Wollstonecraft in turn praised the novel's social aims. In Chapter 4, Jonathan Sadow reads Eliza Fenwick's *Secresy, or, The Ruin on the Rock* (1795) alongside Wollstonecraft's *Maria, or, The Wrongs of Woman* (1798) as a novel that associates sentimental and Gothic tropes with social and personal tyranny. The didacticism in *Secresy* is, however, strangely unclear, which Sadow interprets as a commentary on prevailing notions of romance, education, and the novelistic form. Eleanor Ty and Ada Sharpe focus on *Memoirs of Emma Courtney* (1796) and *The Victim of Prejudice* (1799), both by Mary Hays, another follower of Wollstonecraft, in Chapter 5. Ty and Sharpe argue that Hays's works complicate a clear anti-Jacobin/Jacobin dichotomy and that though she has been traditionally read as a Jacobin, like more conservative didactic authors, she works as a reformer. Hays's vision is grounded in her dissenting religious beliefs and her conviction of the power of rational thought to create social change especially regarding romance and female desire, women's social 'usefulness', and economic roles and the social and economic marginalization of the 'fallen' woman.

Hannah More and Maria Edgeworth are the focal points of the next group of essays, which discuss the largely conservative response of didactic female authors to revolutionary ideals in the first decades of the nineteenth century. Hannah More's *Cœlebs in Search of a Wife* was the first blockbuster novel of the early nineteenth century, and it inspired similarly 'moral-evangelical' novels in the following years, though its successors often improved upon its moral and psychological complexity.[74] The publication of *Cœlebs* heralded the ascendancy of women novelists at the beginning of the nineteenth century. In the 1800s, 362 novels (47 per cent) were published by women, 289 (37.5 per cent) were published by men, and 119 (15.5 per cent) were unattributed. Women were so dominant in the 1810s that even if all of the unattributed novels were written by men, women would still outnumber them: 344 novels (52 per cent) were published by women, 191 (28.8 per cent) were published by men, and 127 (19.2 per cent) were unattributed.[75] In such conditions, More was ideally suited to shine and galvanize, as Patricia Demers argues in Chapter 6. *Cœlebs*'s loquaciousness, which Demers reads as being tinctured boldly with religion and reform, is the chief vehicle of More's didacticism. Despite More's 'aggressive' agenda of female reform, she nevertheless created strong-minded and independent female characters like Miss Sparkes who were not entirely vilified: Miss Sparkes's views of 'Wollstonecraftian' liberation were allowed to be voiced, though they were mitigated by More's presentation of concurrent cultural fears and objections.

More's *Cheap Repository Tracts* (1795–97) also inspire Andrew O'Malley's work on didactic children's literature of the period in Chapter 7. In the wake of the French Revolution, the threat to social order intensified anxieties over children and popular influence. O'Malley addresses the fiction for young readers by one of the key figures of late eighteenth-century children's literature, Maria Edgeworth (*Moral Tales for Young People* (1804)), alongside More's *Cheap Repository Tract* literature, and considers how Edgeworth helped shape the dominant paradigm of didactic, purposeful writing for children. Edgeworth, O'Malley argues, uses didactic forms to both reinscribe the differences between children and adults, while at the same guaranteeing the successful reproduction of adult standards, behaviours, and ways of thinking in the young. Edgeworth was also the author of successful conduct works, including *Essays on Professional Education* (1809), which she wrote with her father Richard Lovell Edgeworth. *Professional Education* is the starting point for Hilary Havens's interpretation of Edgeworth's magnum opus, *Patronage* (1814) in Chapter 8. Although *Patronage* was a critical failure, Edgeworth's didactic treatment of male professionalism and female courtship behaviour blurs political boundaries, as she upholds prevailing British prejudices against the French. In her later revisions, which she undertook after the end of Anglo-French hostilities, Edgeworth removed the most heavy-handed of her didactic scenes and trimmed her patriotic episodes, a move which Havens contends is related to the diminished threat to British nationalism and her changing generic aims.

The final two essays of the collection, Claire Grogan's and Teri Doerksen's, discuss the ways in which the didactic novel is employed to bolster Scottish nationalism and pride. In Chapter 9, Grogan uses Hannah More's

16   *Hilary Havens*

Cheap Repository Tracts as an important intertext for Elizabeth Hamilton's *The Cottagers of Glenburnie* (1808). While both works are positioned as didactic texts aimed at the poorer classes to counter revolutionary writings, Grogan disputes the assumption that Hamilton wrote the same kind of 'popular propaganda for the poor' as More. Through a careful reading of the novel and Hamilton's didactic contexts, Grogan argues that More's primary goal was to quell the working poor, whereas Hamilton's was to inspire them to greater things, beyond individual subsistence and independence to Scottish patriotism. Doerksen similarly links the didactic with the Scottish in novels by Mary Brunton and Susan Ferrier in Chapter 10. Unlike Hamilton's *Cottagers*, Brunton's *Discipline* (1814) and Ferrier's *Marriage* (1818) were directed towards a more general audience as they employed the didactic novel to represent national, religious, and class identity as mutually informing and occasionally conflated concepts. They present Scotland as a locus of poverty and grit, but also of virtue, religion, and simplicity, contrasting both positively and negatively with England's opulence and corruption. Thus in these didactic narratives, 'Marriage', becomes a metaphor for the unequal alliance between nations, forced together in an unhappy union, and 'Discipline' signifies the effort that can finally serve to unite them.

The collection closes with an afterword by Shelley King, who discusses the resurgence of interest in the didactic genre and creates alternate thematic connections between the essays. In particular, she emphasizes the complexity of the didactic novel as a genre, the need to reconsider critical responses to didacticism, and the role played by historical and cultural forces in the composition and reception of didactic texts. These new conversations and comparisons reinforce the importance of studying the didactic novel and its function as an effective avenue for women to participate in public debate, even as women were again outnumbered, but not silenced by male writers with the advent of the 1820s and the end of Anglo-French hostilities.[76]

Notes

1. 'didactic, n. and adj.', *OED Online* (Oxford: Oxford University Press: December 2014), www.oed.com/view/Entry/52341 (accessed 5 February 2015).
2. According to Rebecca Davies, 'In the eighteenth century women were increasingly constructed as the ideal educators of children, due to a cultural belief that maternity was innate in women combined with the notion that education was a key component of the maternal role' (*Written Maternal Authority and Eighteenth-Century Education in Britain: Educating by the Book* (Farnham, Surrey and Burlington, VT: Ashgate, 2014), p. 5).
3. Ibid., pp. 4, 5, my emphasis.
4. In his important study of the eighteenth-century novel, J. Paul Hunter delineates the six key features of early didactic texts: a clear binary between good and evil, a belief in the power of language to affect its readers, a heightened tone and sense of urgency, its direct and personal address, a belief that writing can enact change, and the use of authoritative tones (*Before Novels: The Cultural*

Contexts of Eighteenth-Century English Fiction (New York and London: Norton, 1990), pp. 228–44).

5. E. T. Bannet, *The Domestic Revolution: Enlightenment Feminisms and the Novel* (Baltimore, MD and London: Johns Hopkins University Press, 2000), pp. 11, 10.

6. W. St Clair and I. Maassen, General Introduction, in W. St Clair and I. Maassen (eds), *Conduct Literature for Women, 1500–1640*, vol. 1 (London: Pickering & Chatto, 2000), pp. ix–xli, on p. xvii.

7. The shift in focus of conduct literature towards the feminine is tied to what Michael McKeon calls 'emerging gender difference', where '"gender" [is] sufficiently separated out as a category from "sex" (from that which it defines itself against) to take on the familiar, differential function it performs in modern culture'. The separate term 'gender' 'works to discriminate not only socialized behavior from natural fact, but also masculinity from femininity'; conduct books thus functioned as a means of creating and preserving this new, significant gender difference ('Historicizing Patriarchy: The Emergence of Gender Difference in England, 1660–1760', *Eighteenth-Century Studies*, 28:3 (1995), pp. 295–322, on p. 301). See also S. Augustin, *Eighteenth-Century Female Voices: Education and the Novel* (Frankfurt am Main: Peter Lang, 2005), p. 8.

8. G. S. Halifax, *The Lady's New-Year's-Gift*, in W. St Clair and I. Maassen (eds), *Conduct Literature for Women, 1640–1710*, vol. 2 (London: Pickering & Chatto, 2002), pp. 123–214, on pp. 132–33.

9. N. Armstrong, *Desire and Domestic Fiction: A Political History of the Novel* (Oxford: Oxford University Press, 1987), p. 100.

10. See ibid., pp. 61–62; J. Hemlow, 'Fanny Burney and the Courtesy Books', *PMLA*, 65:5 (1950), pp. 732–61, on p. 732; and M. Poovey, *The Proper Lady and the Woman Writer: Ideology as Style in the Works of Mary Wollstonecraft, Mary Shelley, and Jane Austen* (Chicago, IL: University of Chicago Press, 1984), pp. 15–16.

11. Poovey, *Proper Lady*, p. 15.

12. J. Gregory, *A Father's Legacy to His Daughters*, 2nd edn (London, 1774), p. 5.

13. Ibid., pp. vii–viii.

14. S. Pennington, *An Unfortunate Mother's Advice to her Absent Daughters; In a Letter to Miss Pennington* (London, 1761), p. 1.

15. P. Morris, General Introduction, in P. Morris (ed.), *Conduct Literature for Women, 1770–1830*, vol. 1 (London: Pickering & Chatto, 2005), pp. ix–xxxvii, on pp. xi–xii.

16. Ibid., pp. xxxii–xxxiii.

17. M. Astell, *A Serious Proposal to the Ladies*, ed. P. Springborg (Peterborough, ON: Broadview Press, 2002), p. 60.

18. M. Wollstonecraft, *The Works of Mary Wollstonecraft*, ed. J. Todd and M. Butler, 7 vols (London: Pickering & Chatto, 1989), vol. 4, p. 31.

19. H. More, *Strictures on the Modern System of Female Education*, 2 vols (London, 1799), vol. 1, p. 60.

20. Ibid., vol. 2, p. 2.

21. E. Hamilton, *Letters on the Elementary Principles of Education*, 2nd edn, 2 vols (London, 1801–2), vol. 1, p. 243.

22. G. J. Barker-Benfield identifies the focal point of the 'attack on women's reading' in his magisterial study of eighteenth-century sensibility: 'women could be

18   *Hilary Havens*

sexually aroused by reading novels, thereby readied for seduction' (*The Culture of Sensibility: Sex and Society in Eighteenth-Century Britain* (Chicago, IL and London: University of Chicago Press, 1992), p. 327).

23. William St Clair emphasizes the negative reactions of the conduct authors towards the novel genre: 'The advice books are particularly fearful of novels which are believed to inflame emotions and cause discontent' (W. St Clair, *The Godwins and the Shelleys: The Biography of a Family* (London and Boston, MA: Faber and Faber, 1989), p. 506).
24. Pennington, *Unfortunate Mother's Advice*, p. 39.
25. T. Gisborne, *An Enquiry into the Duties of the Female Sex*, 4th edn (London, 1799), p. 216.
26. Hamilton, *Letters*, vol. 2, p. 88.
27. More, *Strictures*, vol. 1, p. 163.
28. Wollstonecraft, *Works*, vol. 4, p. 49.
29. Gregory, *Father's Legacy*, p. 48.
30. J. Fordyce, *Sermons to Young Women*, 3rd edn, 2 vols (London, 1766), vol. 1, p. 278.
31. See J. Spencer, *The Rise of the Woman Novelist: From Aphra Behn to Jane Austen* (Oxford: Basil Blackwell, 1986), p. 141.
32. S. Richardson, *Pamela*, ed. A. J. Rivero (Cambridge: Cambridge University Press, 2011), p. 2.
33. S. Richardson, *Collection of the Moral and Instructive Sentiments, Maxims, Cautions, and Reflections, Contained in the Histories of Pamela, Clarissa, and Sir Charles Grandison* (London, 1755), p. ix.
34. See P. Morris, General Introduction, in P. Morris (ed.), *Conduct Literature for Women, 1720–1770*, vol. 1 (London: Pickering & Chatto, 2004), pp. ix–xxxii, on p. xxix.
35. Fordyce, *Sermons*, vol. 1, pp. 281–82; cf. vol. 1, p. 279. See also Poovey, *Proper Lady*, pp. 37–38.
36. Armstrong, *Desire and Domestic Fiction*, p. 97.
37. S. Fielding, *The Governess*, ed. C. Ward (Peterborough, ON: Broadview Press, 2005), p. 45.
38. F. Burney, *Evelina*, ed. E. A. Bloom and V. Jones (Oxford: Oxford University Press, 2002), p. 84.
39. Poovey, *Proper Lady*, p. 38.
40. See Augustin, *Eighteenth-Century Female Voices*, p. 35.
41. See Spencer, *Rise of the Woman Novelist*, p. 142.
42. Jane Spencer also argues that women found ways to circumvent the constricting bounds of the didactic genre: 'I suggest that women writers were drawn to the didactic tradition not because they wanted to preach female subordination, but because this tradition could be used for the development of a new and more complex treatment of female character' (*Rise of the Woman Novelist*, p. 143).
43. J. Raven, 'Historical Introduction: The Novel Comes of Age', in J. Raven and A. Forster (eds), *The English Novel 1770–1829: A Bibliographical Survey of Prose Fiction Published in the British Isles*, vol. 1 of 2, *1770–1799* (Oxford: Oxford University Press, 2000), pp. 15–121, on p. 45. The table (Table 6) is in Raven, 'Historical Introduction', pp. 46–47.
44. Ibid., p. 48.
45. Ibid.

Introduction 19

46. St Clair also confirms that anonymous female authorship was on the rise: 'In the romantic period, as many as a third of all novels, including the first published novel by Austen, claimed to have been written "by a Lady"' (W. St Clair, *The Reading Nation in the Romantic Period* (Cambridge: Cambridge University Press, 2004), p. 244).

47. H. T. Dickinson, *The Politics of the People in Eighteenth-Century Britain* (Houndmills and London: Macmillan / New York: St. Martin's, 1995), p. 226.

48. M. Philp, *Reforming Ideas in Britain: Politics and Language in the Shadow of the French Revolution, 1789–1815* (Cambridge: Cambridge University Press, 2014), pp. 74–75. According to Gregory Claeys, these varied responses to the French Revolution solidified into the two-party system, 'which has dominated subsequent modern politics' (*The French Revolution Debate in Britain: The Origins of Modern Politics* (Houndmills and New York: Palgrave Macmillan, 2007), p. 3).

49. J. Barrell, *The Spirit of Despotism: Invasions of Privacy in the 1790s* (Oxford: Oxford University Press, 2006), pp. 14–15.

50. J. J. Rousseau, *Émile, Or on Education*, trans. and ed. C. Kelly and A. Bloom (Hanover, NH: Dartmouth College Press / University Press of New England, 2009), p. 532.

51. E. Burke, *Reflections on the Revolution in France*, ed. Frank M. Turner (New Haven, CT: Yale University Press, 2003), p. 65.

52. Dickinson, *Politics of the People*, p. 184. While denied a 'formal education', women could occasionally 'transgress conventional gendered roles in social life' through the conduit of conversation, according to John Mee (*Conversable Worlds: Literature, Contention, and Community: 1762 to 1830* (Oxford: Oxford University Press, 2011), p. 141).

53. O. de Gouges, 'The Declaration of the Rights of Woman', in D. G. Levy, H. B. Applewhite, and M. D. Johnson (trans. and eds), *Women in Revolutionary Paris, 1789–1795* (Urbana, IL: University of Illinois Press, 1979), pp. 87–96, on pp. 90, 92–93.

54. Wollstonecraft, *Works*, vol. 5, p. 91.

55. Ibid., vol. 5, p. 131.

56. Morris, General Introduction, *Conduct Literature for Women, 1720–1770*, p. xv.

57. St Clair extracts several examples of this from late eighteenth-century instructional writers:

> British ladies, suggests Fordyce, will support plain local fashions, not expensive fripperies from abroad. Pestilential publications from France and the Danube are swarming over Europe, says Mrs More, like the Huns and Vandals of old. The fall of France to the revolutionaries, says Mrs West, was due to the indelicate behaviour of its women.
>
> (St Clair, *Godwins and the Shelleys*, p. 507)

58. St Clair, *Reading Nation*, p. 277.

59. St Clair, *Godwins and the Shelleys*, p. 509.

60. During the revolutionary period, British 'Jacobins' adopted radical principles and supported the corresponding changes to government and social policy; they were heavily influenced by radical French principles. 'Anti-jacobins', in contrast, upheld conservative British ideologies and existing political structures.

20   *Hilary Havens*

61. K. Gilmartin, *Writing Against Revolution: Literary Conservatism in Britain, 1790–1832* (Cambridge: Cambridge University Press, 2007), 153.
62. Davies, *Written Maternal Authority*, p. 8.
63. L. Bellamy, *Commerce, Morality and the Eighteenth-Century Novel* (Cambridge: Cambridge University Press, 1998), p. 157.
64. Mikhail Bakhtin's term 'heteroglossia' comes closest to capturing the competing 'multiplicity of social voice' present within these didactic texts (*The Dialogic Imagination*, ed. M. Holquist, trans. C. Emerson and M. Holquist (Austin, TX: University of Texas Press, 1981), p. 263).
65. G. Kelly, *Women, Writing, and Revolution, 1790–1827* (Oxford: Clarendon, 1993), p. 7.
66. Ibid., pp. 9, 21.
67. Ibid., p. 174.
68. Ibid., p. 191.
69. E. Ty, *Unsex'd Revolutionaries: Five Women Novelists of the 1790s* (Toronto: University of Toronto Press, 1993), p. 20.
70. E. Ty, *Empowering the Feminine: The Narratives of Mary Robinson, Jane West, and Amelia Opie, 1796–1812* (Toronto: University of Toronto Press, 1998), p. vii.
71. M. O. Grenby, *The Anti-Jacobin Novel: British Conservatism and the French Revolution* (Cambridge: Cambridge University Press, 2001), pp. 1–2.
72. L. Wood, *Modes of Discipline: Women, Conservatism, and the Novel after the French Revolution* (Lewisburg, PA: Bucknell University Press, 2003), p. 12.
73. Ibid., p. 15.
74. P. Garside, 'The English Novel in the Romantic Era: Consolidation and Dispersal', in P. Garside and R. Schöwerling (eds), *The English Novel 1770–1829: A Bibliographical Survey of Prose Fiction Published in the British Isles*, vol. 2 of 2, *1800–1829* (Oxford: Oxford University Press, 2000), pp. 15–103, on p. 59.
75. Peter Garside gives these statistics in Table 5 (Garside, 'The English Novel', p. 73), and he summarizes the dominance of female novelists: 'novels by named/identified/implied female authors outnumber those by their male counterparts by 979 (43.4 per cent) to 899 (39.8 per cent), with a residue of 378 (16.8 per cent) titles resisting adequate gender identification' (p. 72).
76. Garside posits that

> The tendency in the 1820s generally reserves what is evident in the 1810s. Novels by male authors now outnumber their female counterparts by 419 to 273, with 132 unknown cases, the male category thus claiming more than half (50.8 per cent) the total number of titles.
>
> (Garside, 'The English Novel', p. 75)

1 Charlotte Smith and the Persistence of the Past

Morgan Rooney

If seeing the term 'didactic' in the title of a collection of essays on the Romantic period strikes us as in any way incongruous, it is perhaps a testimony to the enduring legacy of what Jerome McGann labelled 'the Romantic ideology'.[1] Certainly, many of the 'big six' Romantic poets denounce didacticism in poetry and imaginative literature more broadly. Percy Shelley proclaims in *A Defense of Poetry* (1821) that 'poetry cannot be made subservient' to instruction, while John Keats argues in an 1818 letter that 'We hate poetry that has a palpable design upon us – and if we do not agree, seems to put its hand in its breeches pocket'.[2] Much of the writing of the Romantic era, however, especially in roughly the first half of the period we associate with 'Romanticism' (1790–1805), is infused with didactic intent and provides the backdrop against which Shelley's and Keats's objections are voiced.

This statement is particularly applicable to the novel, and perhaps more so than any other genre in the period. In the wake of the French Revolution, British novelists imaginatively responded to the socio-political arguments first articulated in the speeches, treatises, and pamphlets of statesmen and philosophers. They noisily proclaimed their didactic intent, announcing their designs on readers and positioning their works as interventions in a larger public debate about the nation's future. Not excepting Mary Wollstonecraft or William Godwin, there is arguably no novelist who was more influential and widely read in the 1790s than Charlotte Smith, and who 'is now widely recognized', as Barbara Tarling observes, 'as a central figure in the Romantic canon'.[3] While critics have rightly identified Edmund Burke as the central figure she engages most consistently,[4] they have not traced her considerable literary exchanges with the statesman across her novel corpus.

A prominent recurring target in Smith's fiction is, this essay argues, a Burkean adherence to history-as-inheritance. In *Reflections on the Revolution in France* (1790), Burke argues that attempts to amend British order must be informed by an appreciation of its historically determined nature and a sustained awareness that it is a product of its past.[5] By treating that construct as a corporate inheritance, he contends, Britons ensure that each generation enjoys the socio-political benefits that have accrued over time while leaving open the possibility of improvement by way of alteration or addition. As this essay argues, however, for Smith, this understanding of the

22 *Morgan Rooney*

nation as an inheritance amounts to a deadly commitment to the past that limits the possibility for meaningful change, enables corruption, and stultifies life in the present.

We can trace the evolving nature of Smith's resistance to Burke's understanding of the nation as an inheritance through her three most radical novels, *Desmond* (1792), *The Old Manor House* (1793), and *The Young Philosopher* (1798). While her opposition to Burke remains consistent throughout, the nature of her engagement with his ideas shifts. Her sense of her culture's enmeshment in the past-oriented philosophy she associates with Burke becomes increasingly pronounced, revealing her fading hopes for a Britain free from its grip. In *Desmond*, a young man pursues his 'ideal' (Geraldine), contrary to the caution of his experienced guardian, Bethel, and his country's customs. Disputing Bethel's limited sense of the possible and the patriarchal assumptions of the institutions that render Geraldine the property of a worthless man, Desmond becomes a cipher for a reformed England by forging a future in which his imagined ideal becomes his everyday reality. In *The Old Manor House*, history's hold is re-imagined through an intergenerational lens that gestures toward the complexity of the present's entanglements with the past, but ultimately such forces are surmountable. In *The Young Philosopher*, a Burkean commitment to the past is omnipresent. No longer able to imagine a future Britain free from history's inheritances, Smith's heroes choose exile in America, a land capable of being re-formed, the novel suggests, because of its break from British history. Collectively, these novels chart Smith's evolving conflict with Burkean discourse, in which the past's influence increasingly determines the future while the prospects for change become ever more dire.

'The absurd system you had built': *Desmond*

Modern scholarship, with good reason, situates *Desmond* against the backdrop of the French Revolution debate in Britain. Continuing that critical trend, I focus on the Desmond–Geraldine–Verney relationship as the vehicle through which Smith tracks her hoped-for transformation of Britain from a past-oriented regime to one that accords with the early promise of the French Revolution. Much like James Monteith in Jane West's *A Tale of the Times* (1799), a character who marries a Geraldine of his own,[6] Richard Verney is a representative of the worst features he inherits from the aristocracy. A gambler and profligate, his actions betray his indifference to the family to which he is supposed to be committed and which is in Burke's discourse the nation-building unit that allows for the transmission of value (titles and riches, values and mores). Effectively sold to this man by 'the mercenary hands of her family',[7] whose prejudices mistake wealth for worth, Geraldine demonstrates a capacity for virtue that enthrals Desmond before the narrative begins, but which is oppressed by her husband's influence. The novel depicts the process by which the old-world alliance that systematically enables misery and which stands in for Britain 'as it really is' (Verney/Geraldine) gives way to a prospective marriage that promises to correct the abuses of the old union and which represents Smith's hope for a reformed Britain (Desmond/Geraldine).

Smith sets this fantasy of domestic/national transformation in motion through the narrative's two main male correspondents, Desmond and Bethel. Throughout the novel, Desmond associates Geraldine with 'perfectio[n]' and describes her as 'the very woman [his] imagination had formed'.[8] As Alison Conway observes, his love for Geraldine is aligned with the idealism that conservatives consistently associated with the reform cause.[9] As the experienced Bethel remarks of Desmond's love for Geraldine, 'you expect what you will never find, the cultivated mind and polished manners of refined society, with the simplicity and unpretending modesty of retired life'.[10] But, he cautions, those qualities 'are incompatible – they cannot be united; and this model of perfection, which you have imagined, and can never obtain, will be a source of unhappiness to you through life'.[11] Connected to a longing for perfection and cast as an idealistic vision Bethel insists is unattainable, Desmond's love occupies the same suspect place in the imagination of Bethel as reform discourse does in the writings of the critics of reform.

Long recognized as the novel's fictional counterpart to *Edmund Burke*,[12] *Erasmus Bethel* makes authoritative claims about the world 'as it really is' by virtue of his 'dearly-bought experience'.[13] Like Bethlem Gabor in Godwin's *St Leon* (1799)[14] and a host of other characters in 1790s reformist fiction, Bethel's past experience determines his sense of the present. He dismisses Desmond's idealized 'model of perfection' because his experience confirms for him its impossibility. Hoping to counter Desmond's idealization, Bethel narrates the history of his life. As a young man, he married a woman of 'unaffected innocence and timidity of … manners', who, being corrupted by the 'giddy', 'intoxicating draughts of flattery' of London's polished urban dwellers, eloped with 'a man who disgraces the name he bears'.[15] That early experience colours Bethel's worldview and his sense of the possible. When Desmond proposes that Bethel pursue Geraldine's sister, Fanny, Bethel cites a few reasons for not doing so – the disparity of their ages, her suspected infatuation with Desmond – but, most notably, the thought of taking Fanny as a partner triggers a now deeply engrained prejudice about women's liability to seduction: '*I* could never hope to become acceptable to a young woman surrounded as she is, with flattery and admiration'.[16] Tellingly, too, while the narrative ends with one marriage (Montfleuri/Fanny) and another impending (Desmond/Geraldine), Smith condemns Bethel to a single life: his voice, influence on Desmond, and prospects for a family legacy are simultaneously cut off.

The narrative of *Desmond* is thus structured around a clash between opposing ways of 'knowing', one past-oriented and informed by the logic of precedent (Burke) and the other forward-looking and committed to an ethos of innovation characteristic of many prominent reformers in the period. The hero journeys toward realizing an ideal, contrary to the testimonial evidence of his guardian figure, who himself comes to doubt if his experience applies in Geraldine's case. The text thereby implicitly invites readers to undergo a similar conversion with respect to their opinions of revolutionary France and, by extension, a future reformed England. As the letters that end the novel turn toward the impending realization of the ideal (Desmond/Geraldine's alliance), Bethel's Burkean commitments to 'experience' and 'precedent' make way for the ethic of making new, a point registered formally through the absence of his further correspondence.[17] In the world of the novel, the displacement of one worldview for another is achieved in little over twenty months, and the costs have been, relatively speaking, low. While Desmond experiences hardships, notably wounds from his duel, they remain consistent with the spirit of Comedy: he loses no one he cares about, sustains no lasting physical or mental injury, and retains the key markers of his identity, such as his home, friends, and nation.

While Smith uses Bethel to oppose a philosophy committed to making new, she uses Geraldine and the forces that contributed to her marriage to expose the oppressive potential of Burke's past-oriented worldview. In particular, she targets two institutions at the heart of Burke's metaphor-rich understanding of the nation: inheritance (primogeniture) and marriage (contract). For Burke, 'the idea of inheritance' is the ruling logic of the British family and the nation:

> [it] furnishes a sure principle of conservation, and a sure principle of transmission; without at all excluding a principle of improvement. It leaves acquisition free; but it secures what it acquires. Whatever advantages are obtained by a state proceeding on these maxims, are locked fast as in a sort of family settlement; grasped as in a kind of mortmain for ever. By a constitutional policy, working after the pattern of nature, we receive, we hold, we transmit our government and our privileges, in the same manner in which we enjoy and transmit our property and our lives.[18]

For Burke, inheritance, considered literally as a means for transferring property and metaphorically and more broadly as a vehicle for transmitting socio-political culture, provides the nation's means for the transfer of value through the ages.

In *Desmond*, however, inheritance is configured as the force that puts Geraldine's sufferings in motion. Displaying an 'uncommon indecision of mind' attributed to 'the extreme indulgence of his parents',[19] Geraldine's spoiled brother Waverly is the byproduct of a system that privileges first-born sons. This commitment to primogeniture informs the behaviour of Geraldine's mother, Mrs Waverly, toward all her children. She spends much of the novel scheming to secure a suitable match and then 'an Irish peerage' for her son, but she leaves Geraldine in the hands of an increasingly

Charlotte Smith and the Persistence of the Past 25

authoritarian Verney, who commands her to make a perilous journey into revolutionary France accompanied by a man to whom her husband has sold her to settle his 'debts of honour'.[20] As her sister Fanny comments, such indifference towards Geraldine is entirely in keeping with Mrs Waverly's character:

> Wrapt up as her whole soul has ever been in my brother, she has always thought, that in marrying her daughters in what is called a prudent way, that is, to men of large fortune, she had taken sufficient trouble about them. She never considered whether there were any other sources of unhappiness than want of money.[21]

Mrs Waverly is not so much a villain as a product of her culture and its inherent structure of values. Instead, her behaviour toward Geraldine – selling her to Verney and leaving her to his authority without attending to her well-being afterwards – is the consequence of a mind conditioned by the logic of inheritance.

If Smith uses Geraldine's situation to expose the oppressive byproducts of primogeniture, she also uses it to reveal the destructive potential of the permanent and unchanging social contract that reformers attributed to Burke. Burke's sceptical readers sometimes lost sight of his commitment to the necessity of change,[22] but, undoubtedly, he supplied them with materials that facilitated such interpretations:

> Society is indeed a contract.... [It is] a partnership not only between those who are living, but between those who are living, those who are dead, and those who are to be born.... The municipal corporations of that universal kingdom are not morally at liberty at their pleasure, and on their speculations of a contingent improvement, wholly to separate and tear asunder the bands of their subordinate community, and to dissolve it into an unsocial, uncivil, unconnected chaos of elementary principles.[23]

For reformers, the ideas that the 'living' and 'those who are to be born' are tied to the 'dead', and that the 'living' cannot attempt change 'on their speculations of a contingent improvement', translated into a static philosophy that cut the nation off from reform. Burke's interpretation of the Glorious Revolution of 1688 in particular raised, for them, the spectre of an unchanging England: 'So far is it from being true, that we acquired a right by the Revolution to elect our kings', he argues, countering Richard Price's account of the Glorious Revolution, 'that if we had possessed it before, the English nation did at that time most solemnly renounce and abdicate it, for themselves and for all their posterity for ever'.[24]

Recalling Paine's dismissal of this sentiment as '[t]he vanity and presumption of governing beyond the grave',[25] Smith's rendering of the Verney/

Geraldine marriage is an imaginative response to Burke's declaration that their ancestors of 1688 had made a binding decision for all future generations. Similarly situated in an inviolable contract, Geraldine exemplifies the abuses such an arrangement facilitates. Verney's tyranny and Geraldine's powerlessness parallel Smith's sense of the oppressive nature of France's (and, by implication, Britain's) socio-political realm as it was constituted.[26] Conscious that she has no will independent of 'the unfortunate man whose property [she is]',[27] Geraldine has two paths open to her: obey her husband's commands, regardless of the danger his poor judgement presents to his family, or suffer social death. Mrs Waverly makes this point when she learns that Geraldine, after receiving Verney's command to journey into revolutionary France, is traveling to Bath to seek her mother's protection: she offers financial assistance 'to grant [Geraldine] any little accommodation for [her] journey – though, certainly, not to support [her] in a wilful separation from [her] husband, which nothing can excuse, and no mother, who has a due sense of propriety, will encourage'.[28] Thus circumstanced, Geraldine becomes 'a complete martyr to [her] duty',[29] submitting herself to the will of an arbitrary husband whose judgement cannot be legitimately opposed. As in the private sphere, the novel suggests, so in the public: the static social contract Burke proposes, Smith argues, enables the same kind of corruption and oppression as the marriage contract that binds Geraldine. Thus imagined, the social contract is, for Smith, unjust and a lie. She makes both charges amply clear in the novel through, respectively, Verney's tyranny and death: the former lays bare the oppressive potential of a society so constituted, while the latter confirms that the duration of any man's influence is tied to his lifespan.

'I never saw this like of this old house': *The Old Manor House*

Critics of *The Old Manor House* have not always appreciated that the work is (as Loraine Fletcher, Smith's most recent biographer writes) the 'most subtle of [Smith's] novels'.[30] Almost thirty years ago, one scholar, reflecting on what she apparently regarded as current critical consensus, wrote that in this novel Smith 'set aside French questions in a story resembling the sentimental narratives of her early period'.[31] In fact, Smith uses sentimental narrative to explore some of the fundamental issues raised by the French Revolution, returning, in particular, to the Burkean configuration of the nation as an inheritance, a key preoccupation in *Desmond*.

Smith's *The Old Manor House* subverts Burkean discourse by exploiting one of Burke's favourite images, the estate, using it to characterize his appeal to history as a deadly entrapment by the past.[32] Through a network of associations, Smith suggests a symbolic relationship between Rayland Hall and its inner workings with the British nation and its politics. Rayland Hall is presided over by Mrs Rayland, an eccentric spinster whose dedication to the past recalls Burke's. Because she has the power to determine

Charlotte Smith and the Persistence of the Past 27

who inherits the estate, she exerts control over subsequent generations. This intergenerational influence is depicted in the novel as paralytic, encouraging stasis among the younger generations instead of action, sycophancy instead of self-determination, and anxiety instead of security. The novel reveals that a commitment to the past such as Mrs Rayland's, rather than producing the ordered society Burke imagines, enables various manipulative, exploitative, and criminal behaviours. Tyrannical and long lasting as it is, Mrs Rayland's control is limited to her lifetime, which suggests that the past's determining power is similarly constrained. At the same time, Smith's sense of the complexities associated with bringing about a reformed Britain are more pronounced in *The Old Manor House* than in *Desmond*, with Mrs Rayland's reign being longer and the psychological and human costs of her displacement more substantive than those associated with Verney's.

The Old Manor House is set in the 1770s, but the novel's narrative centres, Mrs Rayland and Rayland Hall, are products of the previous century. Smith pursues a number of strategies to identify Mrs Rayland, her estate, and the order they represent with an antiquated past, Burkean discourse, and the British nation. Rayland Hall, the narrator reveals, 'had not received the slightest alteration, either in its environs or its furniture, since it was embellished for the marriage of [Mrs Rayland's] father Sir Hildebrand, in 1698'.[33] Similarly, its owner Mrs Rayland is introduced as 'a specimen of the magnificence of the last century': her conduct is determined by 'the notable maxims of her mother'; her writing style is comically archaic, 'spelling as her father spelt, and distaining those idle novelties by which a few superfluous letters are saved'; and her understanding of the present is limited by her propensity to read current events in light of historical parallels.[34] Surrounded by her ancestors' portraits and taking a 'peculiar satisfaction in relating the history of the heroes and dames of her family',[35] Mrs Rayland and the house she occupies are a microcosm of the late seventeenth century preserved and unnaturally extended into the present moment.

In organizing her plot around a manor that has not been altered in almost one hundred years and which is presided over by a past-oriented proprietor, Smith invites readers not only to read the manor as a figure for the British nation, but also to recall the post-1688 constitutional settlement and the ways it was invoked in the early stages of the French Revolution debate. Burke's opponents objected to the reading of the events of 1688 that he articulated in the *Reflections*, particularly, as mentioned, his claim that 'the English nation did at that time most solemnly renounce and abdicate [the right to elect kings], for themselves and for all their posterity for ever'.[36] *The Old Manor House* novelizes this political theme of the previous generation 'governing beyond the grave',[37] with Smith showing how Mrs Rayland's control over the estate allows one antiquated figure to control the lives of the rising generation.

Smith develops her critique of the past's control over the present in a variety of ways. Orlando Somerive, the novel's (passive) romantic hero, is

28 *Morgan Rooney*

rendered static and subservient because Mrs Rayland refuses to name her successor, thus putting his future on hold. He is largely immobilized in the novel's first three volumes, torn between his desire to secure his family's finances and his desire to pursue his happiness in the form of Monimia, whose lowly social status makes her, from the elitist Mrs Rayland's perspective, an unthinkable match. The entire Somerive family, in fact, is held hostage by Mrs Rayland: permanently anxious about his family's financial future, Mr Somerive counsels his children, against his conscience, to pursue those things that stand to bring them security. Such moral compromises and ongoing anxieties overtake Mr Somerive before the novel's end, and he dies, we are told, of 'a broken heart',[38] the casualty of an intergenerational struggle precipitated by Mrs Rayland's power over her younger relations.

In addition to configuring the past as a life-denying force, Smith extends her criticism of Burke's configuration of the nation as an inheritance by detailing the disorder and abuse Mrs Rayland's backward-looking imagination and ancient house make possible. For all her power, Mrs Rayland is governed by her servant, Mrs Lennard, who manipulates her mistress by acquiescing to and distracting her with her reverence for the past. Because of Mrs Rayland's susceptibility to manipulation, Rayland Hall has become involved in a smuggling operation. In a purposeful travesty of the state/estate metaphor used by Burke and consciously mobilized in the novel, Smith implicates the architecture of the house, and particularly its substructure, in the perpetuation of this corruption: it is, after all, the secret cellars and doors that 'nobody knows nothing about'[39] that allow the smuggling operation to thrive. Ironically, too, that same 'rotten' architecture that facilitates this corruption is crucial to the novel's envisioning of a future distinctly different from the oppressive past: the secret passageway between the base of one of the manor's turrets and Monimia's room enables the lovers to come together and, eventually, to succeed Mrs Rayland as the Hall's owners.

If the secret passageways in *The Old Manor House* imply that this past-oriented order is vulnerable to the kind of subversion that Orlando and Monimia's relationship represents, then Mrs Rayland's death makes a similar point, suggesting that its duration is limited. When Orlando returns from America to discover that his patroness has died, he is finally free to pursue his heart's desire, Monimia, whom he promptly marries. As inept a romance hero as Orlando is, his decision to marry Monimia is a remarkable instance of self-determination, of looking forward to a future he can define rather than backward to a past that shapes it for him. Mrs Rayland's ability to influence Orlando's future in ways that contradict his deepest desires is circumscribed by her death: 'The little withered figure, bent down with age and infirmity', the narrator claims, is 'the last of a race ... which in a few years, perhaps a few months, might no more be remembered'.[40] The novel ends in a gesture loaded with reformist implications, with Orlando and

Monimia taking possession of the Hall and re-decorating it to bring it into the eighteenth century: 'without spoiling that look of venerable antiquity for which it was so remarkable, [Orlando] collected within it every comfort and every elegance of modern life'.[41] Such narrative elements in *The Old Manor House* suggest that meaningful reform in Britain remains possible.

At the same time, however, bringing about the reformed order that Orlando/Monimia's marriage represents demands considerable time and suffering, placing pressure on the otherwise Comedic ethos of *The Old Manor House*. In *Desmond*, Verney is the only character connected to the lovers who dies and, standing in for an old order whose demise Smith anticipates, his death is necessary in the novel's economy. Mrs Rayland is a counterpart to Verney in this sense, and yet, before her death, she and the system of inheritance she represents substantially mar the lives of the lovers and their circle. Convinced 'early in life' that he 'must have the Rayland estate', Orlando's older brother Philip develops 'violent passions, and an understanding very ill suited to their management'.[42] Formed by the inheritance laws that privilege first-born sons, Philip is a self-devoted being with no concern for any members of his family who, he concludes, 'must scramble through the world as well as they can'[43] while he enjoys the spoils of his forefathers. His character thus (de)formed by the logic of inheritance, Philip dies after he has 'too plainly evinced, that to his own selfish gratifications he would always sacrifice the welfare, and even the subsistence of his family'.[44] Philip contributes to the death of his father, Mr Somerive, who is 'the novel's most evocative exploration', as Ina Ferris argues, 'of the … deleterious effects' of the Burkean understanding of the nation as an inheritance.[45] Permanently anxious because of his family's uncertain fate, Mr Somerive's health finally fails when he learns on his sickbed 'that Philip was actually in treaty … for the sale of his future interest in the [Somerive] estate at West Wolverton'.[46]

The toll Mrs Rayland's 'legacy' exacts is also, as Simon Parkes has shown, etched onto Orlando's person.[47] After returning from America, Orlando is described as so 'changed by the hardships he had undergone' that he is mistaken by strangers 'for a Frenchman'.[48] Orlando has been branded, as it were, by the hereditary prejudices that sent him to America. Dependent upon Mrs Rayland's favour, Orlando pursues a military career because she approves of it for predictably backward-looking reasons – because her grandfather 'appeared with distinguished honour in the service of his master in 1685, against the rebel Monmouth', and because she views the American war as 'a quarrel with people whom she considers as the descendants of the Regicides, against whom her ancestors drew their swords'.[49] Orlando emerges at the end of *The Old Manor House* with his chosen wife and Rayland Hall, signalling the displacement of Mrs Rayland and the backward-looking philosophy she represents, but that transition has been achieved at the staggering cost of members of the Somerive family as well as Orlando's identity.

'Human nature unadulterated by *inhuman* prejudices': *The Young Philosopher*

In *The Young Philosopher*, Smith depicts a British nation in which a pervasive adherence to the Burkean logic of inheritance deforms all socio-political, legal, and familial relations. The many characters who oppose the novel's heroes (George Delmont, Mr and Mrs Glenmorris, their daughter Medora, and Armitage) are motivated by considerations stemming, directly or indirectly, from Burkean discourse. Some characters obstruct the Glenmorris circle because they believe wealth should be centred in the eldest offspring, while others intervene from fears that the Glenmorris party will redirect the line of inheritance and damage their self-interest. Still other characters offer resistance because they resent the heroes' failure to follow precisely in their forefathers' footsteps, or are motivated by a dedication to the hierarchal order Burke defends and which requires an adherence to class boundaries the Glenmorris party defies, or hope to redirect to themselves the inheritance due to Medora. In all cases, the Glenmorris circle's members are harassed, their interests thwarted, and their existence threatened by a society in which a commitment to a backwards-looking system distorts human relations. Smith's sense of the pervasive influence of this past-oriented philosophy in *The Young Philosopher* is complemented by her conviction that resistance is difficult, costly, and, in Britain's case, perhaps futile. The few who resist this influence are exceptional, having been shaped by Godwinian philosophy or cosmopolitan forces, and the price of their resistance is steep: persecution, defamation, exile, and potentially permanent mental scarring. In *The Young Philosopher*, Britain is so infused with a Burkean commitment to inheritance that it is unliveable and incapable of reform.[50]

The motivations of the 'formidable phalanx'[51] that opposes Medora's rightful claim to a share of Lady Mary De Verdon's fortune stem directly from the notion of inheritance Burke celebrates. The behaviour of Laura Glenmorris's mother, Lady Mary, is shaped by the logic of primogeniture, but with a twist. Lacking a son, she becomes 'entirely engrossed by [Laura's] sister', Guilielmina, for whom 'she formed the project of giving to her eldest daughter a larger portion of their fortune, on the condition that whoever became her husband should take the name of De Verdon'.[52] As Laura notes, Lady Mary 'seemed not to have room enough in her heart' for her second daughter and 'expelled [her] from her affections long before [she] could have done any thing to forfeit them'.[53] Her accumulation of a large inheritance for her eldest daughter for the purpose of aggrandizing the family is complemented by her inflated sense of the family name's worth. Convinced that 'her illustrious blood was derived from Geoffry [*sic*] Plantagenet', she is absorbed by 'all ideas of antiquity'.[54] She convinces her husband to buy a gothic fortress stuffed with 'the rubbish left from generation to generation' and other 'relics of ancient chivalry' 'because it had, above two hundred years ago, been the principal seat of her family'.[55] Laura's elopement with the obscure Glenmorris aggravates Lady Mary's sense of the family's high social standing

Charlotte Smith and the Persistence of the Past 31

while the idea that their equally obscure daughter, Medora, could mar her cherished project to leave the De Verdon fortune to one descendent (Mary Cardonnel, Guilielmina's only daughter) spurs on Lady Mary's opposition.

The other characters who forward Lady Mary's cause are influenced by similarly backward-looking considerations. Like Mrs Rayland, Delmont's aunt Mrs Crewkherne is a relic of a time long passed and is directly aligned with Burke, 'having once dined in company with the great and commanding writer and orator, who ... preached a crusade against "the Gallic savages"'.[56] She laments how 'times are strangely altered since [her] father ... and [her] brother ... lived'; derives her sense of her family's worth from her ancestors, 'the very first people since the conquest'; and measures her relations' worth based on their adherence to their ancestors' examples.[57] Holding a similar sense of 'the elevated hereditary respectability of her ancestors' and aligned with Burke through her praise of 'salutary prejudices', Mrs Grinsted plots against the Glenmorris party because she believes 'that the high-born and affluent only were worth her consideration, or worthy to be ranked in the same class of beings'.[58] Even the lowly lawyers Lady De Verdon enlists are fuelled by such considerations. One lawyer, Brownjohn, urges his brother-in-law Darnell to kidnap Medora to secure her fortune for the family, while Sir Appulby Gorges is spurred to legal chicanery in pursuit of his 'ambitious projects for his grandson'.[59] The cabal aimed at the Glenmorris party is not motivated solely by greed so much as by assumptions about family aggrandizement and human worth that Smith identifies as byproducts of Burke's worldview.

In addition to this cabal, the Glenmorris party faces others who oppose their interests for similar reasons. A guest in Delmont's home, Dr Winslow becomes his enemy when he perceives his host has attracted the notice of his wealthy niece, whom he has been plotting to marry to his milksop son. Aligned with Burke through his 'profoun[d] respect' for 'all sorts of prejudices ... "because they were prejudices"' and his love of 'ancient opinions', Dr Winslow 'never thought of any object but exactly as his predecessors, his masters, had told him to think'.[60] Like Philip Somerive, Delmont's older brother Adolphus repeatedly obstructs the Glenmorris party because of '[i]deas of his own consequence'.[61] Having 'imbibed so early, that if not the whole world, at least all his own family, were to sacrifice every thing to any want or wish of his, as a matter of course',[62] Adolphus demands his brother's time and fortune to fend off his creditors. 'He persisted', the narrator relates,

> in considering George as one born only to promote his views and obey his mandates. Impressed with ideas of primogeniture at a very early age, he could never submit to any mention of equality even among brethren.... [H]e thought it scandalous that in any country, the younger branches of a family should be suffered to diminish the property of the elder.[63]

Smith clarifies that, much like Mrs Waverly in *Desmond*, Adolphus is not entirely to blame; rather, his thinking here is a byproduct of his culture.

32   *Morgan Rooney*

Laura's persecutors betray similarly warped understandings of the world around them. Hoping 'to scrape together every thing she could amass' for her eldest son',[64] Lady Kilbrodie kidnaps a pregnant Laura, distressing her so much that she loses her newborn son. Meanwhile, Mrs Mackirk looks on Laura with 'bitterness' and 'aversion'[65] because she sees that her brother, Lord Macarden, whose protection Laura seeks after escaping the Kilbrodies, loves her. For Mrs Mackirk, Lord Macarden's love for Laura threatens to redirect the line of inheritance away from her children. In these instances, characters with no stake in the legal battle over the De Verdon inheritance oppose the Glenmorris party, with their opposition betraying a familiar grounding in Burkean discourse.

While the opposition the Glenmorris party faces demonstrates the dehumanizing effects such a past-oriented philosophy has on human relations, Smith's characterization of her heroes establishes the difficulties associated with escaping the cultural matrix that perpetuates the evils they face. In *The Young Philosopher*, the only qualities strong enough to bypass the Burkean model are rooted in independent reason[66] or a cosmopolitan education. The novel's 'young philosopher', Delmont, is taught by his mother 'to reason on every thing he learned, instead of seeing all objects, as they are represented, through the dazzling and false medium of prejudice, communicated from one generation to another'.[67] His reading teaches him, as it often did reformers, that history is little more than 'the annals of fraud and murder, of selfish ambition, or wicked policy, involving millions in misery for the gratification of a few'; accordingly, he 'never voluntarily sat down to read' such accounts 'after he was nine or ten years old'.[68]

Lacking mother figures that foster such independent thinking, Laura and her husband Glenmorris instead require an experiential, cosmopolitan education to 'dives[t]' themselves 'not only of local prejudice, but ... of all prejudices'.[69] Through exposure to continental Europe and America, Laura and her husband acquire a vantage point that gives them access to 'human nature unadulterated by *inhuman* prejudices', thus rendering transparent the hereditary status of British opinions and values.[70] In their daughter Medora, Smith collects together these features – an education that prioritizes reason over inherited knowledge, a disgust for the past's follies, a non-British identity,[71] and a cosmopolitan upbringing – to create a character who displays a remarkable capacity for resisting the past's influence. Never attracted to the prospect of inherited wealth and, like Smith, critical of British socio-political order, Medora is unfazed by the allures and threats of a social structure grounded in Burke's framework. One memorable instance in which she displays this capacity for resistance is her description of the room in which the Darnells hold her captive:

> There were two doors in the room where I was left to my contemplations; one from a passage by which I entered, the other I unbolted, and found it led into a closet which was lined with arras, while the room

adjoining, where the bed stood, was of dark wainscot in little pannels, and ornamented only with two full length pictures of some former squire and his spouse, possessors of the mansion ... they were superb, and probably it was expected they would impress me with veneration; but the only sentiment they inspired was fearful curiosity to know if they did not conceal behind them any door or entrance to the room.[72]

Her captors have placed her in a chamber with these portraits in hopes that they will inspire her with the 'veneration' for their family and so induce her to marry Darnell. Because she was raised by reform-minded parents who sought exile in America, however, Medora is immune to such feelings. Rather than inspiring her with respect for her abductor and his marriage offer, the paintings raise only the suspicion that they hide a secret passage that, she fears, might be used for a more nefarious purpose. '[T]here was no restraining a nymph', as Adolphus remarks, 'who had been reared on the broad basis of continental freedom'.[73]

Immersed in a culture that disfigures all relations, and standing outside of it only because of their exceptional educations, the members of the Glenmorris party pay a high price for resisting the past's influence. The closing scenes of *The Young Philosopher* depict Delmont and Medora married, their enemies overcome, and Mary Cardonnel committed to 'a just and amicable division of the disputed part of her inheritance',[74] thereby signalling the expected Comedic resolution. But that ending is undermined by unresolved tensions, denying readers a clear signal that a backwards-looking order has been displaced by a future-oriented one, as Verney's and Mrs Rayland's deaths do in *Desmond* and *The Old Manor House*, respectively. Whether or not Laura's intellects will recover 'from the shock she had sustained' remains uncertain.[75] As Medora laments, too, Laura's fractured mental status reflects the frayed condition of the Glenmorrises generally: 'I fear, I know not why, that the calm and contented state we then enjoyed [in America], we shall never recover. Oh! no! I feel that my mind is hurt, my temper embittered'.[76] Scarred, perhaps permanently, by their experience in Britain, the Glenmorris party chooses expatriation to America, 'for a little while at least'.[77] While the ambiguity surrounding the duration of Laura's disordered state and the family's 'embittered temper' and exile leave open the possibility of a reformed Britain, Smith offers no guarantees of a Britain freed from the past's influence in this novel.[78] The nation remains, as Glenmorris concludes, a place where 'the miseries inflicted by the social compact greatly exceed the happiness derived from it'.[79]

* * *

Focusing on questions of gender more than national identity, James Holt McGavran, Jr, recently argued that, with *The Old Manor House*, Smith 'became finally a brilliantly clear-eyed, cold-eyed woman of no illusions

34 *Morgan Rooney*

who saw Burkean chivalry and ancestor-worship for the cheats they were'.[80] While accounts such as McGavran's reflect the essence of Smith's relation to Burkean discourse, focusing on only one novel in Smith's oeuvre can also elide the complex, evolving nature of that relation. An examination of Smith's didacticism in her most radical novels reveals an author who consistently engages with a past-oriented philosophy she loathes but which she views increasingly as more pervasive, entrenched, and powerful. Immersed in an imagined Britain in which Burkean discourse thrives to varying degrees, each set of heroes in the novels studied here struggles with the oppressive offshoots of a cultural adherence to 'the principle of inheritance'; the price of resistance grows higher in each novel, that is, while the prospects for change at home become increasingly dire. Reading Smith's best-known radical novels in light of Burke not only contextualizes the transference of her hopes for political reform from France and England to America that critics have recently noted,[81] but it also provides a powerful example of 'the sense of loss and confusion' that, modern scholarship reports, overcame British reform movements at the turn of the nineteenth century.[82]

Notes

1. J. J. McGann, *The Romantic Ideology: A Critical Investigation* (Chicago, IL: University of Chicago Press, 1983).
2. R. Ingpen and W. E. Peck (eds), vol. 7 of *The Complete Works of Percy Bysshe Shelley* (New York: Gordian Press / London: Ernst Benn, 1965), p. 122; H. E. Rollins (ed.), vol. 1 of *The Letters of John Keats* (Cambridge, MA: Harvard University Press, 1958), p. 224.
3. B. Tarling, '"The Slight Skirmishing of a Novel Writer": Charlotte Smith and the American War of Independence', in J. Labbe (ed.), *Charlotte Smith in British Romanticism* (London: Pickering & Chatto, 2008), pp. 71–86, on p. 71.
4. I. Ferris (ed.), *The Old Manor House*, in S. Curran (ed.), vol. 6 of *The Works of Charlotte Smith* (London: Pickering & Chatto, 2006), pp. vii–xxii; L. Fletcher, *Charlotte Smith: A Critical Biography* (Basingstoke, UK: Macmillan / New York: St. Martin's Press, 1998) and 'Charlotte Smith's Emblematic Castles', *Critical Survey*, 4 (1992), pp. 3–8; E. Ty, *Unsex'd Revolutionaries: Five Women Novelists of the 1790s* (Toronto, ON: University of Toronto Press, 1993); J. H. McGavran, Jr, 'Smuggling, Poaching and the Revulsion against Kinship in *The Old Manor House*', *Women's Writing*, 16 (2009), pp. 20–38; M. Wheeler, 'Charlotte Smith's Historical Narratives and the English Subject', *Prism(s)*, 10 (2002), pp. 7–18; and Tarling, '"The Slight Skirmishing of a Novel Writer"'.
5. See J. G. A. Pocock, Introduction, in J. G. A. Pocock (ed.), *Reflections on the Revolution in France* (Indianapolis, IN: Hackett, 1987), pp. vii–lvi, on pp. vii and xlvi.
6. For a reading of West's *A Tale of the Times* as a response to Smith's *Desmond*, see S. A. Ford, 'Tales of the Times: Family and Nation in Charlotte Smith and Jane West', in A. O. Herrera, E. M. Nollen, and S. R. Foor (eds), *Family Matters in the British and American Novel* (Bowling Green, OH: Bowling Green State

University Popular Press, 1997), pp. 15–29. See also M. Woodworth, Chapter 2 of this volume, p. 47.

7. C. Smith, *Desmond*, ed. A. Blank and J. Todd (Peterborough, ON: Broadview Press, 2001), p. 49.

8. Ibid., pp. 48 and 296.

9. Bethel's description of 'his ward's passion as "the absurd system you [have] built"', Conway notes, 'call[s] into question both the revolution and Desmond's love and mak[es] clear the connection between the two "events"' (A. Conway, 'Nationalism, Revolution, and the Female Body: Charlotte Smith's *Desmond*', *Women's Studies*, 24:5 (1995), pp. 395–409, on p. 401).

10. Smith, *Desmond*, p. 59.

11. Ibid., p. 59.

12. See A. Mellor, *Mothers of the Nation: Women's Political Writing in England, 1780–1830* (Bloomington and Indianapolis, IN: Indiana University Press, 2000), p. 107; A. Blank and J. Todd (eds), Introduction to *Desmond* (Peterborough, ON: Broadview Press, 2001), p. 22; S. J. Wolfson, *Romantic Interactions: Social Being and the Turns of Literary Action* (Baltimore, MD: Johns Hopkins University Press, 2010), p. 292, n. 9; and M. L. Wallace, 'Crossing from "Jacobin" to "Anti-Jacobin": Rethinking the Terms of English Jacobinism', in J. Cass and L. H. Peer (eds), *Romantic Border Crossings* (Aldershot, UK and Burlington, VT: Ashgate, 2008), pp. 99–112, on p. 105.

13. Smith, *Desmond*, p. 54.

14. See G. Handwerk, 'Historical Trauma: Political Theory and Novelistic Practice in William Godwin's Fiction', *Comparative Criticism*, 16 (1994), pp. 71–92, and 'History, Trauma, and the Limits of the Liberal Imagination: William Godwin's Historical Fiction', in T. Rajan and J. M. Wright (eds), *Romanticism, History, and the Possibilities of Genre: Re-Forming Literature 1789–1837* (Cambridge: Cambridge University Press, 1998), pp. 64–85.

15. Smith, *Desmond*, pp. 62, 64, and 65.

16. Ibid., p. 313.

17. For an insightful reading of Bethel's role in the novel, see W. Fuson, 'Cosmopolitanism and the Radical Politics of Exile in Charlotte Smith's *Desmond*', *Eighteenth-Century Fiction*, 25:1 (2012), pp. 37–59.

18. E. Burke, *Reflections on the Revolution in France*, in P. Langford (ed.), vol. 8 of *The Writings and Speeches of Edmund Burke* (Oxford: Clarendon Press, 1981–), pp. 83–84.

19. Smith, *Desmond*, p. 50.

20. Ibid., pp. 317 and 122.

21. Ibid., p. 229.

22. See Burke, *Reflections*, pp. 72 and 146–47.

23. Ibid., pp. 146–47.

24. Ibid., p. 70.

25. T. Paine, *Rights of Man* (1791–92), in M. Philp (ed.), *Rights of Man, Common Sense, and Other Political Writings* (Oxford and New York: Oxford University Press, 1995), p. 92.

26. For early readings that consider Smith's use of the domestic sphere to comment on the public, see D. Bowstead, 'The Epistolary Novel as Ideological Argument', in M. A. Schofield and C. Macheski (eds), *Fetter'd or Free?: British Women Novelists, 1670–1815* (Athens, OH and London: Ohio University Press, 1986),

pp. 237–63; K. Binhammer, 'Revolutionary Domesticity in Charlotte Smith's *Desmond*', in L. Lang-Peralta (ed.), *Women, Revolution, and the Novels of the 1790s* (East Lansing, MI: Michigan State University Press, 1999), pp. 25–46; A. W. Flanders, 'An Example of the Impact of the French Revolution on the English Novel: Charlotte Smith's *Desmond*', in C. E. Lucente and A. C. Labriola (eds), *The Western Pennsylvania Symposium on World Literatures, Selected Proceedings: 1974–1991, A Retrospective* (Greenburg, PA: Eadmer, 1992), pp. 145–50; J. D. Miller, 'The Politics of Truth and Deception: Charlotte Smith and the French Revolution', in A. Craciun and K. E. Lokke (eds), *Rebellious Hearts: British Women Writers and the French Revolution* (Albany, NY: State University of New York Press, 2001), pp. 337–63; and E. Wikborg, 'Political Discourse versus Sentimental Romance: Ideology and Genre in Charlotte Smith's *Desmond*', *English Studies*, 78:6 (1997), pp. 522–31.
27. Smith, *Desmond*, p. 333.
28. Ibid., p. 292.
29. Ibid., p. 384.
30. Fletcher, *Charlotte Smith*, p. 170. See also Miller, 'The Politics of Truth and Deception', p. 344.
31. E. R. Napier, 'Charlotte Smith', in M. C. Battestin (ed.), vol. 2 of *British Novelists, 1660–1800*, vol. 39 of *Dictionary of Literary Biography* (Detroit, MI: Gale, 1985), pp. 433–40, on p. 437.
32. See Fletcher, 'Charlotte Smith's Emblematic Castles'.
33. Smith, *The Old Manor House*, ed. J. Labbe (Peterborough, ON: Broadview Press, 2002), p. 40.
34. Ibid., pp. 43, 47, 102, 238, and 160.
35. Ibid., p. 49.
36. Burke, *Reflections*, p. 70.
37. Paine, *Rights of Man*, p. 92.
38. Smith, *The Old Manor House*, p. 429.
39. Ibid., p. 153.
40. Ibid., p. 49.
41. Ibid., p. 521.
42. Ibid., p. 42.
43. Ibid., p. 58.
44. Ibid., p. 506.
45. Ferris (ed.), *The Old Manor House*, p. xv.
46. Smith, *The Old Manor House*, p. 429.
47. S. Parkes, '"More Dead Than Alive": The Return of Not-Orlando in Charlotte Smith's *The Old Manor House*', *European Romantic Review*, 22:6 (2011), pp. 765–85.
48. Smith, *The Old Manor House*, pp. 391 and 395.
49. Ibid., pp. 238 and 160.
50. For a similar reading, see L. Maunu, '"Home Is Where the Heart Is": National Identity and Expatriation in Charlotte Smith's *The Young Philosopher*', *European Romantic Review*, 15:1 (2004), pp. 51–71.
51. Smith, *The Young Philosopher*, ed. Elizabeth Kraft (Lexington, KY: University Press of Kentucky, 1999), p. 340.
52. Ibid., p. 83.
53. Ibid., pp. 106 and 271.

Charlotte Smith and the Persistence of the Past   37

54. Ibid., pp. 93 and 92.
55. Ibid., pp. 93 and 91.
56. Ibid., p. 54.
57. Ibid., pp. 15 and 41.
58. Ibid., pp. 210, 186, and 211.
59. Ibid., p. 341.
60. Ibid., pp. 47–48.
61. Ibid., p. 163.
62. Ibid., p. 156.
63. Ibid., p. 199.
64. Ibid., p. 109.
65. Ibid., p. 135.
66. For an account of the novel's 'romantic' educations, see M. K. Fulk, 'Mismanaging Mothers: Matriarchy and Romantic Education in Charlotte Smith's *The Young Philosopher*', *Women's Writing*, 16:1 (2009), pp. 94–108.
67. Smith, *The Young Philosopher*, p. 30.
68. Ibid.
69. Ibid., p. 169.
70. Ibid., p. 352. For Smith's increasing identification with America as a site of utopic possibility, see W. D. Brewer, 'Charlotte Smith and the American Agrarian Ideal', *English Language Notes*, 40:4 (2003), pp. 51–61; N. E. Johnson, '"Seated on Her Bags of Dollars": Representations of America in the English Jacobin Novel', *Dalhousie Review*, 82:3 (2002), pp. 423–39; E. Kraft (ed.), Introduction to *The Young Philosopher*, pp. xxviii–xxix; and Tarling, '"The Slight Skirmishing of a Novel Writer"', p. 86.
71. Smith, *The Young Philosopher*, pp. 172 and 152.
72. Ibid., p. 314. Kraft reads Laura and Glenmorris's escape from Sandthwaite Castle in similar terms, noting how they 'invoke and impersonate the ghosts of the past in order to escape a restrictive present in which they are limited by family prejudice and notions of aristocratic pride' (E. Kraft, 'Encyclopedic Libertinism and 1798: Charlotte Smith's *The Young Philosopher*', *The Eighteenth-Century Novel*, 2 (2002), pp. 239–72, on p. 261).
73. Smith, *The Young Philosopher*, p. 265.
74. Ibid., pp. 350 and 354.
75. Ibid., p. 353. See also Kraft, 'Encyclopedic Libertinism and 1798', p. 266.
76. Smith, *The Young Philosopher*, p. 350.
77. Ibid., p. 352. The narrator also refers to Delmont's impending exile as 'his temporary absence' (p. 353).
78. Maunu, '"Home Is Where the Heart Is"', p. 57, and Kraft, 'Encyclopedic Libertinism and 1798', p. 266.
79. Smith, *The Young Philosopher*, p. 352.
80. McGavran, 'Smuggling, Poaching and the Revulsion against Kinship', pp. 21–22.
81. See note 70 above.
82. N. E. Johnson, *The English Jacobin Novel on Rights, Property and the Law: Critiquing the Contract* (Basingstoke: Palgrave Macmillan, 2004), p. 155.

2 'Vehicles for Words of Sound Doctrine'

Jane West's Didactic Fiction

Megan Woodworth

Jane West is principally known as a contributor to the flood of anti-Jacobin fiction that swamped England in the 1790s. As a writer perceived to be on the wrong side of history in the liberal revolutions of the late eighteenth century, West and her work have been relegated to the status of back-bench reactionary villains. Even as scholars reconsider the political allegiances of other writers of the period whose works had been assumed conservative, opinion of West is slow to change. Claire Grogan's assessment is typical: her introduction to Elizabeth Hamilton's *Memoirs of Modern Philosophers* characterizes Hamilton as ideologically closer to Mary Wollstonecraft than Loyalist writers, including West, who reject reform, enshrine female inferiority, and defend the status quo.[1] Twentieth-century scholars more interested in radical writers dismiss West's novels as, to use Eleanor Ty's words, 'thinly disguised conduct books with obvious lessons'.[2] Even David Thame, who argues that greater attention should be paid to the complexities of West's seven novels, suggests, 'no one can deny her anti-Jacobin credentials'.[3] Despite a slight increase in critical interest in West in the last decade, the body of criticism remains small.

West's novels are undoubtedly didactic and narrator Prudentia Homespun's concerns about fiction, 'sophism', 'infidelity', and 'the times' seem stridently anti-Jacobin; however, her novels also contain threads of resistance to Homespun's reactionary bluster. Part of the problem with properly evaluating West's fiction, and novels from the 1790s more generally, is, as Miriam L. Wallace notes, the Jacobin/anti-Jacobin dichotomy that frames such discussions. Though these terms come from the 1790s, they were neither neutral nor uncontested. The labels constitute 'pro-government' propaganda; however, '[m]odern scholarship has contributed to reiterating and solidifying this over-determined opposition between English Jacobins and anti-Jacobins by accepting the polemical terms of *The Anti-Jacobin Weekly* and *Review*, and by using these publications to define the very terms at stake'.[4] Wallace offers a corrective, calling for novels of the 1790s to be 'read attentively' for how they use 'political romance and parody, how they engage larger political and social debates, and how they render both parodic and stock figures'; furthermore, she suggests that by ignoring the Jacobin/ anti-Jacobin dichotomy, 'we stand to develop a richer sense of how narrative

'*Vehicles for Words of Sound Doctrine*' 39

fiction contributed to constructing an engaged and engaging public sphere of ideological debate'.[5]

With this in mind, I will offer a reading of *The Advantages of Education* (1793) and *A Tale of the Times* (1799) that focuses on the narrative strategies employed and the kind of reading that the texts demand of their readers. April London suggests that Homespun 'marshals good and bad readers (both actual and fictional) in order to reinforce the need for critical engagement with the text' and illustrates her contention with an analysis of the interpolated tale within *A Gossip's Story* (1796).[6] The ability to read and interpret the story properly is associated with virtue, as the heroine Louisa Dudley is the only auditor able to uncover the story's moral. Homespun as narrator is almost more interesting to critics than West's novels themselves. As Lisa Wood observes, 'Prudentia's liminal status becomes the source of her narrative authority and the condition that enables and impels the narrative itself'.[7] However, her position also problematizes her claims to authority. As Susan Allen Ford argues, she gives domestic advice – particularly about the submission of wives – though she has no 'domestic ties of her own'.[8] Homespun's problematic authority also concerns Thame, who laments the conflation of Homespun and West and argues that the paired heroines typical of West's novels provide an instructive model for understanding the relationship between West and Homespun.[9] In drawing a further distinction between West and Homespun, I want to suggest that Homespun is an unreliable narrator whose anti-Jacobin ideology is routinely undermined by the actual events of the stories she narrates. The texts, I will demonstrate, consistently privilege private action over public speech. I contend that the actions of the text – which belong to West – are similarly privileged over Homespun's histrionics.

Essentially, I am suggesting that Homespun's moral pronouncements are weakened by the novels' 'tendency'. William Godwin employs this term to distinguish the author-defined moral from the tendency, the 'actual effect' the work is 'calculated to produce upon the reader'. Though Godwin suggests that tendency can elude authorial control and can only be 'completely ascertained' by the 'experiment' of reading,[10] in West's works the doubled author – West controlling the text behind the scenes and Homespun conspicuously on stage – allows West to encode a tendency for attentive readers. Careful reading was a particular concern of both eighteenth-century literary theory and conduct literature, which, as Katie Halsey explains, correlated the kind of reading undertaken to the value derived from that reading. Halsey borrows Samuel Coleridge's terms to note there was concern that 'much-reading' dominated 'hard-reading'.[11] Hannah More feared 'the indolent repose of light reading' would 'soften the mind' and 'impair' its 'general powers of resistance'.[12] Similarly, Mary Wollstonecraft deplored the effects of shallow reading and superficial learning and linked rational education to the 'progress of human virtue'.[13] The solution, Halsey notes, is not simply to read more difficult books but to engage 'meaningfully' with the text.[14]

The idea that West's novels contradict Homespun's stated morals is borne out by contemporary critical reaction to *A Tale of the Times*. As Thame notes, the *Analytical Review* disparaged the 'strange' 'contradictions between the statements of facts, the motives assigned for them, and the inferences deduced', which gave 'the whole history of Lady Monteith the air of a studied palliation to the conduct of some actual demirep'.[15] They recognize West's sympathy for and mitigation of faults in a character many critics argue is sacrificed in order to support conservative morality.

West's earliest work also complicates any easy identification of her social and political thought with 1790s conservative ideology.[16] Pamela Lloyd, author of the only critical biography of West, points to *Miscellaneous Poems, and a Tragedy* (1791), a collection that embraces liberty and independence and cites Britain as an inspiration for France's rejection of tyranny. 'Ode IV, 1789' discusses the importance of the 'rights of man, / Not built on variable laws, / But at his first creation giv'n' and describes them as a 'priviledge bestow'd by heaven' which is the source of man's 'generous love of independence'.[17] The poem expresses hope that France's newly-gained liberty and independence will inspire Spain, Asia, and the rest of the world still toiling in the bondage of mental and physical slavery to throw off a system in which 'Man's inherent right [of liberty] from brother Man requires'.[18] This ode, along with another entitled 'To Independence', suggests that West had ideas not quite consonant with her reputation as a reactionary.[19] Lloyd accounts for the influence of West's conduct books, published in 1801 and 1806, in establishing her reactionary credentials among twentieth-century scholars.[20] Perhaps Homespun's role as conservative orator is a pragmatic choice on West's part that enables her to dress her reformist message in conservative drapery to ensure readership: as Lisa Wood's data suggests, anti-revolutionary novels were more lucrative.[21] This coincides with Thame's claim that West was preoccupied with the sale and 'consumption' of her novels.[22] Furthermore, the possibility that West wrote stories encouraging reform despite Prudentia Homespun's conservative commentary aligns with Gerald Newman's contention that many apparently conservative novels did 'much more to subvert the established order than to uphold it'.[23]

This chapter looks beyond the question of partisan politics and explores the tendencies of West's first novel, *The Advantages of Education* (1793), and her third and most successful, *A Tale of the Times* (1799). West's primary concern is that readers of novels, of people, and of the world are properly able to decode what they encounter and, through reflection, make the correct choices based on that information. This end – of teaching both her characters and readers to read properly – is achieved through texts that play with stock characters and conventions from popular forms – romance, sentimental, and seduction narratives – and rely on a readership well versed in the plots of popular novels. Only careful readers can uncover West's more specific lessons about proper education, the right ordering of society, and the roles of men and women. The tendency revealed by such an interpretation is not a loyalist endorsement of the status quo but a careful corrective to abuses of power, the poor education of women, and the corrupting power of fashion.

Delight and Instruct: Balancing the Didactic and the Fictive in *Advantages of Education*

> [L]et us acknowledge, that next to those moral essays which breathe the wisdom of a Johnson or the suavity of an Addison, a well written novel is the best introduction to the knowledge of life and manners.[24]

Despite her own endorsement, West's novels are frequently ambivalent – and sometimes hostile – about the novel form. Homespun concludes a *Tale of the Times* by adverting to the novel's dangerous use as a weapon for the revolution, yet *The Advantages of Education*, a novel often regarded as less political than some of West's later fiction,[25] features a perfect marriage between form and didactic purpose and demonstrates fiction's positive effects in the hands of good readers.

The novel has been dismissed as a 'thinly fictionalized conduct book' by Claudia Johnson,[26] and this, combined with the notion that conservative didacticism must produce inferior fiction, means that there is little critical engagement with the novel. Daniel Schierenbeck's essay 'Reason and Romance: Rethinking Romantic Era Fiction Through Jane West's *The Advantages of Education*' stands out as the novel's only chapter-length study. He highlights the similarities between West's and Mary Wollstonecraft's philosophies of female education, rejection of romance, and promotion of reason in order to destabilize the critical constructs that obscure connections between apparently disparate texts. However, he continues to place West as an anti-Jacobin, though with a more fluid position on the conservative spectrum. By exploring the relationship between Homespun and West and exposing the gaps between their ideological positions, I will further destabilize West's conservative identity.

The Advantages of Education is certainly a novel of education. It is also a novel about novels, one aware of its own constructedness. Homespun reflects on her creative process, revealing her intentions to write an anti-novel with a plain heroine called Polly.[27] Homespun is forced to alter her plans in order to find an audience, but she continually reminds her readers of the difference between unrealistic popular confections and her text, which shelters its heroine from the usual plots and problems of sentimental novels. Instead, Maria is provided with examples of heroines West's readers would recognize from contemporary texts: her best friend Charlotte Raby and her mother Amelia Williams. Both women were educated by their fathers after their mothers died, though the fashionable Charlotte has no useful education, while Mrs Williams has an unusually masculine education. Each tries to influence Maria. Charlotte seeks to introduce Maria to the

42 *Megan Woodworth*

world – beginning with an invitation to a country-town masquerade – in order to help her secure a good husband. Mrs Williams redirects this 'young lady's entrance into society' narrative, gently guiding her daughter to recognize the emptiness of such fashionable ambitions and instead choose a life of benevolent action by teaching her to read beyond the surface.

In addition to demonstrating the damaging effects of a superficial education,[28] Charlotte is used to critique the idea that sentiment and sentimental narratives necessarily encourage right feeling and action. Charlotte responds to all kinds of distressing events with 'violent' floods of tears.[29] The account of her masquerade disappointments is one such event, and her 'mournful tale' rouses sympathy in naive Maria.[30] Homespun fills the role of Wollstonecraftian critic, gently mocking Maria for being moved by her friend's tale, which was neither 'unfortunate' nor 'distressing'.[31] Mrs Williams, conversely, tells a better story, one more worthy of engaging her daughter's sympathy, and, crucially, she explains the correct response to it. She details a charitable visit to an impoverished family afflicted by smallpox. The truly distressing scene – a corpse covered in a 'sack', ill and dying children, 'half naked' children, and a mother 'emaciated by famine'– inspires appropriate tears from Maria.[32] Mrs Williams's response goes beyond tears: she procures remedies and appeals to the parish officers to help the family, despite the fact that the father had been unworthy.[33] Maria learns to distinguish true from false distress and comes to understand that worthy narratives should not merely rouse emotions but spur ameliorative action.

Maria also learns that readers need proper preparation – through a good education – to respond properly. She relates the story to Charlotte who 'lamented exceedingly that she had not time to visit the poor herself; was shocked to hear that so much misery existed near her, which she knew nothing of'; and subsequently agrees to donate money.[34] Significantly, Maria administers aid to the needy, while Charlotte continues to shed indiscriminate sentimental tears. Charlotte receives Maria's tales of poverty the way she does any diverting tale of woe (particularly the ones she constructs for herself): she reads for the tears and does not reflect on why she cries. The money she donates is akin to her meaningless tears as each produces fleeting pleasure but fails to create any real sense of social responsibility. Thus when she finds herself short of funds, Charlotte recasts herself as the victim of tragedy. Maria's application is a 'torment' that causes 'vehement' distress.[35] Mr Raby satisfies his daughter's debt, but on Maria's departure, he begs her 'never more to tell his poor girl any melancholy stories, for her temper was too meek to bear them; and as he perceived that they deeply hurt her spirits, he positively must not have her made unhappy'.[36] This statement is more than a misreading; it is a twist on parental censorship of reading material since Mr Raby bans the 'stories' of his neighbours' sufferings because they cannot give pleasure.

The contrasting heroines have dissimilar parents. Mr Raby's attitude accounts for Charlotte's superficiality and her self-absorption. More problematically,

'Vehicles for Words of Sound Doctrine' 43

his position parodies fashionable attitudes to women's education and utility. While Mrs Williams takes care to show Maria the hardships of life and give her a sense of social purpose, Mr Raby does nothing to curb his daughter's desires. On the contrary, he creates an artificial environment in which her every whim is indulged, her petulance and extravagance are unpunished, and, most significantly, her ignorance is cherished as innocence. His parenting philosophy boils down to bribing Charlotte's affections: 'old people should not contradict and thwart their children's desires, for if they did, how could they expect the young ones should love them'.[37]

This idea seems consonant with Homespun's frequently drawn connections between filial obedience and affection,[38] but the reality is not so straightforward. As Gilbert West's epigraph on the title page indicates, all the 'pious duties which we owe / Our parents, friends, our country and our God' are the result of 'discipline alone and early culture'. The results of Mr Raby's and Mrs Williams's different parenting methods are exposed in the novel's inevitable conflicts over matrimony. Charlotte's suitor, Major Pierpont, is a man for whom 'gold had entirely usurped what ought to have been the seat of the softer passions', and who 'never thought of the fair sex but as an occasional amusement' and a 'means to recruit a decayed fortune'.[39] Mr Raby, suspecting a fortune hunter, objects to the match and dismisses him, much to Charlotte's disappointment. He orders a better suitor from his banker, one to be endowed with good temper, good conduct, and a good fortune: 'the last excellence was principally insisted upon'.[40] A vapid nabob is produced, but he is no match for Major Pierpont's practiced – and deceptive – social graces. Charlotte suffers an attack of lovesickness, producing 'violent hystericks', and Mr Raby's 'indulgent love' finally capitulates to Charlotte's matrimonial wishes despite his (somewhat) better judgement.[41]

Mrs Williams uses Charlotte's marriage to teach Maria about the proper foundations of conjugal love. She asks Maria to delve below the surface of Charlotte's attachment and analyse what qualities the Major possesses 'upon which love may, with propriety, be founded?'[42] Mrs Williams emphasizes that his 'specious' knowledge and 'negligent behaviour' is distressing to Charlotte, and though he is evidently handsome, Mrs Williams dismisses 'advantages, merely personal, as a motive for love'.[43] In exposing Charlotte's love as vanity, Mrs Williams teaches her daughter to see past the stories people tell about themselves and focus instead on what their actions reveal. These will prove important lessons for Maria's own brush with romance, the ostensible subject of the novel.

Maria's suitor, Sir Henry Neville, emerges on the scene like the knight of romance, chivalrously escorting her home and begging the good rustics for her name. However, he is undercut at every turn both by Prudentia Homespun's heavily ironic tone and the rational education and careful guidance Maria receives from Mrs Williams, who doubts 'the merit of his character, and the nature of his designs'.[44] Neville expects to be treated like a romance hero, with his contrived identity giving him an attractive air of mystery. As Homespun tartly observes, 'The lover, who had a few *aristocratic* notions (I use that word to prove my knowledge of modern politics), seemed to think it impossible that Mrs Williams should object, when acquainted with his rank and character'; however, because Mrs Williams 'judge[s] from principles very different from what influenced the generality of the world',[45] she is not taken in by romance, mystery, or convention. Neville is frequently allowed to look ridiculous. He acts 'the passionate lover; he lamented, sighed, gazed, swore it was impossible to abandon her; raved about sacrificing his own life to her scruples with indifference'.[46] His performance includes rushing back to the neighbourhood when Charlotte writes that Maria is dying of love; he is appropriately 'mortified' when Charlotte tells him Maria's fever has taken a favourable turn since the 'irruption' of measles.[47] He is also rendered ridiculous by Mrs Williams's ability to see through his seduction plot: her presence 'check[s]' his 'vivacity' and produces a 'gloomy reserve, or confused hesitation' in his manner.[48] The mother, usually absent from these plots, is a dragon safeguarding her daughter from the erring baronet.[49]

Mrs Williams guards her daughter primarily through narrative. The story of her youthful encounter with fashionable life and the near-tragedy of her unequal marriage counters Neville's elaborate constructions of character and plot. By this means, Mrs Williams exposes the dangers presented by fashionable men and unequal marriages. The episode illustrates Mrs Williams's – and the novel's – contention that young people would learn better from 'plain and unadorned' stories.[50] In some ways, Mrs Williams is the heroine of a sentimental novel. She is raised in isolation in a 'romantic part of Yorkshire' and educated by her father, whose death leaves her an 'unprotected orphan'.[51] He has left her with an important gift, however: 'instead of permitting me to avail myself of the indulgencies [*sic*] commonly granted to our sex, he insisted that I should think justly and reason correctly'.[52] Unfortunately, as Schierenbeck also notes,[53] even masculine education is insufficient to save her from the snares of fashionable life and the problems associated with being dependent on people who live beyond their means and supplement their income by gambling.

The pitfalls of inferior training are explored in the history of Maria's father, who attained his fortune as a minor and was manipulated by 'base flatterers', 'miscreants' who 'initiated' him into an 'early course of dissipation'.[54] He initially tries to seduce his future wife; however, unlike the more villainous Neville who has a 'bad heart', Williams possessed a 'compassionate heart, and a generous disposition'.[55] He offers to marry her instead, despite the disparity in their fortunes, and in her desperation she agrees.

Mrs Williams's history illustrates the undesirability of unequal marriage. Mr Williams, conscious of his own superiority, tries to compensate for his wife's lowly status by forbidding her to resume her friendship with a tradesman's wife.[56] The injustice of his pretended superiority is particularly striking to the reader who is familiar with Mrs Williams's 'generous, exalted, and independent mind'.[57] These events undercut Mrs Williams's assertions about the need for socio-economic equality between potential spouses and reveal that moral and intellectual equality are imperative. Further, Mrs Williams's history illustrates a crisis in male education and its disastrous consequences for women, which in some cases cannot be mitigated by female education.

While Mrs Williams has received an excellent masculine education, many of the novel's male characters have not. Significantly, a man's educational attainment is directly correlated to his respect for women. Those poorly-educated characters – Mr Williams, Sir Henry Neville, Major Pierpont, and Mr Raby (all of whom move in fashionable circles, by virtue of birth or fortune) – regard women as lesser creatures: either as beings who exist for their sexual or financial gratification or as fragile creatures who must be kept happy at all costs. Neither position acknowledges the human dignity, immortal soul, and above all, the subjectivity of women. Edmund Herbert is the remedy to this patriarchal blindness. His worthy professional-class parents instilled within him solid English virtues, identical to those West extols in her poetry. His 'characteristic frankness', indicating 'manly virtue which acts with full force upon a heart of conscious independence, and glowing with courage and honour', presents a sharp contrast to Neville's duplicity and artful prevarications.[58] Herbert's refreshingly unfashionable values are further illustrated by his 'blunt habit', which disconcerts the 'fine gentlemen of his acquaintance' accustomed to flattery from their inferiors in fortune and status, but secures the 'esteem of the discerning few, who knew how to value integrity and truth'.[59] He refuses to collude with unscrupulous men and instead provides information about Neville's true character that could save Maria from ruin, unlike Major Pierpont who is 'too much a modern man of honour' to 'spoil the Baronet's design'.[60] The villagers, among the discriminating few, identify Herbert as a 'friendly honest fellow',[61] and Maria herself demonstrates the success of her education by recognizing the value of Herbert's honest affections and the emptiness of Neville's passionate demonstrations.

Maria chooses to save herself, armed with a thorough education in practical hermeneutics and a parent who exercises her authority with a light hand. Indeed, Mrs Williams well knows that '[p]arental opposition generally increases love'[62] – a truth illustrated in Charlotte Raby's experience. West takes the power from the seducer by enabling her heroine to say no. The seduction narrative is inverted into a revenge-fantasy as the seducer is punished with death while the heroine lives. Indeed, Neville is as much altered as any fallen woman: he was 'no longer the man of ease and address, the ornament of society, and the delight of all who knew him'. Caught 'in the net which he had spread for the destruction of others', he chooses to take his own life rather than suffer the consequences of his actions.[63]

Throughout the novel, the forward momentum of Maria's quest for knowledge stalls at crucial points in order to teach her how to read the world around her. The digressions – particularly her mother's history – supplement the deficiencies of her sheltered upbringing by giving her vicarious experience;

moreover, the novel demonstrates the didactic power of realistic narratives to help its heroine navigate the snares of courtship. The didactic form of *The Advantages of Education* justifies its existence and demonstrates its superiority over standard novels, which Homespun constantly criticizes. What results is not the endorsement of the status quo expected from a writer of West's anti-Jacobin reputation, but a call for improved education for women so that they can be equals in marriage to worthy men – and a call for men to be better educated so they can treat women properly.

The political consequences of failure are hinted at in *The Advantages of Education*. A worthy young woman, educated to be useful and charitable, is saved from a useless life as the wife of a corrupt man of fashion – or worse. Instead she is united to what Homespun calls a 'practical reformer', and together they work to improve their community, both materially and morally.[64] West would go on to explore the contrast of reformist ideas with the disastrous consequences of failure in her sensational 1799 bestseller, *A Tale of the Times*.

Complicating the Pattern: Re-evaluating *A Tale of the Times* (1799)

In *The Advantages of Education*, Mrs Williams reflects on her difficult history noting, '[r]ectitude of intention will not protect inexperience and credulity from many glaring errors'.[65] This maxim proves true in the tragic story of Geraldine Powerscourt, the beautiful, intelligent daughter of a Welsh baronet who marries a Scottish earl and is ruined by a scheming villain. Significantly, the lessons of *Advantages* also prove true: those who read well and can successfully interpret what they read are able to navigate the snares of the world. Geraldine's cousins, Henry Powerscourt and Lucy Evans, are the novel's exemplary readers.

Reading *A Tale of the Times* in the context of *Advantages* highlights the connections between the two texts and helps to elucidate *Tale*'s didactic thrust, which despite its anti-revolutionary language, is again about proper reading practices. West's didactic and reformist purposes can be uncovered by paying careful attention to the novel's form and characters, which serve to undermine Homespun's political pronouncements. Recognizing that West is not merely 'writing as' Homespun, as though it is a pseudonym,[66] is essential to separating Homespun's hysterical conservatism from West's subtle shifting of power from ineffective aristocrats to well-educated members of the middle classes.[67]

Homespun signals her disregard for fictional convention by beginning with the expected end of most sentimental, didactic, and domestic fictions: a wedding. Digressions are then used to explore the family histories of the bride and bridegroom, bringing a sense of impending doom to the festivities. James Macdonald, the bridegroom, is the latest in a succession of problematic earls of Monteith. His father died in a duel with his mother's lover,

'Vehicles for Words of Sound Doctrine' 47

while his mother died shortly thereafter, as Homespun mockingly phrases it, because 'the necessity of seclusion and oeconomical retrenchment, barbed the mortal dart of woe in the bosom of the fair inconsolable'.[68] Monteith is clearly the scion of a thoroughly vitiated family, and though incapable of deep thought or feeling he is not naturally bad. He was 'intended ... by nature to be humane and beneficent; but neglect of discipline and constant indulgence had introduced an indolent selfishness'.[69] Finally, he is a natural follower, not a leader, but '[u]nhappily for him, his birth and fortune obtruded him into notice, and placed him in situations to which his natural talents were unequal'.[70]

The head of the Powerscourt family is equally, though differently, problematic. Sir William seems to be a good conservative patriarch, far removed from the dissipated, spendthrift Macdonalds of Monteith. He is a 'singular character' who distinguishes himself from his peers in viewing himself as the 'conscientious guardian' of his estate 'rather than a self-accountable owner'.[71] His goodness is never in doubt; however, his judgement is frequently faulty. At forty he is told that a local well-bred woman is dying of love for him. He naively has no notion of her mercenary intentions, so he marries her according to the 'same principles which governed all his actions' – he could not bear to make (or see) 'a fellow-creature miserable'.[72] Lady Powerscourt's happiness depends on fashionable home décor and moving in the first circles. Sir William's capitulation to his wife's whims resembles the indulgence with which Mr Raby treats his daughter in *The Advantages of Education*. His unequal marriage threatens his stewardship of his ancestral seat and demonstrates the limits of his conscientiousness.

Together Sir William and Lord Monteith illustrate Thomas Paine's critique in *Common Sense* (1776) of hereditary power, which can raise 'rogues and fools' to power.[73] Those who are 'born to reign' are of a sphere that differs so 'materially' from 'the world at large', that they are 'frequently the most ignorant and unfit [to govern] of any throughout the dominions';[74] moreover, Lord Monteith illustrates the ruler 'poisoned' by the idea of his own importance, while Sir William's isolation and naivety suggest a man acting in a world that 'differs so materially' that he fails to understand other peoples' 'true interests'.[75] By presenting these flawed patriarchs, West reinforces many of the revolutionary critiques of aristocratic power. In *Advantages*, Homespun discourages the reader from attributing Mrs Williams's suspicions of Neville to prejudice against his class, distinguishing her from those 'querulous beings' who 'hate affluence and quality, merely because of its name and ever annex to the idea of a superior in fortune, that of an inferior in virtue'. Moreover, Homespun reveals that when Mrs Williams moved in fashionable circles she frequently witnessed 'the most exalted sentiments and consistent conduct, added to the lustre of wealth and nobility'. Despite Homespun's assurances, she provides no textual evidence that such beings exist.[76] *A Tale of the Times* furthers the critique of aristocracy as Lady Arabella Macdonald sinisterly takes

48 *Megan Woodworth*

Marie-Antoinette's apocryphal let-them-eat-cake indifference a step further, suggesting that the poor be put out of their misery – 'shoot them, as one does worn-out horses'.[77]

Anti-Jacobin interpretations of *A Tale of the Times* focus on the fate of the heroine and frequently ignore her flaws. Homespun lists those 'shades' in her character, which include a wit verging on levity, a desire for adulation, and a consciousness of her beauty.[78] While Geraldine is Homespun's tragic heroine, she is not West's heroine. The same paragraph in which Homespun brings 'my Heroine upon the stage' also introduces Lucy Evans, whose character was 'perfectly her own', 'cast in nature's most artless mould, and finished by the unremitting attentions of an intelligent mother and an exemplary father'.[79] Lucy is further distinguished for having 'read much' and 'thought more',[80] qualities that West's readers should recognize as desirable and important. Geraldine's failure to cultivate her understanding leads to her unequal marriage, in part because Geraldine plays Pygmalion, transforming a handsome young man she met at the Chester race ball into a paragon. She becomes 'deeply enamoured' with this 'creature of her own imagination',[81] illustrating a flaw that Geraldine regards as a gift: her propensity to determine 'characters from a mere outline,… condemning or admiring in the gross'.[82] She pities those people, like Mrs Evans, her teacher and surrogate mother, and Lucy, her cousin, who 'must judge from experience and consideration' while she is able to draw 'as clear inferences from an intuitive art of guessing'.[83]

The competing motives of these three characters appear once Lord Monteith makes his first matrimonial overtures. Monteith is decisively rejected by Sir William, whose reasoning reveals his tenacious grip on patriarchal prerogative: Sir William would rather Geraldine marry a 'worthy man who would keep up my family, than sink my name and fortune in that of any peer in the three kingdoms'.[84] Complicating matters, Sir William has already selected that 'worthy man': his young cousin Henry Powerscourt. Sir William has secretly planned to use Geraldine to bestow his fortune on this 'modest good lad' who he assumes will 'enjoy his fortune better, and know how to do more good with it, for having been without one when he was young'.[85] He has no inkling that Geraldine might object and takes her obedience for granted. As much as Geraldine's thoughtlessness contributes to her poor marriage choice, Sir William's demand for obedience exacerbates it. Remember Mrs Williams's observation from *The Advantages of Education* that '[p]arental opposition generally increases love'.[86] Geraldine is caught in a difficult position because Mrs Evans has instilled in her 'a veneration for her father's character' – though Homespun notes that 'her respect for such a father could only be founded on the persuasion which she had imbibed in her early youth of the natural superiority of his uncultivated understanding'.[87] Rather than submit or attempt to convince her father, she privately asks Henry to refuse Sir William's offer. Henry's diffidence and love of Geraldine prompt him to acquiesce.

'*Vehicles for Words of Sound Doctrine*'   49

The novel provides interpretive commentary at this juncture. Mrs Evans, discussing the conflict with Lucy, expresses some 'disapprobation', yet her 'uniform respect' for Sir William's character – no doubt the legacy of his generous relief of their distress – prevented her from 'expressing any doubt of the propriety or practicability of the scheme'.[88] Her 'artless openhearted' daughter, however, has no such qualms and is so convinced of the plan's 'impropriety' that she is compelled to reprobate 'the absurdity of allowing her friend so little influence in an affair so infinitely momentous to her own happiness'.[89] Though Mrs Evans cautions her daughter to 'conform a little to the notions of other people' and temper her 'tenacity of opinion',[90] Lucy is correct. Mrs Evans attempts to excuse Sir William, who is 'not apt to make observations on people or incidents which do not immediately affect himself', such as his daughter.[91] His myopic perception of the world damages the things he has sworn to protect.

The novel's promised villain, Edward Fitzosborne, is another crucial element in the anti-Jacobin interpretation of the text, yet his revolutionary credentials are not as clear-cut as Homespun would have us believe. He is the next iteration of the Gothic villain, suited to a tale that features 'no other labyrinth than the wiles of systematic depravity' nor 'any object more soul-harrowing than a deceived and entangled, but ultimately penitent heart'.[92] Eleanor Ty argues that Fitzosborne is one of the most compelling anti-heroes of the period, a 'satanic destroyer of domestic bliss' drawn from 'Milton's devil, Shakespeare's Iago, Richardson's Lovelace, a French *philosophe*, and a Godwinian'.[93] These numerous allusive debts complicate Homespun's veiled assertion that she owes her villain to a certain 'class of writers' noted for their 'liberality'.[94] Though she does not identify them, it is easy to assume these writers are Jacobins in general and Godwin in particular. Godwin ruefully noted that *An Enquiry Concerning Political Justice* (1793) had become standard fodder for popular novels,[95] but Fitzosborne's sentiments bear the stamp of controversial English Enlightenment figures, including Bolingbroke and Shaftesbury (who, incidentally, are the influential – and named – bogeymen responsible for corrupting West's eponymous *Infidel Father* (1802)).

As Fitzosborne manipulates Geraldine into dwelling on her unhappy marriage, he makes what Homespun flags as dangerous, revolutionary statements. In the first instance, Fitzosborne meditates on the advantages of redistributing property: 'Is it not a general advantage, that property should be transferred from an indolent sensualist to an active intelligent enterprising citizen?'[96] While this statement perhaps represents Godwin's idea that property should be put to better use, it is very different in spirit. Godwin imagines a 'community of men, who ... communicate instantly and unconditionally, each man to his neighbour that for which the former has not and the latter has immediate occasion'.[97] The exchange is freely given; there is no scheming nor is there a sense of entitlement to another's possessions. In contrast, Fitzosborne's philosophy is far more cynical. As Homespun reveals,

50   Megan Woodworth

'Private vices are public benefits' is one of the 'principles' that 'sanction' his 'more monstrous activities'.[98] This statement, which dates at least to Bernard Mandeville's *The Grumbling Hive* (1705), allies Fitzosborne with a longer tradition of corruption. Furthermore, his doubled character recalls both Bolingbroke, who saw no reason why his bad morals overshadowed his public service, and Chesterfield.

Chesterfield's advice to his son about how to succeed in public life seems to have provided a perfect pattern for Fitzosborne. For Chesterfield, 'the height of abilities is to have … a frank, open and ingenuous exterior, with a prudent and reserved interior; to be upon your guard, and yet, by a seeming natural openness, to put people off theirs'.[99] Fitzosborne models Chesterfield's 'man of sense', who 'sees, hears, and retains every thing that passes where he is'. Chesterfield cautions his son to 'mind not only what people say, but how they say it' as 'their looks frequently discover what their words are calculated to conceal'.[100] This perfectly describes how Fitzosborne detects that Geraldine's 'ruling foible' is vanity.[101] Fitzosborne continues to follow Chesterfield's advice in his persecution of both Geraldine and her transparent husband: 'Search everyone for his ruling passion' and once it has been uncovered, '[work] upon him by it, if you please; but be on your guard yourself against it'.[102] Like the earlier reformers who found fault with these sentiments, West works to expose discrepancies between public presentation and private character. In *Advantages*, Homespun cautions that public actions are 'equivocal': '[w]e all act and speak well, when in the presence of those, whose esteem we are anxious to acquire';[103] thus, private actions – when individuals are free from 'the restraint of observation' – serve as a better barometer of a person's 'natural aspect'.[104] Careful readers should be able to detect the difference, but Geraldine's propensity to form judgements on superficial information – her unwillingness to read thoroughly and critically – makes her easy prey for Fitzosborne.

The second instance is filtered through Geraldine's consciousness and demonstrates how far Fitzosborne's manipulations have been successful. She finds herself losing faith in a society that can produce such misery and begins to see the justice of Fitzosborne's claim that an 'intelligent reformer' is required by 'the present order of things'.[105] Homespun disdainfully declares she will leave 'lady Monteith's conclusion to disprove itself';[106] however, West provides a 'practical reformer' in Henry Powerscourt, who, united with Lucy Evans, will begin the task of improving the ruling class as regents of Powerscourt and educators of the Monteith children.

The conservative interpretation of *A Tale of the Times* focuses on Fitzosborne's seduction of Geraldine.[107] In Eleanor Ty's reading, fallen Geraldine represents 'what England could and would become if the Jacobins prevail'.[108] Ty recognizes *Paradise Lost* as the novel's most significant intertext. An epigraph from the poem sets the scene for Geraldine's rape, and afterward, Ty suggests, Geraldine's home is 'deftly recast' into 'a state of Eden that it never was': 'all the limitations of Monteith's character, his neglect, even his infidelity, albeit engineered by Fitzosborne, become forgotten. Instead the events after the fall focus on Geraldine's irrevocable error and the impossibility of returning to the prelapsarian state'.[109] This idealization of a flawed past, however, is similar to the conservative valorisation of pre-revolutionary days. While Homespun is quick to demonstrate her 'knowledge of modern politics',[110] the revolutionary characteristics she ascribes to her villain are, upon closer inspection, vices derived from English sources, demonstrating that before its invasion by Jacobins and radicals England was deeply flawed, morally and politically. To support the status quo – represented either by Sir William Powerscourt or Lord Monteith – is irresponsible. After they and Geraldine are removed from the narrative, Lucy and Henry Powerscourt replace them. In order to avoid the dangerous 'infidelity' of controversial philosophies old and new, West makes her 'practical' reformers explicitly Christian reformers.

An attention to secondary characters in *A Tale of the Times* reveals the narrative's reformist heart. Geraldine's deathbed wish is for Henry and Lucy to raise her children. The cycle of corruption that has haunted the Macdonald family since the reign of Charles II – which symbolizes England's own corruption, unmitigated by the naive goodness of country booby squires – will be broken. Though Ford suggests that, while Lucy and Henry's virtues are indisputable, the ending is ambivalent about the success of their blended family,[111] her evidence, Homepsun's worry that the 'opening graces' of these 'lovely children' will be undercut by their mother's (biological) legacy, is complicated because spoken by an unreliable narrator. It is true that Lucy and Henry's power is limited. The events of the novel show that they cannot undo the effects of poor education. Though they are properly educated and acquainted with the world but not corrupted by it, they cannot save Geraldine from the effects of her vanity and wilful blindness. Nor are they needed to bring Fitzosborne to justice (like his villainous predecessors, he destroys himself). Their true purpose is to shape the next generation of rulers. The problems of hereditary power will be mitigated by a practical education in quiet country living and Christian virtues. While the future seems to suggest a society that will be structurally similar – despite Homespun's fears about the 'annihilation of thrones and altars'[112] – it eschews the repression of women, uncritical deference to hereditary and patriarchal authority, and an unquestioning acceptance of tradition.

Conclusions

Swept up by Prudentia Homespun's overwrought statements about the dangers of 'sophism', 'infidelity', and the novel, it is easy to overlook the ways in which West's texts undermine her authority; moreover, Homespun's anti-Jacobin declamations obscure the alternative sources of apparently revolutionary contagion. At the end of *A Tale of the Times*, Homespun laments the state of popular novels, manipulated so that their 'insinuating

52   Megan Woodworth

narrative[s] and interesting description[s]' will 'fascinate the imagination without rousing the stronger energies of the mind'.[113] She concludes with the strong aspersion that the popular novel is 'an offensive weapon directed against our religion, our morals, or our government, as the humour of the writer may determine his particular warfare'.[114] However, West has been carefully training her readers to read beyond the surface – to consider the discrepancies between public statements (Prudentia) and private actions (the events of the plot) – as she warns in *Advantages*, private actions are the only ones that can be trusted. Public displays are far too often calculated to produce a certain effect; this also applies to narratives. The fact that some of the hidden depths of West's fiction have largely remained buried is evidence of the far-reaching consequences of allowing the 'Jacobin' and 'anti-Jacobin' labels to define the terms of our exploration of 1790s texts.

Notes

1. C. Grogan, Introduction to *Memoirs of Modern Philosophers* (Peterborough, ON: Broadview Press, 2000), pp. 9–26, on pp. 9, 21, 12.
2. E. Ty, *Empowering the Feminine* (Toronto, ON: University of Toronto Press, 1998), p. 102.
3. D. Thame, 'Cooking Up a Story: Jane West, Prudentia Homespun, and the Consumption of Fiction', *Eighteenth-Century Fiction*, 16 (2004), pp. 217–42, on p. 225.
4. M. L. Wallace, 'Crossing from "Jacobin" to "Anti-Jacobin": Rethinking the Terms of English Jacobinism', in P. Cass and L. H. Peer (eds), *Romantic Border Crossings* (Aldershot, UK and Burlington, VT: Ashgate, 2008), pp. 99–112, on p. 100.
5. Ibid., p. 112.
6. A. London, 'Jane West and the Politics of Reading', in A. Ribeiro and J. G. Basker (eds), *Tradition in Transition: Women Writers, Marginal Texts, and the Eighteenth-Century Canon* (Oxford: Clarendon, 1996), pp. 56–74, on p. 61.
7. L. Wood, *Modes of Discipline* (Lewisburg, PA: Bucknell University Press, 2003), p. 99.
8. S. Allen Ford, 'Tales of the Times: Family and Nation in Charlotte Smith and Jane West', in in A. O. Herrera, E. M. Nollen, and S. R. Foor (eds), *Family Matters in the British and American Novel* (Bowling Green, OH: Bowling Green State University Popular Press, 1997), pp. 15–29, on p. 18.
9. Thame, 'Cooking Up a Story', pp. 225–26.
10. W. Godwin, *The Enquirer* (London, 1797), p. 136.
11. Quoted in K. Halsey, *Jane Austen and Her Readers, 1786–1945* (London: Anthem, 2012), p. 33.
12. Ibid., p. 32. See also P. Demers, Chapter 6 of this volume, p. 107.
13. Ibid.
14. Ibid., p. 34.
15. Quoted in Thame, 'Cooking Up a Story', p. 234.
16. Increasingly, critics have produced more nuanced evaluations of West's work: Caroline Gonda (1996), Pamela Lloyd (1997), David Thame (2004), Daniel Schierenbeck (2009), Angela Rehbein (2011), Richard de Ritter (2011), Woodworth (2011) and Fiona Price (2012) have uncovered many ways that her work

is more complicated and less stridently anti-revolutionary than previously supposed. Lloyd's unpublished dissertation remains the only book-length study.

17. J. West, 'Ode IV: for the year 1789 Written on New Year's Day 1790', in *Miscellaneous Poems, and a Tragedy* (York, 1791), pp. 25–33, lines 46–50.

18. Ibid., line 110.

19. As I have argued elsewhere (*Eighteenth-Century Women Writers and the Gentleman's Liberation Movement* (Aldershot, UK and Burlington, VT: Ashgate, 2011)), West's attention to independence in the early 1790s problematizes her association with conservatism. As Matthew McCormack notes, independence would not become a loyalist theme until after 1800 (*The Independent Man* (Manchester, UK: Manchester University Press, 2005), p. 126, 143).

20. P. Lloyd, 'Jane West: A Critical Biography' (PhD diss., Brandeis University, 1997), p. 101.

21. Wood, *Modes of Discipline*, p. 77.

22. Thame, 'Cooking Up a Story', p. 219.

23. G. Newman, *The Rise of English Nationalism: A Cultural History, 1740–1830* (London: Weidenfield, 1987), pp. 233–38.

24. J. West, *Letters to a Young Lady* (New York, 1806), p. 320.

25. See also D. Schierenbeck, 'Reason and Romance: Rethinking Romantic-Era Fiction Through Jane West's *The Advantages of Education*', in M. L. Wallace (ed.), *Enlightening Romanticism, Romancing the Enlightenment: British Novels from 1750 to 1832* (Aldershot, UK and Burlington, VT: Ashgate, 2009), pp. 69–84.

26. C. Johnson, *Jane Austen: Women, Politics, and the Novel* (Chicago, IL: University of Chicago Press, 1988), p. 6.

27. J. West, *The Advantages of Education* (London, 1793), vol. 1, p. 5.

28. See Schierenbeck, 'Reason and Romance', pp. 82–83.

29. West, *Advantages of Education*, vol. 1, p. 58.

30. Ibid., vol. 1, p. 59.

31. Ibid., vol. 1, p. 60. Schierenbeck cites the following passage, which illustrates Wollstonecraft's critical approach in reviews:

The best method, I believe, that can be adopted to correct a fondness for novels is to ridicule them; not indiscriminately, for that would have little effect; but, if a judicious person, with some turn for humour, would read several to a young girl, and point out both by tones, and apt comparisons with pathetic incidents and heroic characters in history, how foolishly and ridiculously they caricatured human nature, just opinions might be substituted instead of romantic sentiments. (vol. 5 of *The Works of Mary Wollstonecraft*, ed. J. Todd and M. Butler, 7 vols (London: Pickering & Chatto, 1989), p. 185) See also J. Sadow, Chapter 4 of this volume, p. 78.

32. West, *Advantages of Education*, vol. 1, p. 61.

33. Ibid., vol. 1, p. 62.

34. Ibid., vol. 1, p. 69.

35. Ibid., vol. 1, pp. 73–74.

36. Ibid., vol. 1, pp. 74, 75.

37. Ibid., vol. 1, pp. 52–53.

38. Ibid., vol. 1, pp. 36, 97.

39. Ibid., vol. 1, p. 112.

40. Ibid., vol. 1, p. 98.

41. Ibid., vol. 1, pp. 109, 110.
42. Ibid., vol. 1, p. 117.
43. Ibid., vol. 1, p. 117.
44. Ibid., vol. 1, p. 204.
45. Ibid., vol. 1, p. 158, West's emphasis.
46. Ibid., vol. 1, p. 159.
47. Ibid., vol. 1, p. 187.
48. Ibid., vol. 1, p. 216.
49. Ibid., vol. 1, p. 232.
50. Ibid., vol. 1, p. 170.
51. Ibid., vol. 2, pp. 100, 103.
52. Ibid., vol. 2, p. 97.
53. Schierenbeck, 'Reason and Romance', p. 84.
54. West, *Advantages of Education*, vol. 2, p. 111.
55. Ibid., vol. 1, p. 191; vol. 2, p. 111.
56. Ibid., vol. 2, p. 119.
57. Ibid., vol. 1, p. 237.
58. Ibid., vol. 1, p. 203.
59. Ibid., vol. 2, p. 35.
60. Ibid., vol. 2, p. 3.
61. Ibid., vol. 1, p. 208.
62. Ibid., vol. 1, p. 204.
63. Ibid., vol. 2, pp. 161–62.
64. Ibid., vol. 2, p. 203.
65. Ibid., vol. 2, p. 114.
66. E. Ty, *Unsex'd Revolutionaries: Five Women Novelists of the 1790s* (Toronto, ON: University of Toronto Press, 1993), p. 15.
67. *A Tale of the Times* has arguably received the most critical attention because of its politically-charged plot and characters (including Homespun). The novel frequently figures as an example of anti-Jacobin fiction in monographs about some element of Romantic-era fiction. The most famous examples include Marilyn Butler in *Jane Austen and the War of Ideas* (Oxford: Clarendon, 1975), pp. 103–5) and Claudia Johnson in *Jane Austen: Women, Politics and the Novel* (pp. 6–9). Their analyses of West's endorsement of Burkean values have been tremendously influential. Longer readings of the novel are relatively rare. Eleanor Ty links Geraldine's fate with that of the nation in *Empowering the Feminine* (1998); Susan Allen Ford sees *Tale* as a conservative re-working of Charlotte Smith's *Desmond* in 'Tales of the Times' (1997); Woodworth also considers the affinities between Smith and West in *Eighteenth-Century Women Writers and the Gentleman's Liberation Movement* (2011); Morgan Rooney devotes a substantial portion of a chapter to exploring the novel's use of Burkean historical discourse in *The French Revolution Debate and the British Novel, 1790–1814: The Struggle for History's Authority* (Lewisburg, PA: Bucknell University Press, 2013).
68. West, *Tale of the Times*, vol. 1 p. 20.
69. Ibid., vol. 1, p. 194. See also M. Rooney, Chapter 1 of this volume, p. 22.
70. Ibid., vol. 1, p. 195.
71. Ibid., vol. 1, p. 28.
72. Ibid., vol. 1, pp. 30, 61.

73. T. Paine, *Common Sense* in *Rights of Man, Common Sense, and Other Political Writings*, ed. M. Philp (Oxford: Oxford University Press, 2008), pp. 1–59, on p. 15.
74. Ibid., p. 17.
75. Ibid.
76. West, *Advantages of Education*, vol. 1, pp. 196–97. It is not until *The Infidel Father* (1802) that West presents any well-behaved, properly educated, suitably serious, and religious aristocrats.
77. West, *Tale of the Times*, vol. 2, p. 126.
78. Ibid., vol. 1, p. 102.
79. Ibid., vol. 1, p. 104.
80. Ibid., vol. 1, p. 105.
81. Ibid., vol. 1, p. 113.
82. Ibid., vol. 1, p. 225.
83. Ibid., vol. 1, p. 234.
84. Ibid., vol. 1, p. 122.
85. Ibid., vol. 1, p. 124.
86. West, *Advantages of Education*, vol. 1, p. 204.
87. West, *Tale of the Times*, vol. 1, pp. 130–31.
88. Ibid., vol. 1, p. 141.
89. Ibid.
90. Ibid., vol. 1, p. 142.
91. Ibid., vol. 1, p. 145.
92. Ibid., vol. 1, p. 6.
93. Ty, *Empowering the Feminine*, p. 106.
94. West, *Tale of the Times*, vol. 1, p. iv.
95. Grogan, 'Introduction', pp. 10–11.
96. West, *Tale of the Times*, vol. 2, p. 294.
97. W. Godwin, *An Enquiry Concerning Political Justice* (London, 1793), vol. 2, p. 836.
98. West, *Tale of the Times*, vol. 2, p. 294.
99. P. D. S. Chesterfield, *Lord Chesterfield's Letters* (Oxford: Oxford University Press, 1998), p. 105.
100. Ibid., p. 29.
101. West, *Tale of the Times*, vol. 2, p. 129.
102. Chesterfield, *Letters*, p. 44.
103. West, *Advantages of Education*, vol. 2, p. 202.
104. Ibid., vol. 2, p. 202.
105. West, *Tale of the Times*, vol. 3, p. 208.
106. Ibid.
107. See E. Ty and W. Stafford, *English Feminists and Their Opponents in the 1790s: Unsex'd and Proper Females* (Manchester, UK: Manchester University Press, 2002), pp. 89–90.
108. Ty, *Empowering the Feminine*, p. 102.
109. Ibid., p. 109.
110. West, *Advantages of Education*, vol. 1, p. 158.
111. Ford, 'Tales of the Times', p. 25.
112. West, *Tale of the Times*, vol. 2, p. 275.
113. Ibid., vol. 3, p. 388.
114. Ibid.

3 Epistolary Exposés

The Marriage Market, the Slave Trade and the 'Cruel Business' of War in Mary Robinson's *Angelina*

Sharon M. Setzer

After publishing her first major volume of poems in 1791, Mary Robinson made her sensational debut as a novelist in 1792 with *Vancenza; Or, the Dangers of Credulity*. Reputedly selling out before noon on the first day of publication, the two-volume novel set in fifteenth-century Spain reads, in some places, much like a Radcliffian re-telling of Robinson's scandalous love affair with the Prince of Wales in 1780.[1] As Robinson later told the story in her *Memoirs*, the Prince declared his love shortly after he saw her play the role of Perdita in a command performance of Shakespeare's *Winter's Tale* at Drury Lane.[2] If *Vancenza* exemplifies Robinson's tendency to revise the story of her life and turn it into novelistic capital, however, the cautionary tale also evinces her desire to claim moral authority in a public sphere where she had earlier won somewhat dubious celebrity as an actress, a royal mistress, and a flamboyant woman of fashion. By the end of *Vancenza*, Robinson's didactic voice is almost indistinguishable from that of her fictional Marchioness de Vallorie, a 'gracefully majestic' figure who not only warns against 'the dangers and calamities to which [unprotected women] are exposed' but also recommends 'the laudable pursuits of mental cultivation' over 'the tinsel blandishments of fashionable folly'.[3] More importantly perhaps, the Marchioness echoes the radical discourse of the 1790s as she decries the 'empty distinctions' of rank and wealth. Characterized as an 'affectionate monitress' and an 'excellent preceptress', the Marchioness figures Robinson's reinvention of herself as a moralist, one who would ultimately claim affiliation with the radical school of Mary Wollstonecraft rather than with the conservative camp of Hannah More.[4]

After *Vancenza*, Robinson made more controversial bids for moral authority as she wove explicit critiques of contemporary social and political injustices into the sentimental fabric of six subsequent novels set in the turbulent 1790s: *The Widow* (1794), *Angelina* (1796), *Hubert de Sevrac* (1796), *Walsingham* (1797), *The False Friend* (1799), and *The Natural Daughter* (1799). According to conservative commentators in the late 1790s, Robinson's fame as a poet was seriously compromised by her association with Joseph Johnson's circle of radical authors, which included Wollstonecraft, Mary Hays, and William Godwin. In his satiric poem *The Pursuits of Literature*, Thomas

Epistolary Exposés 57

James Mathias associated Robinson with Charlotte Smith, Elizabeth Inchbald, and other nameless women writers who were so 'frequently *whining* and *frisking* in novels' that 'girls' heads turn wild with impossible adventures, and now and then are tainted with democracy'.[5] Taking inspiration from Mathias, the Reverend Richard Polwhele included Robinson in a despicable Jacobin band of 'unsex'd females' led by Wollstonecraft.[6]

Although recent scholarship has called attention to the emergence of a radical feminist voice in Robinson's fiction, her epistolary novel *Angelina* typically receives no more than a passing nod.[7] One noteworthy exception is Adriana Craciun's overview of Robinson's radical politics, which includes a consideration of *Angelina* as a 'feminist meditation on arbitrary power, one in dialogue with Godwin and written by a close friend who addressed him as "my dear Philosopher"'.[8] While this characterization of *Angelina* usefully foregrounds the radical sentiments expressed in the novel, it distorts the chronology of Robinson's friendship with Godwin. Citing evidence in Godwin's diary, biographers concur that he did not meet Robinson until 9 February 1796, more than a month after the publication of *Angelina*.[9] A more substantive issue, however, is the complete effacement of Wollstonecraft's influence in the textual genesis of *Angelina*. Although I do not dispute Craciun's claim that it enters into 'dialogue' with Godwin's *Caleb Williams* (1794), I aim to show how *Angelina* is also a fictional mobilization of radical precepts articulated in Wollstonecraft's *Vindication of the Rights of Woman* (1792). As I read the novel, it is ultimately not so much a 'meditation on arbitrary power' as it is a polemical intervention in the 1790s war of ideas.

In 1795, the year in which *Angelina* was composed, the war of ideas between conservatives and radicals was inextricably related to the war between England and France, which had begun in February 1793. On 30 December 1794, the King addressed the House of Lords with a speech urging 'a vigorous prosecution of the just and necessary war'.[10] Although the King's will was endorsed by a majority vote in Parliament, heated debate continued throughout 1795 as the ruinous effects of the war became increasingly apparent. While opposition newspapers routinely reported the numbers of casualties, they also editorialized on the government's callous indifference to suffering and its disregard for the will of the people, which was formally registered in numerous petitions to broker a peace with France. On a number of occasions, the daily papers also published charges that the King's ministers were amassing private fortunes as they selfishly promoted an '*unjust* and *unnecessary* war' that threatened to bankrupt and starve the nation.[11] The economic disparity between the few who dictated government policies and the masses that suffered from the consequences only exacerbated the resentment that erupted in street riots protesting the rising cost of bread and the nefarious practice of crimping (kidnapping young men to serve as soldiers).[12] Civil unrest came to a head on 20 October 1795, when an angry mob attacked the King's coach. Responding to the crisis, the Prime Minister, William Pitt, whipped up support for the notorious 'Two Bills' against

58   *Sharon M. Setzer*

Seditious Meetings and Treasonable Practices in November, and they were signed into law on 18 December 1795, less than two weeks before the publication of *Angelina*.

While the war with France played out on the Continent, it also extended to the Caribbean and forestalled efforts to abolish the slave trade. In 1792, the House of Commons had passed a compromise resolution to abolish the slave trade by 1796. But the measure stalled in the House of Lords and quickly lost support in the lower house as well after England became embroiled in war with France in 1793. By 1794, the Abolitionist movement, which had been initiated by Quakers in the 1780s, became associated, in loyalist circles, with pernicious Jacobin doctrines. When a modified version of the bill to abolish the slave trade was taken up in the House of Lords on 2 May 1794, for example, the Earl of Abingdon declared that it was 'founded upon French principles' and that it would produce 'all the direful effects necessarily flowing from, such principles, namely, those of insubordination, anarchy, confusion, murder, havock, devastation, and ruin'.[13] As the context indicates, Lord Abingdon feared that slave rebellions in the French colonies would spill over into English colonies in the West Indies. But he also harboured suspicions that the proposition to end the slave trade was a pretext for fomenting rebellion at home. Although William Wilberforce was the chief sponsor of the bill in Parliament, Lord Abingdon identified Thomas Paine's *Rights of Man* (1791–92) as the 'chief and best support' of a bill that contained 'seeds of other abolitions, different and distinct from that which it professes'.[14] After another unsuccessful effort to pass legislation against the slave trade in February 1795, Wilberforce took the floor in the House of Commons on 15 December 1795, to remind his colleagues that they had previously agreed to end the slave trade by 1 January 1796. Issuing this reminder in the midst of parliamentary debate over Pitt's Two Bills or 'Gagging Acts', Wilberforce remarked that 'a more proper time could not be chosen by the House, to shew their just regard to the Rights of Man, than when they were adopting measures to restrain the principles of anarchy and licentiousness'.[15] Having voted in favour of the Two Bills, Wilberforce, at this point, was clearly trying to distance himself and the Abolitionist cause from charges of Jacobinism. Robinson, meanwhile, might well have been wondering if government watchdogs would detect seditious passages in her forthcoming novel, *Angelina*, which clearly linked Abolitionist sentiments with radical support for the rights of man and woman.

Given the general antipathy towards women venturing into the realm of politics, Robinson had good reason to package her radical sentiments under the cover of a novel titled *Angelina*. As biographers have suggested, the thirty-six-year-old eponymous heroine is in some respects a beatific version of Robinson herself.[16] Although Angelina has no epistolary voice of her own in the novel that bears her name, other characters, repeatedly praising her virtues and her genius as well as her beauty, participate in the communal construction of a female ideal that encompasses much more than corporeal attributes. Wollstonecraft is now generally credited with writing the extremely positive assessment published in the *Analytical Review*, which praised Robinson's 'portrait of Angelina' for exhibiting 'an assemblage of almost every excellence which can adorn the female mind, beaming mildly through clouds of affliction and melancholy'.[17] Nonetheless, Angelina is still essentially a passive heroine living in retirement amid the ruins of an ancient castle in South Wales.[18]

Robinson's epistolary heroine, Sophia Clarendon, on the other hand, is a Wollstonecraftian re-creation of Rousseau's Sophia, the submissive heroine of *Émile*. As Wollstonecraft observed, the education of Rousseau's Sophia was based upon the erroneous principles that a woman should be taught the 'grand lesson' of obedience with 'unrelenting rigour' and that she should 'never, for a moment, feel herself independent'.[19] Although Robinson's Sophia has a tyrannical father who shares these principles, she also has a bluestocking aunt, Juliana Pengwynn, who supervised her education since infancy and cultivated her powers of reason, reflection, and resistance. Throughout much of the novel, these powers are severely tested as Sophia's father tries to coerce her into marrying a man that she does not love. Sophia asserts her independence, however, by running away from her father's home before sunrise on the morning appointed for the wedding, and she undergoes many subsequent trials including robbery, abduction, imprisonment, and temporary madness. Before the end of the first volume, she emerges as the Wollstonecraftian heroine of a novel that might have been more aptly titled *Sophia*, *The Runaway Daughter*, *Filial Disobedience*, or *Virtue in Resistance*.

Writing for the *Analytical Review*, Wollstonecraft (or someone who has been misidentified as Wollstonecraft) called attention to the radical thrust of *Angelina* by remarking:

> its principal object is to expose the folly and the iniquity of those parents who attempt to compel the inclinations of their children into whatever conjugal connections their mercenary spirit may choose to prescribe, and to hold forth to just detestation the cruelty of those, who scruple not to barter a daughter's happiness, perhaps through life, for a sounding title or a glittering coronet.[20]

With this trenchant account of Robinson's didactic purpose, the *Analytical Review* implicitly acknowledges *Angelina* as a fictional supplement to Wollstonecraft's polemical commentary on tyrannical parental authority and trifling aristocratic distinctions. Given the long-standing analogy between the family and the nation, knowing readers might have guessed that parental tyranny represented political tyranny.[21] Their expectations almost certainly would have been heightened by the review's approbation for the 'just, animated, and rational' sentiments that 'breathe a spirit of independence, and a dignified superiority to whatever is unessential to the true respectability and

60   *Sharon M. Setzer*

genuine excellence of human beings'.[22] Where other contemporary reviews apparently presupposed that *Angelina* targeted an audience of 'poor romantic girl[s]'[23] or 'ladies' who sought vicarious thrills from 'tales of wonder about caverns, rocks, woods, lakes, castles, abbies, and manor-houses',[24] the *Analytical Review* simultaneously dignified *Angelina* and its potential readers by suggesting that the novel had a purpose. As correspondents in the epistolary novel pick up various strains of Wollstonecraft's argument for the rights of women, they also condemn the slave trade and voice impassioned opposition to the British government's prosecution of the enormously costly war with France. Taken together, the overlapping exposés of the marriage market, the slave trade, and the 'cruel business' of war constitute a sweeping indictment of the moral bankruptcy threatening the nation.

Robinson lays the foundation for her critique of the marriage market in the first letter of the novel as Lord Acreland, writing to his friend Sir George Fairford in Wales, openly acknowledges his intention to profit from a lucrative traffic in women. Although he boasts 'one of the most splendid estates in the kingdom', Acreland confides that he is in want of a 'rich wife' to rescue his ancestral property from 'incumbrances' brought on by his 'folly on the turf' and 'connections among women of the most profligate description'.[25] According to Acreland, noblemen in his desperate straits have the 'blessed consolation' of knowing that they can always barter social rank for financial capital, especially in the 'overgrown metropolis' of London, where 'we constantly behold young women of little birth, and great fortune, as indelicately exposed to sale, as our horses or our hounds'.[26] After only one month of surveying the available goods, Lord Acreland reports that he has made a 'convenient bargain' to marry Sophia Clarendon, the eighteen-year-old daughter of a wealthy London merchant who 'pants for an alliance with nobility'. According to the legal documents subsequently drawn up to ratify the bargain, Lord Acreland stands to gain 'seventy thousand [pounds] down' upon his marriage to Sophia as well as the extensive property of Clarendon Abbey after her father's death.[27] Sir Edward Clarendon, for his part, stands to gain the social consequence of having a daughter who bears the title of Countess. While the men congratulate themselves upon having struck 'no bad bargain', Sophia decries the ambition of a 'blind and mistaken parent' who would seek to 'ennoble his family' through 'the purchase of a title for an only daughter'.[28]

Lord Acreland's analogy between young women and horses or hounds gives a sportsman's inflection to Wollstonecraft's observation that nothing can be 'more indelicate than a girl's *coming out* in the fashionable world' because it is essentially bringing 'to market a marriageable miss'.[29] Wollstonecraft's implied analogy between the marriage market and the African slave trade was later pushed to ridiculous, and arguably offensive, extremes in Hannah More's satiric 'Hints towards Framing a Bill for the Abolition of the White Female Slave Trade, in the Cities of London and Westminster'. There, More observes, 'a multitude of fine fresh young slaves are annually imported at the age of seventeen or eighteen, or, according to the phrase of the despot [Fashion], *they come out*.[30] Despite their important philosophical and political differences, Wollstonecraft and More both suggest that the marriageable miss/slave willingly participates in the degrading spectacle of her own commodification. Robinson's Sophia, however, repeatedly expresses her aversion to being 'bartered for like a slave'.[31] The analogy, in her case, carries particular force because her tyrannical father is also a 'black trader' and the proud owner of plantations and slaves in the West Indies.

Although Thomas Paine, following John Locke and others, had famously declared that 'man has no property in man',[32] Sir Edward Clarendon never questions his right to own slaves or to claim ownership of his daughter. On more than one occasion he explicitly refers to Sophia as his 'property', and he insists upon his right to 'dispose' of her as he pleases.[33] Expecting unconditional obedience from his daughter, as from his slaves, Sir Edward reproaches Sophia for having written 'verses on Independence' with a diamond on a window of the hermitage at Clarendon Abbey. Incensed by the topic of her verses as well as by the very act of 'scribbling poetry', Sir Edward blusters,

> what have you to do with independence?... Are you not obliged to me ... for your daily subsistence? Do you know that independence is a sort of freedom – and freedom is liberty – and liberty spurns all constraints, as a body may say![34]

Evincing a Burkean terror of 'French' liberty, which had inspired slave revolts in the West Indies, Sir Edward subsequently seems to be translating the plantocratic proscription against slave literacy into a rule for female conduct when he declares, 'Women have no business either to write or to read'.[35] Sir Edward's association of Sophia with his slaves rises to the surface much later in the novel, after his sister, Lady Watkins, expresses admiration for Sophia's 'independent spirit'. Sir Edward arrogantly replies,

> independence is the stalking-horse for all sorts of absurdities. I should like to know what would become of my plantations if such doctrines were encouraged.... Hav'n't I made a fortune by slavery? And I warrant independence had nothing to do in the profits of *black* traffic.[36]

As Sophia's Aunt Juliana observes, there is not simply an analogy between Sir Edward's attitudes towards his slaves and his daughter but a causal connection. Taking Sir Edward to task for his inhumanity on both counts, Juliana asserts, 'the detestable human, or rather inhuman traffic, by which you have ... enhanced your fortune, contaminated your heart, till all its feelings are deadened to the supplications of helpless innocence'.[37]

While Robinson's representation of Sir Edward Clarendon strips away the mask of respectability worn by many slave owners living in England, her representation of Sophia promotes the virtue of resistance to tyrannical authority. After her epistolary confidante, Mrs Horton, asserts that 'reason,

62   *Sharon M. Setzer*

nature, justice, and humanity, forbid the alliance' with Lord Acreland,[38] Sophia responds,

> I never will become a voluntary victim.... My father has the free disposal of my fortune; but my mind is still unshackled! I may be driven from his house; – stung by his reproaches, condemned by the world; but will there not be virtue in resistance? If I consented to marry Lord Acreland, I should detest him; I should consider him in no other light, than that of my destroyer; I should shrink from his gaze, as the slave does from his tyrant; I should be the purchased object of his fancy, the legal mistress of his caprice; the disgrace of my family, – and perhaps, at last, the victim of some beloved seducer![39]

Sophia's language here resonates with the revolutionary doctrines articulated in Wollstonecraft's two *Vindications*. In *The Rights of Men*, Wollstonecraft averred,

> A father may dissipate his property without his child having any right to complain; – but should he attempt to sell him for a slave, or fetter him with laws contrary to reason; nature, in enabling him to discern good from evil, teaches him to break the ignoble chain.[40]

In the *Rights of Woman*, Wollstonecraft emphasized mental bondage when she criticized the 'absurd duty, too often inculcated, of obeying a parent only on account of his being a parent'. Such blind obedience, Wollstonecraft declared, 'shackles the mind, and prepares it for a slavish submission to any power but reason'. On the Continent, where women are 'particularly subject to the views of their families, who never think of consulting their inclinations', Wollstonecraft suggests, it is almost axiomatic that 'dutiful daughters become adulteresses'.[41] By implication at least, Sophia's Wollstonecraftian claim that her 'mind is still unshackled' arises from a consciousness that filial obedience could ultimately render her susceptible to the blandishments of 'some beloved seducer'.

Although he has no direct communication with Sophia, Sir George Fairford picks up the slave analogy as he urges Lord Acreland to extricate himself from the bargain that he has struck with Sir Edward Clarendon. Insofar as Sophia's fortune comes from her father's sordid dealings in the West Indies, Acreland's willingness to make the bargain in the first place exemplifies the moral compromises made by many members of a ruling class who depended upon the profits from colonial slavery to maintain their country estates in England.[42] As Fairford tells Acreland, however, any financial gains will be more than offset by his loss of honour and peace of mind:

> You will be some thousands the richer; but you will have millions of self-wounding reproaches, when you behold your lovely wife, disgusted with your attentions, shrinking from you, as the slave does from

Epistolary Exposés 63

his tyrant; pining under the misery of compulsive obedience – a purchased victim!... The only sensation that fills the bosom of a devoted slave – is hatred.[43]

In presenting these 'hard truths' to dissuade his friend from entering into a mercenary marriage, Fairford makes it very clear that the problem is not simply the tainted source of Sophia's fortune but the moral turpitude of a bargain that replicates the power structure of colonial slavery and degrades everyone involved. Although the immediate purpose of Fairford's analogy between Sophia and a chattel slave is to chasten Lord Acreland, the letter also carries a clear Abolitionist message, one that contests the plantocratic narrative of the benevolent master and the grateful slave.

As Karen Sánchez-Eppler and many others have observed, 'the alliance attempted by feminist-Abolitionist texts is never particularly easy or equitable'. In any 'metaphoric linking of women and slaves', there is always the potential to efface 'the particularity of black and female experience, making their distinct exploitations appear as one'.[44] More problematic still, as Susan Fraiman suggests, is the 'imperialist' tendency 'to exploit the symbolic value of slavery, while ignoring slaves as suffering and resistant historical subjects'.[45] Although Robinson is not entirely blameless on either account, she nevertheless goes out of her way on a number of occasions to remind readers that slavery is not simply a trope for female subjugation but a brutal reality. Juliana Pengwynn, for example, scolds Sir Edward Clarendon for participating in the 'barbarous traffic' that has enabled him to amass treasure 'sullied by the tears, if not the blood of persecuted slaves'.[46] When he boasts of the profits that he has made through '*black* traffic', Lady Watkins issues an even stronger rebuke:

> Can the colour of a human creature authorize inhumanity? I wish the colour of all hearts could be scrutinized, and the black ones sent to expiate their crimes on the scorching sands of Africa. They would then behold the miseries they deride; they would then confess, that the poor negro can feel the scourge – can faint in the burning rays of noon – can hope, can fear – can shrink from torture, and sigh for liberty as well as the European![47]

Although she does not completely dismantle a value-laden opposition between the colours black and white, Lady Watkins radically destabilizes the prevailing dichotomy between the savage African and the civilized European as she boldly challenges the plantocratic narrative that slaves feel little, if any, pain. Refusing to be silenced by Sir Edward's angry directive to 'mind [her] own business', Lady Watkins asserts, 'This is my business ... 'tis the business of every friend to humanity'.[48]

Such heated exchanges over the slave trade in *Angelina* are certainly more radical than the well-known dinner-table conversation in Hays's *Memoirs*

64   Sharon M. Setzer

of Emma Courtney, published later in 1796. As Katie Trumpener notes, the scene in *Emma Courtney* not only shows '[t]he parallels between West Indian slavery and the domestic oppression of European women', but also demonstrates '[t]he clear mandate of the abolitionist ... to speak out for what is right: to bring hidden connections to light, to break a tacit silence about the subject of slavery, and to break the more general taboo against political argument in mixed company'.[49] Interestingly, however, Hays does not show Emma actually participating in the debate over the slave trade. By her own account, she only 'listened with delight' and 'secretly gloried' in 'the virtue and abilities' of her beloved Augustus as he 'exposed and confuted the specious reasoning and sophistry of his antagonist'.[50] Robinson, in contrast, represents two women who directly confront a slave owner in their own family, and she puts their exact words on the page, offering models for active engagement in the debate over the slave trade. By doing so, of course, Robinson leaves herself open to charges of using characters as 'mouthpieces for doctrine'.[51] If Robinson's approach is more heavy-handed than Hays's is, however, it is also more consistent with the feminist ethos of women writers who wanted to encourage other women to enter into political debate, to exert their influence in the home and beyond even if they had no voice in Parliament.

While Sophia's aunts are pleading with Sir Edward Clarendon, Robinson herself is clearly pleading with a much larger audience, one that included her lover, Banastre Tarleton, an MP from Liverpool who represented the slaving interests of the city and his own family. On 23 February 1796, the *Morning Post* reported that Tarleton had spoken out in the House of Commons on the dangers of preaching '*the Rights of* MAN to NEGROES!' Taking Tarleton to task, the *Post* inquired, 'How does the Honourable Member reconcile the barbarity of this sentiment to his vaunted principles of Liberty and Patriotism?' On 24 February, the *Post* quoted Lady Watkins's stern rebuke of Sir Edward immediately after another pointed question: 'Has General TARLETON ever read in the ANGELINA of his Philanthropic Friend, the following emphatic passage?' Given Robinson's connections with the *Morning Post*, it is likely that she had something to do with the newspaper's quotation and application of the 'emphatic passage' from *Angelina*. If that were in fact the case, it was not only a very public admonishment of Tarleton but also a virtual declaration of Robinson's own independence. Their often-stormy liaison, dating back to 1782, ended finally in 1797, leaving Robinson free to exert her influence as a 'Philanthropic Friend' without any compromising connection to Tarleton.

Although Robinson is arguably more successful than Hays in keeping the historical reality of the slave trade in view, it is also true that slavery functions as a pervasive metaphor in *Angelina*, linking the degradation of the marriage market to the 'cruel business of war'. The subject of war is broached very early in the novel when Sir George Fairford relates his encounter with an old man keeping a turnpike-gate in Wales. After sharing his jug of ale with Fairford and proposing a toast to 'peace and prosperity', the old man exclaims, 'O! this war is a cruel business, your Honour!' Fairford evinces a naivety that may have been shared by many of Robinson's readers, when he responds, 'How can you suffer by it ... your situation cannot be materially affected by political events; what can you possibly lose by the war?'[52] As the old man explains in the ensuing inset narrative, his son was the innocent victim of the cruel and underhanded tactics routinely used by crimpers to enlist soldiers in the army. In this particular case, a crimper, posing as a kindly stranger, offered the man's son a shilling to buy a pint of wine for his dying mother. Before he could take it to her, however, 'the men-trappers rushed in, and they forced him away ... in spite of all his entreaties to take a last farewell of his dying mother'. The sad story concludes as the old man explains how she expired later the same day, 'calling on her poor son, and praying for his safety'.[53]

The old man's reference to the 'men-trappers' who carried away his son taps into tendentious contemporary analogies between crimping and the slave trade. On 23 January 1795, for example, a paragraph in the *Morning Post* declared,

> It is really shocking to suppose, that in a Civilized Country there are lock-up Dungeons, where unfortunate men have been found in CHAINS; dragged from their parents and relations, used more cruelly than the natives of Africa, and secluded, for weeks, from the world, subject to the torments inflicted on them by those miscreant dealers in human flesh.

On 24 July 1795 the *Post* published an article titled 'Slave Trade', which asserted that 'the habits of Crimping, so notorious of late, must stimulate all the passions against this worse than African Slavery practised on ourselves'. The article concluded with the bold assertion that such flagrant disregard for 'the glorious Constitution of our Ancestors' exposed the baseness of Pitt's administration and rendered the 'Monarchy odious'.

Insofar as it exposes the abuse of power and elicits sympathy for the oppressed, the old man's story exemplifies the kind of inset narrative that Miriam L. Wallace and others have identified as a characteristic feature of radical fiction in the 1790s. As Wallace suggests, such narratives and the responses they evoke from characters within a novel contribute to a 'double movement' in radical fiction, which seeks 'to represent the development of political consciousness in fictional characters while creating a real political consciousness in the reader'.[54] The development of Fairford's political consciousness is quite striking as he moves from the easy assumption that the old man could not possibly be affected by the war to an understanding that his suffering represents that of thousands more. Quick to find a radical moral in the story, Fairford exclaims, 'Insatiable ambition!... these are thy ravages! Thus to augment the power of a few individuals, thousands and

66   *Sharon M. Setzer*

tens of thousands perish unregarded'.[55] As a figure of the reader within the text, however, Fairford supplements his immediate visceral response to the story with more extended reflections upon 'the helpless millions who are destined to fall, that the more powerful may rise'.

Much later in the novel, the philanthropic Sir James Montagu envisages an appalling scene of devastation as he strolls towards the ramparts at Portsmouth in the moonlight and listens to the waves crashing against the fortress. As Mary Favret has emphasized, 'the displacement of fighting onto foreign lands and waters' during the 1790s 'meant that the immediate activity of war ... remained for the most part outside the visual experience of the English population'.[56] According to Samuel Coleridge, physical distance from the theatre of war made it all too easy for readers on the home front to maintain a psychic distance, to assume that those who fell in battle '[p]assed off to Heaven, translated and not killed'.[57] Sir James Montagu undermines that easy assumption, however, as he evinces a poet's ability to see and hear 'absent things as if they were present':[58]

> I naturally thought on those who had perished; I fancied that I could hear their dying groans; see their deep wounds, and trace the torrents of blood, that, gushing from them, ran in mingling streams along the decks. I then started, as if roused by the thundering cannon; I almost believed that the air thickened with the clouds of sulphur rising from the floating bulwarks. My ideas then were filled with the cries of helpless infants, left to bewail a gallant father. I saw, in fancy, the despairing widow, the aged parent, hosts of kindred, weeping, raving, lamenting, perhaps, their only hope! While he, a mangled corpse, was consigned to the howling deep – sinking fathoms down the terrible abyss – cold – insensible![59]

Like many poets of the period, Sir James Montagu reveals what Favret calls an 'affiliation between the mortal, mangled body of the fighting man ... and the vulnerable, often injured bodies of those removed from public life on the domestic front – the beggar, widows, orphans and elderly'.[60] As Favret observes, the suffering of the survivors ultimately exposes 'the fiction motivating the war effort: that it will keep violence from coming home'.[61]

While the reflections of Sir George Fairford and Sir James Montagu articulate a radical resistance to loyalist narratives about 'a just and necessary war', they also model 'a process of reflective and active reading' which, as Wallace argues, 'aim[s] at nothing less than reconstituting the reader as a politically resistant subject'.[62] Sophia provides a particularly interesting example of this process at the end of the second volume, as she contemplates the story of Eleanor Plantagenet, 'The Damsel of Brittany', held captive by John I. As Sophia explains,

> [the story] has awakened a thousand reflections on events of past ages, the sufferings of the innocent, and the tyranny of rulers. It shews the

danger of authority when placed in the hands of minions, who, instead of being the protectors of the people, become the scourges of mankind: it paints the hardy virtue of the barons, and evinces, that the resistance of firm and patriotic spirits may, at all times, repel the encroachments of arbitrary power, and rescue the human race from the shackles of oppression.[63]

Sophia's reflections bring into view the same contentious period of English history that George Watson-Taylor represented in his play *England Preserved*, first performed at Covent Garden on 21 February 1795. On 23 February, the government-backed *Morning Chronicle* reported that the historical play, with its obvious parallels to the current conflict with France, was intended 'to animate the loyalty of the People of England against that dreadful nation the French, our inveterate and *natural* enemy'. On 25 February, the anti-ministerial *Morning Post* agreed that circumstances during the reign of King John were particularly 'applicable to the present day', but it took great exception to the way in which *England Preserved* represented the barons 'in an odious light ... as Rebels' rather than as honourable 'men fighting to free themselves and their posterity from the most sanguinary and detestable Tyranny'. The competing interpretations of the barons' revolt against King John were, of course, an extension of the competing interpretations of the Glorious Revolution (1688–89) offered in Richard Price's *Discourse on the Love of Our Country* and Edmund Burke's *Reflections on the Revolution in France*.[64] Considered within the context of partisan debate in 1795, Sophia's reflections are clearly aligned with the opposition politics of Price and the *Morning Post* rather than with the loyalist sympathies of Burke and the *Morning Chronicle*.

At the close of *Angelina* the political debate of the 1790s is mirrored in the conflicting assessments of Sophia's conduct. According to the haughty Lady Arranford, Sophia's refusal to marry Lord Acreland is not simply a shameless defiance of parental authority; it is also evidence of 'an impertinent disrespect for the consequence of nobility'. As much as she detests the vulgar presumption of Sir Edward, Lady Arranford realizes that insubordination in the family threatens the whole social and political hierarchy. Therefore, she affirms Sir Edward's rights 'to command obedience' and 'to dispose of his own', as well as his right to 'inflict such penance as would reduce [Sophia] to a proper sense of her duty'. She also impugns the 'moral character' of Mrs Delmore and others who have supported Sophia 'in the violation of every duty, human and divine!'[65] In her response, the philanthropic Mrs Delmore displaces Lady Arranford's model of governance by divine right with a model of governance by social contract. As Wollstonecraft suggested in the *Rights of Woman*, the social contract had an analogue in the 'reciprocal duty, which naturally subsists between parent and child'. If parents fulfil their duty, Wollstonecraft argued, 'they have a strong hold and sacred claim on the gratitude of their children'. Sir Edward Clarendon, however, is clearly one of those parents who, in Wollstonecraft's words, 'demand blind obedience, because they do not merit a reasonable service'.[66] By Mrs Delmore's Wollstonecraftian reckoning, he forfeited his right to expect 'filial obedience' when he 'overstepped the bounds' of 'parental authority'.[67]

Although the stark contrast between the positions of Lady Arranford and Mrs Delmore invites readers to engage in the debate over Sophia's conduct and to consider its larger political implications, Robinson ultimately closes down the debate by giving the last words on the subject to Sophia's epistolary confidante, Mrs Horton. Looking back over Sophia's trials after she is happily married to Charles Belmont, the young man she truly loves, Mrs Horton concludes:

> Fastidious observers may say, that the encouragement given to Mrs. Belmont by a circle of compassionating friends, was immoral, as tending to countenance filial disobedience: that I deny. The crime was Sir Edward's; the vanity, the ambition, and the avarice were also his: she was marked as a victim; her resistance was dictated by truth, and consistent with reason: she had to choose between the single act of disobedience, and the degradations of falsehood, perjury, meanness, sordid, legal prostitution! I cannot believe that the matron, the philosopher, or the philanthropist, will venture to condemn her.[68]

The finality of this verdict might well have inspired the last sentence of Jane Austen's *Northanger Abbey*, which leaves 'whomsoever it may concern' to decide whether the general 'tendency' of the novel is 'to recommend parental tyranny, or reward filial disobedience'.[69] Mocking the moral imperative to identify the 'tendency' of a novel,[70] Austen wryly presents two false choices, with the confidence that most of her readers will understand that she is actually promoting the ideal of reciprocal duty. Although Robinson is arguably committed to the same ideal, *Angelina* reflects a world in which the principle of reciprocity has been abrogated by heads of families and heads of state. In such instances, Robinson suggests, it is reasonable to invoke the second principle of the Glorious Revolution articulated by Richard Price: 'the right to resist power when abused'.[71]

For conservatives like Hannah More, of course, Sophia's resistance would not have been 'a new and glorious feature in her character',[72] but a lamentable example of 'the revolutionary spirit in families'. Sophia, in fact, is precisely the kind of young woman that provoked More to opine, 'Who can forbear observing and regretting in a variety of instances, that not only sons but daughters have adopted something of that spirit of independence, and disdain of control, which characterize the times?'[73] Sophia, however, is only a prototype of Martha Morley, the heroine of Robinson's last novel, *The Natural Daughter*. Characterizing Martha as

Epistolary Exposés 69

'a decidedly flippant female, apparently of the Wollstonecraft school', the conservative *British Critic* expressed unqualified contempt for a novel that 'inculcated and held up for imitation' the 'morals and manners which tended to produce' the French Revolution.[74] While such reviews exemplify the conservative panic over the 'New Morality' spawned by revolutionary France, they also implicitly confirm Robinson's status as a radical didactic novelist.

Notes

1. According to her posthumously published *Memoirs*, *Vancenza* 'owed its popularity to the celebrity of the author's name, and the favourable impression of her talents given to the public by her poetical compositions, rather than to its intrinsic merit' (M. Robinson, *Memoirs of Mrs. Mary Robinson*, ed. H. Davenport, vol. 7 of *The Works of Mary Robinson*, 8 vols (London: Pickering & Chatto, 2009–10), p. 280). For discussions of the autobiographical elements in the novel, see P. Byrne, *Perdita: The Literary, Theatrical, Scandalous Life of Mary Robinson* (New York: Random House, 2004), pp. 275–77; and H. Davenport, *The Prince's Mistress: A Life of Mary Robinson* (Stroud, UK: Sutton, 2004), pp. 167–69.
2. Robinson, *Memoirs*, pp. 253–57. According to most sources, Robinson's affair with the Prince lasted only about a year. Robinson gives an account of her estrangement from the Prince and her subsequent public humiliation in a letter published in the *Memoirs*, pp. 261–67.
3. M. Robinson, *Vancenza; Or, The Dangers of Credulity*, ed. D. Vernooy-Epp, vol. 2 of *The Works of Mary Robinson*, pp. 255, 304, 306.
4. In her *Memoirs* (p. 197), Robinson indicates that she briefly attended a school in Bristol run by 'the Misses More'. Hannah was one of the five sisters who contributed to the enterprise. In her *Letter to the Women of England, on the Injustice of Mental Subordination* (1799), Robinson, writing under the pseudonym of Anne Frances Randall, declared that she was 'avowedly of the same school' as Wollstonecraft (*The Works of Mary Robinson*, vol. 8, p. 131). The pamphlet appeared later in 1799 under Robinson's own name as *Thoughts on the Condition of Women, and on the Injustice of Mental Subordination*.
5. T. Mathias, *The Pursuits of Literature, A Satirical Poem in Four Dialogues*, 7th edn (London, 1798), p. 58.
6. R. Polwhele, *The Unsex'd Females: A Poem* (London, 1798), p. 16.
7. For discussions of radical/feminist voices in Robinson's novels, see M. Adams, *Studies in the Literary Backgrounds of English Radicalism with Special Reference to the French Revolution* (New York: Greenwood Press, 1968), pp. 104–29; W. Brewer, 'The French Revolution as a Romance: Mary Robinson's *Hubert de Sevrac*', *Papers on Language and Literature*, 42:2 (2006), pp. 115–49; A. Close, 'Into the Public: The Sexual Heroine in Eliza Fenwick's *Secresy* and Mary Robinson's *The Natural Daughter*', *Eighteenth-Century Fiction*, 17:1 (2004), pp. 35–52; A. Markley, 'Banished Men and the "New Order of Things": The French Emigré and the Complexities of Revolutionary Politics in Charlotte Smith and Mary Robinson', *Women's Writing*, 19:4 (2012), pp. 387–403; S. Russo, '"Where Virtue Struggles Midst a Maze of Snares": Mary Robinson's *Vancenza* (1792) and the Gothic Novel', *Women's Writing*, 20:4 (2013), pp. 586–601;

S. Setzer, 'Romancing the Reign of Terror: Sexual Politics in Mary Robinson's *Natural Daughter*', *Criticism*, 39:4 (1997), pp. 531–55; S. Setzer, 'The Dying Game: Crossdressing in Mary Robinson's *Walsingham*', *Nineteenth-Century Contexts*, 22:3 (2000), pp. 305–28; E. Ty, separate chapters on *Walsingham*, *The False Friend*, and *The Natural Daughter*, in *The Narratives of Mary Robinson, Jane West, and Amelia Opie* (Toronto, ON: University of Toronto Press, 1998), pp. 42–84; M. Zunac, '"An Immediate and Final Separation": Allegory and the Colonial Condition in Mary Robinson's *The Widow*', *Pennsylvania Literary Journal*, 2:2 (2010), pp. 25–46.

8. A. Craciun, *British Women Writers and the French Revolution: Citizens of the World* (New York: Palgrave, 2005), p. 83.

9. See Byrne, *Perdita*, pp. 321–22; and Davenport, *The Prince's Mistress*, p. 203. According to Godwin's diary, he read *Angelina* between 13 February and 22 March 1796 (*The Diary of William Godwin*, ed. V. Myers, D. O'Shaughnessy, and M. Philp (Oxford: Oxford Digital Library, 2010), at http://godwindiary.bodleian.ox.ac.uk (accessed 30 August 2014)). It is generally assumed that Godwin introduced Robinson to Wollstonecraft sometime later the same year.

10. *The Parliamentary History of England, from the Earliest Period to the Year 1803*, 31 (1794–95), col. 959.

11. Letter to the Editor, *The Morning Post*, 6 August 1795.

12. For an account of the riots, see J. Barrell, *The Spirit of Despotism: Invasions of Privacy in the 1790s* (Oxford: Oxford University Press, 2006), pp. 42–47.

13. *The Parliamentary History of England*, 31 (1794–95), col. 467.

14. *The Parliamentary History of England*, 31 (1794–95), cols 467–68.

15. Proceedings in the House of Commons were reported in the column 'British Parliament' in *The Morning Post*, 16 December 1795. For more extended discussion of the debate over slavery and the slave trade in the 1790s, see M. Ferguson, *Subject to Others: British Women Writers and Colonial Slavery, 1670–1834* (New York: Routledge, 1992), pp. 165–248.

16. See Byrne, *Perdita*, pp. 316–17; and Davenport, *The Prince's Mistress*, p. 170.

17. *Analytical Review*, 23 (1796), pp. 293–94. The unsigned review is included without any editorial caveat in *The Works of Mary Wollstonecraft*, ed. J. Todd and M. Butler, 7 vols (London: William Pickering, 1989), vol. 7, pp. 461–62. As M. Myers notes, however, the evidence for ascribing the review to Wollstonecraft is not 'conclusive' ('Mary Wollstonecraft's Literary Reviews', in C. Johnson (ed.), *The Cambridge Companion to Mary Wollstonecraft* (Cambridge: Cambridge University Press, 2002), pp. 82–98, on p. 95). See J. Sadow, Chapter 4 of this volume, p. 78.

18. For a discussion of Welsh settings in Robinson's novels and in her *Memoirs*, see M. Darnley, *Distant Fields: Eighteenth-Century Fictions of Wales* (Cardiff: University of Wales Press, 2001), pp. 172–89.

19. M. Wollstonecraft, *A Vindication of the Rights of Woman*, vol. 5 of *The Works of Mary Wollstonecraft*, p. 94.

20. *Analytical Review*, 23 (1796), p. 293.

21. For a useful account of the philosophical grounds of the family/state analogy in radical fiction, see N. E. Johnson, *The English Jacobin Novel on Rights, Property and the Law: Critiquing the Contract* (New York: Palgrave, 2004), pp. 25–55.

Epistolary Exposés 71

22. *Analytical Review*, 23 (1796), p. 294.
23. *Critical Review*, 16 (1796), pp. 397–400, on p. 397.
24. *Monthly Mirror*, 1 (1796), p. 290.
25. M. Robinson, *Angelina*, ed. S. Setzer, vol. 3 of *The Works of Mary Robinson*, 8 vols (Pickering & Chatto, 2009–10), p. 3.
26. Ibid., p. 4.
27. Ibid., p. 48.
28. Ibid., p. 6.
29. Wollstonecraft, *A Vindication of the Rights of Woman*, p. 242.
30. H. More, 'Hints towards Framing a Bill for the Abolition of the White Female Slave Trade, in the Cities of London and Westminster', *Christian Observer*, 3 (1804), pp. 156–59, on p. 157.
31. Robinson, *Angelina*, p. 281.
32. T. Paine, *The Rights of Man: Being an Answer to Mr. Burke's Attack on the French Revolution* (London, 1791), p. 9.
33. Robinson, *Angelina*, pp. 28, 184.
34. Ibid., p. 29.
35. Ibid., p. 30.
36. Ibid., p. 240.
37. Ibid., p. 119.
38. Ibid., p. 8.
39. Ibid., p. 21.
40. M. Wollstonecraft, *A Vindication of the Rights of Men*, vol. 5 of *The Works of Mary Wollstonecraft*, p. 14.
41. Wollstonecraft, *A Vindication of the Rights of Woman*, pp. 225–26. In her *Memoirs*, Robinson invites readers to consider her own life as a telling case in point. By her account, she reluctantly consented to marry Thomas Robinson on 12 April 1774, after considerable pressure from her family. She was only fifteen or sixteen years old at the time (*Memoirs*, pp. 208–11).
42. This issue has figured prominently in discussions of Jane Austen's *Mansfield Park* following Edward Said's provocative commentary on the novel in *Culture and Imperialism* (New York: Knopf, 1993), pp. 80–97. See, for example, G. Boulukos, 'The Politics of Silence: *Mansfield Park* and the Amelioration of Slavery', *Novel: A Forum on Fiction*, 39:3 (2006), pp. 361–83; S. Fraiman, 'Jane Austen and Edward Said: Gender, Culture, and Imperialism', *Critical Inquiry*, 21:4 (1995), pp. 805–21; and K. Trumpener, *Bardic Nationalism: The Romantic Novel and the British Empire* (Princeton, NJ: Princeton University Press, 1997), pp. 172–84.
43. Robinson, *Angelina*, p. 66.
44. K. Sánchez-Eppler, 'Bodily Bonds: The Intersecting Rhetorics of Feminism and Abolition', *Representations*, 24 (1988), pp. 28–59, on p. 31.
45. Fraiman, 'Jane Austen and Edward Said', p. 831.
46. Robinson, *Angelina*, p. 120.
47. Robinson expressed similar sentiments in her poems 'The Storm' (1796), substantially revised as 'The Negro Girl' (1800), and 'The African' (1798), later incorporated into the *Progress of Liberty*. See *The Works of Mary Robinson*, vol. 1, pp. 375–76, 318–20, and vol. 2, pp. 166–69. For an overview of Robinson's anti-slavery poetry, see Ferguson, *Subject to Others*, pp. 175–78.
48. Robinson, *Angelina*, p. 240.

72   *Sharon M. Setzer*

49. Trumpener, *Bardic Nationalism*, pp. 173–74.
50. M. Hays, *The Memoirs of Emma Courtney*, ed. M. L. Wallace (Glen Allen, VA: College Publishing, 2004), p. 173.
51. B. G. MacCarthy levels this general charge against didactic novelists in the 1790s who employed the novel as a 'means of propaganda' rather than as a form of more elevated 'artistic' expression (*The Female Pen: Women Writers and Novelists, 1621–1818* (1946–47; New York: New York University Press, 1994), pp. 420–21). After a brief summary of *Vancenza* in a chapter on the 'The Novel of Sentiment and Sensibility', MacCarthy summarily dismisses all of Robinson's novels as 'a curious mixture of vulgarity, ignorance, and poetic feeling' (p. 327).
52. Robinson, *Angelina*, p. 13.
53. Ibid., p. 14.
54. M. L. Wallace, *Revolutionary Subjects in the English Jacobin Novel, 1790–1805* (Lewisburg, PA: Bucknell University Press, 2009), p. 14.
55. Robinson, *Angelina*, p. 14.
56. M. Favret, 'Coming Home: The Public Spaces of Romantic War', *Studies in Romanticism*, 33:4 (1994), pp. 539–48, on p. 539.
57. S. Coleridge, 'Fears in Solitude', *The Poems of Samuel Taylor Coleridge*, ed. E. Coleridge (Oxford: Oxford University Press, 1931), p. 260, line 121.
58. In his Preface to the second edition of *Lyrical Ballads*, Wordsworth observed that the poet has 'a disposition to be affected more than other men by absent things as if they were present' (*Wordsworth: Poetical Works*, ed. T. Hutchinson, rev. E. De Selincourt (Oxford: Oxford University Press, 1985), p. 737).
59. Robinson, *Angelina*, p. 205.
60. Favret, 'Coming Home', p. 544. Robinson's poems 'The Old Beggar' and 'The Widow's Home', both published in 1800, illustrate the same affiliation. See *The Works of Mary Robinson*, vol. 2, pp. 105–6 and pp. 157–60.
61. Favret, 'Coming Home', p. 547.
62. Wallace, *Revolutionary Subjects*, p. 21.
63. Robinson, *Angelina*, p. 213.
64. As R. White explains, 'the Magna Carta in 1215 is often hailed as the originating document for "rights" in England', but

> it was essentially an agreement between the major barons and King John, curbing the monarch's power. Its significance lies in its power as a symbol or myth rather than a reality, for it hardly established rights for ordinary people.... The origin of demands for more popular rights stem from the English civil war and the commonwealth period. (*Natural Rights and the Birth of Romanticism* (New York: Palgrave, 2005), p. 30)

65. Robinson, *Angelina*, p. 278.
66. Wollstonecraft, *A Vindication of the Rights of Woman*, p. 224.
67. Robinson, *Angelina*, p. 279.
68. Ibid., p. 331.
69. J. Austen, *Northanger Abbey*, ed. B. Benedict and D. Le Faye (Cambridge: Cambridge University Press, 2006), p. 261.
70. See M. Woodworth, Chapter 2 of this volume, p. 39.

71. R. Price, *A Discourse on the Love of Our Country, Delivered on Nov. 4, 1789, at the Meeting-House in the Old Jewry to the Society for Commemorating the Revolution in Great Britain* (London, 1789), p. 34.
72. Robinson, *Angelina*, p. 280.
73. H. More, *Structures on the Modern System of Female Education*, 2 vols (London, 1799), vol. 1, pp. 134–35.
74. *British Critic* 16 (1800), pp. 320–21.

4 Moral and Generic Corruption in Eliza Fenwick's *Secresy*

Jonathan Sadow

Women's didactic fiction of the late eighteenth century largely acted as a form of political dialogue; nevertheless, part of that political and gendered discussion was a self-conscious inquiry into the nature, use, and value of fictional modes. As Hilary Havens points out, the didactic novel and its conduct-book cousin are the single genre seen to be grudgingly acceptable for both women writers and readers: novels should be either instructional or avoided. Still, as Morgan Rooney and others in this collection aptly demonstrate, the didactic novel was an excellent form to embed or disguise complex or subversive views not easily expressed in other venues.[1] And, as Havens notes, some 'female novelists used the didactic genre to criticize constricting conceptions of virtuous women'.[2] Additionally – as the survey of the eighteenth-century novel's didacticism in the introduction to this volume makes obvious – the potential subversion of more overt forms of instruction readily existed as part of the novel's history. Complex generic opportunities existed along with the accompanying constraint, and sometimes a subtlety of approach expanded the potential limitations of the so-called didactic novel. On the surface, the lurking question was a simple one: If, as the standard complaint went, fiction was potentially a dangerous, misleading, or worthless pursuit, why write 'better' novels or engage with the form at all?

Mary Wollstonecraft understood the difficulty of this problem; the heroine of her novel *Maria: Or the Wrongs of Woman* (1798) finds solace in Rousseau's *La Nouvelle Héloïse* (1761) even as it offers her false promise. It is precisely the figure of Rousseau – Rousseau, the social theorist and Rousseau, the sentimental novelist – that best embodies this conundrum in some of the radical didactic fiction of the 1790s. Though Nicola J. Watson and Janet Todd remind us that the novel, hardly ever seen as a form suitable for women, seemed problematic during this period,[3] it is perhaps the solidifying of women's didactic fiction as an established practice that caused increased anxiety. Watson has also shown us that *La Nouvelle Héloïse* and *Émile* (1762) formed the locus of social concern for a number of post-revolutionary women novelists. For radical women writers like Wollstonecraft and her friend Eliza Fenwick, this in some sense creates a sense of formal and political limitation. As Isobel Grundy points out, 'Wollstonecraft's rebuttal of Rousseau in her *Vindication* is a major influence on *Secresy*'.[4] It is certainly

Moral and Generic Corruption in Eliza Fenwick's Secresy   75

true that Wollstonecraft's rejection of educational isolation, female subservience, and class privilege serves as partial template for Valmont's misguided education of his niece, Sibella. However, I will try to show that Fenwick's and Wollstonecraft's relationship to Rousseau's critical and fictional heritage is tinged with both admiration and frustration. As Marilyn Butler and Jennifer Golightly have pointed out, 'they are hindered ... by the forms they inherit and which they seem unable to transcend'.[5]

Hindered, yes. But is fiction doing the hindering? It is true that the contemporary possibilities of the novel as a form matched the dismal social prospects for women. The endpoint for each is either conventional patriarchal marriage or ruin, and, indeed, both *Maria* and *Secresy: or The Ruin on the Rock* (1795) end in the latter, unhappy possibility. Nevertheless, the self-conscious understanding of genre exhibited by these works – Eliza Fenwick's *Secresy* in particular – suggests, if not transcendence, a generic complexity that is often ignored in studies of didactic fiction. Ellen Malenas Ledoux has demonstrated that *Secresy* participates in a gradual expansion of the novel's possibilities for female protagonists.[6] I believe *Secresy*'s relationship to *Émile* and *La Nouvelle Héloïse* goes beyond, in Watson's formulation, the 'aesthetic and political deadlock which displays the crippling effect of the epistolary mode upon the urgent feminist project of distinguishing between sensibility as debilitating conservative ideology and as the powerhouse of a new feminist vision'.[7] Alongside this complication lies a keen critical consciousness of the novel's past and future potential. Genre awareness tends to lead to parody, an often-ignored element of *Secresy* and even *Maria*. Our own awareness of this phenomenon may help us understand how didactic writers of the 1790s understood their own projects. For Fenwick the novel, at least in its more morally acceptable form, ends up being an entirely compatible vehicle for a social agenda that includes women's education, 'rational' virtue, and other reformist goals. In short, the secret of *Secresy*'s parody and 'mixture' lies in a modulated view wherein questions of genre, especially discrepancies between didacticism and romance, are clearly part of a larger inquiry about the benefits and pitfalls of novels. I contend that the generic questions that Fenwick poses through her novel's characters and their accompanying moral judgements give rise to subtle generic and moral parody, largely to discern the useful from the suspect. Ultimately, the importance of these questions hinges on the associated questions raised about social theory such as Rousseau's, since the novel warns about the wholesale adoption of an educational system that contains both virtues and drawbacks. Therefore, Fenwick's nuanced attitude toward fiction ultimately exists in service to the question of whether the novel can depict a nuanced attitude toward women's rational and moral development.

Though integral to the work, this kind of reflective hedging can create some confusion about the novel's essentially progressive ideology and may be the reason that *Secresy* has received limited and mixed attention and evaluation. At its most basic level, it is a didactic epistolary novel about

76 Jonathan Sadow

female friends that plays out a reasonably overt parable of the virtues and perils of Rousseauian educational theory. Isobel Grundy regards it as a pseudo-Gothic centring on the virtues and drawbacks of various forms of female education.[8] Its various oddball qualities are sometimes disliked; Terry Castle regarded it as an 'excruciating' incoherent melodrama in her well-known review entitled 'Sublimely Bad'.[9] Others have seen *Secresy* as profound: Julia Wright suggests Pierre Bourdieu as a lens for understanding the novel's social tableau, and Christopher Bundock believes that *Secresy* is an exploration of community and subjectivity best understood through a theoretical dialogue between Jean-Luc Nancy, Maurice Blanchot, and Martin Heidegger.[10] Calley Hornbuckle points out that there is 'much more at work in *Secresy* than a Rousseauian experiment'.[11]

That is undoubtedly true, but without disputing any of these readings – and with a debt to Hornbuckle, Wright, and Julia Douthwaite – I would like to make a more straightforward observation about *Secresy* as a supplement to my argument. Although we often think of the novel as a strange genre confection, I believe that it is a good exemplar of the essential historical unity between what we now think of as sentimental, didactic, and Gothic fiction. It does not present a generic conundrum because – as Fenwick understood – the elements on which it draws were never particularly distinct in the first place; its conflicts and anxieties are primarily reflective and didactic. *Secresy* is a knowing novel and is knowing about the novel.

Though *Secresy*'s appropriations have been well-documented, I believe that its satirical qualities – and the relationship of those qualities to an implied investigation of the state of the novel – have been largely ignored by critics. Terry Castle's review claims that the novel will appeal to lovers of 'camp',[12] but that description only raises the pleasures of the unintentionally bad. I am quite convinced that *Secresy* is instead (or, at least, in addition) a purveyor of 'intentional' satire, and that any reading of *Secresy* ought to take the text's satirical elements into account. Ultimately, as I argue above, these elements point to the potential of novelistic discourse even as they mock many reactionary fictional conventions. Fenwick and Wollstonecraft correctly understand the novel as an essentially didactic form; the primary question for these writers was whether it was a sufficiently improvable one and whether novels were ultimately compatible with their moral and political beliefs. This was not a 'new' concern, and it is part of my goal to claim that didactic novels of the period simply and self-reflectively continued the eighteenth century's already self-reflective concerns about the didactic potential and pitfalls of novels.

We regard novels like *Secresy* as generic oddities, but the 1790s did not. Whether or not *Secresy* is primarily a 'Gothic' or a 'didactic' novel, or a 'blend' of the two, was not an issue that concerned the novel's contemporary reviewers and readers. The didactic novel and the Gothic are sometimes thought of as later eighteenth-century developments, but these tendencies are closely linked to the sentimental novel. Frances Sheridan's

Moral and Generic Corruption in Eliza Fenwick's Secresy 77

1767 *The Memoirs of Miss Sidney Bidulph* is a good case in point. Although posing as a didactic epistolary work, it contains a variety of elements we often think of as 'Gothic': fragmented frame narratives, an aura of horror, a curse that will be passed on to succeeding generations. At the same time, it is fittingly dedicated to Richardson. That novel's endless series of terrors 'bridge' the Richardsonian novel and the Gothic, suggesting their essential continuity. *Sidney Bidulph* also demonstrates that a well-understood sub-text of 1790s fiction – that unending female terror is a product of the legal system, the family, and a violent and discriminatory social order – exists as a potential of the didactic, sentimental, libertine, and Gothic novel much earlier than ordinarily recognized. For Sheridan, there is no spectralization of the phenomenon that produces terror; it only needs to be presented in its overwhelming, literally maddening, and seemingly unchangeable form. More simply: female persecution and terror (and an evolving social critique that accompanies it) are a constant theme of the eighteenth-century novel, with or without a haunted castle. Though we are sometimes used to thinking of a history of the Gothic that depends on Horace Walpole and William Beckford, many novelists of the 1790s saw themselves as inheritors of the entire form of the romance. Writers like Fenwick and Wollstonecraft understood Ann Radcliffe's Gothic as part of an existing tradition where new and fashionable elements are added to a broadly existing genre with mixed success. Supernatural or not, a story of female terror ought to be judged on whether it is effectively deployed for the improvement of female readers. Our own bafflement by *Secresy*'s 'genre mix' may be an artefact of our own retrospective sense of genre.

Like *Secresy*, Wollstonecraft's 1797 *Maria* (published in 1798 as part of the *Posthumous Works*) treats the problems of the sentimental and Gothic as more or less the same. *Maria* opens:

> Abodes of horror have frequently been described, and castles, filled with spectres and chimeras, conjured up by the magic spell of genius to harrow the soul, and absorb the wondering mind. But, formed of such stuff as dreams are made of, what were they to the mansion of despair, in one corner of which Maria sat, endeavouring to recall her scattered thoughts![13]

This, of course, announces Gothic romance. Chapter two, though, finds Maria reading *La Nouvelle Héloïse*:

> it seemed to open a new world to her – the only one worth inhabiting ... she flew to Rousseau, as her only refuge ... she read on the margin of an impassioned letter, written in the well-known hand – 'Rousseau alone, the true Prometheus of sentiment, possessed the fire of genius necessary to portray the passion, the truth of which goes so directly to the heart'.[14]

78 Jonathan Sadow

This novelistic world – the Gothic, the sentimental, the epistolary – is a deceptive lure that may lead one down an irrational and emotional path (the fragments at the end of the novel indicate that Maria's lover will eventually betray her); however, Wollstonecraft, who reviewed novels for the *Analytical Review* and spent the last year of her life writing *Maria*, was critical but serious when it came to the form and potential of the novel. A look at her *Analytical Review* articles reminds one of her commitment to the apprehension and critique of contemporary fiction. On the one hand, she was entirely in line with contemporary thought about the novel's moral dangers: she comments in her review of Charlotte Smith's *Emmeline* (1788) that

> few of the numerous productions termed novels, claim any attention . . . the false expectations these wild scenes excite, tend to debauch the mind, and throw an insipid kind of uniformity over the moderate and rational prospects of life, consequently *adventures* are sought for and created, when duties are neglected, and content despised.[15]

Her praise for Helen Maria Williams's *Julia* (1790) lies in the fact that '[Williams's] mind does not seem to be *debauched*, if we may be allowed the expression, by reading novels'.[16] On the other hand, Wollstonecraft is certainly interested in *good* novels, even fanciful ones. Her review of Radcliffe's *The Italian* (1797) proposes that a reader familiar with her technique will end up 'leaving the aching sight searching after the splendid nothing'. Her generic breakdown, such as it is, is standard for the period: 'The nature of the story obliges us to digest improbabilities, and continually to recollect that it is a romance, not a novel, we are reading'. As Anne Chandler comments in her discussion of these pieces, Wollstonecraft 'is better equipped [than Samuel Johnson] to imagine an enlightened novelistic realism that would be informed by, while moving beyond, sentiment'.[17] Chandler also points out that Wollstonecraft is especially annoyed by hackneyed novelist conventions such as the 'found manuscript'; she is strongly concerned with the novel's moral seriousness while possessing a varying attitude toward its conventions.[18] Her review of *The Italian* continues by proposing that 'the restless curiosity it excites is too often excited by something like a stage trick', but this does not prevent her from gushing over that trick's effectiveness.[19] A work's relation to sentiment is very important to her, though she is not especially concerned with whether or not an individual work acts as a coherent exemplar of one generic tendency; her reviews are more concerned with whether an author's appropriation of fictional convention works as a whole. The conceptual outlook of *Maria* is quite similar: as a piece of fiction, it acts as a self-conscious, critical survey of the contemporary romance landscape. As such, it is less a wholesale rejection of Gothic and sentimental convention than a sardonic corrective.

As we shall see, this practical attitude toward the uses and abuses of convention is shared by Fenwick. A so-called mixture of elements, with the same

Moral and Generic Corruption in Eliza Fenwick's Secresy   79

essential subtext, forms the basic structure of *Secresy. Secresy* might be seen as a kind of generic successor to *Sidney Bidulph* and a companion to *Maria* in the sense that the adoption of didactic, sentimental, and Gothic tendencies are entirely self-conscious and immaterial as far as genre is concerned; mixed modes were common, and – in these works – the appropriation of a variety of styles and clichés serves an artistic agenda that nods holistically to the state of the novel. Though we have no direct critical commentary from Fenwick at the time of *Secresy*, every serious reader has observed her intellectual and personal entanglement with Wollstonecraft.[20] (William Godwin writes that 'Mrs. Fenwick, author of an excellent novel, entitled Secresy',[21] nursed Wollstonecraft on her deathbed.) Various other novels of the 1790s contain all of these elements as well; Charlotte Smith's fiction is a good example. Similarly, many novels of the period didactically reflect on the sentimental dangers of the romance. This, too, is generically unremarkable – what eighteenth-century novel does *not* engage in this reflection?

Douthwaite points out that *Secresy* is marked by a striking 'didactic division into two registers: Gothic romance and philosophical diatribe. These two voices are strung along in an epistolary exchange between two female alter-egos': the 'rational' Caroline and the 'tempestuous' Sibella.[22] This register shift is certainly jarring, and yet it is not entirely unusual in fiction of the 1790s for different narrative registers to be associated with characters of differing moral or aesthetic natures; the sections associated with libertine and clergyman characters in Radcliffe's *The Romance of the Forest* (1791) are a good example. Really, *Secresy* is not so much a generic 'mix' as a self-conscious appropriation of novelistic plot elements, generally speaking. Wright notes that it contains many stock plots: heroine trapped in a castle by an evil relative or suitor; an epistolary and advisory friendship between two women; a rake seeks a financially useful marriage; a virtuous woman provides for the moral education of those around her; a hero risks all to save beloved from villain.[23] It also contains the obligatory masquerade scene and many other standard elements from eighteenth-century fiction. Certainly, Gothic sublimity is a central concern, and Radcliffe's romances and, as Wright also points out, Laclos's novels are contemporary objects of interest. Ultimately, though, *Secresy* takes on the sentimental romance as a whole.

I have said that Fenwick's pragmatic attitude toward the novel is inextricable from its relationship to social theory, and it is notable that the French novel in particular seems iconic for both Wollstonecraft and Fenwick. The 1795 *British Critic* review of *Secresy* wrote that it was

> one of the wildest romances we have met with, yet not very original in the ground-work of its plan ... the *morality* which pervades these volumes; a morality worthy enough of modern *France*, but far removed (we trust) from the approbation of Englishmen.[24]

For Fenwick's critics, the 'foreign' nature of her politics and literary form were inseparable. In some sense, the problem of the novel for female Jacobin

80 *Jonathan Sadow*

novelists was a simple one: how to write a novel with a form and content that accorded with reformist or revolutionary ideals. There was, however, an ideological complication when it came to the influence of those same French novels on their work: though Rousseau and Laclos are associated with Jacobin thought, neither *La Nouvelle Héloïse* nor *Les Liaisons Dangereuses* (1782) are in any way reformist texts. As Watson asks: 'How, then, was a revolutionary polemic premised upon the heartstrings to be metamorphosed from solitary effusion to social programme?'[25] Watson sees *Secresy* as a capitulation: a sentimental or libertine plot cannot escape its own ideological nature. Watson and Wright have documented the many self-conscious nods that the novel makes to Laclos – including the names of Valmont and Sibella, as well as many plot parallels[26] – and, indeed, one might ask how the morally vexed *Les Liaisons Dangereuses* can serve as a major artistic influence for a novel whose central didactic concern is a radical analysis of female education. Others have provided a more optimistic view: Wright believes that 'Fenwick has much broader concerns that extend Wollstonecraft's interest in the duplicity that patriarchy requires of women to Laclos's interest in the conflict between public and private personae'.[27] Nevertheless, *Secresy*'s politics do on some level necessitate a critique of libertine fiction even as it adopts some of its strategies; it is precisely through a satirical and selective adoption of the libertine figure that this contradiction is, perhaps, resolved.

I believe more positively than Watson that *Secresy*, like *Maria*, is a re-examination of the broad novelistic landscape. How can this be, given the novel's standard, tragic course? Though ultimately almost as dire as *Maria*, *Secresy* possesses a somewhat lighter and more expansive relationship to standard novel plots. *Secresy*'s social theory is conveyed through a free use of stock elements, regardless of the ideology of their source material. Or, one could say, precisely because of that ideology; *Maria* and *Secresy* operate by repurposing compelling but suspect motifs, and by trying to sort good from bad in form and content. *Secresy*'s and *Maria*'s relationship to form and formal systems might be summed up by Wollstonecraft's remarks on David William's *Lectures on Education*:

> Mr. W. avails himself of the excellent advice contained in that celebrated novel [Rousseau's *Émile*], without being dazzled by brilliant beauties, or disgusted with gross errors; he neither blindly swallows conceited paradoxes, nor joins in the laugh raised by ignorance.... [He] appears, to us, to be a little too severe on the faults of a writer, whose production, if it is not considered as a complete system, yet affords much valuable desultory information, and persuasive expostulations.[28]

Secresy and *Maria* share an interest and scepticism toward theory and method, and this statement also provides a useful condensation of both novels' relationship to Rousseau. Wollstonecraft writes that 'Rousseau's mistake was the mistake of genius, ever eager to trace a well-proportioned system'

Moral and Generic Corruption in Eliza Fenwick's Secresy   81

and claims that he was 'blinded by his prevailing idea'.[29] This describes Wollstonecraft's relationship to *La Nouvelle Héloïse*, as well; the epigraph to *Mary: A Fiction* (1788) is taken from that novel, even as Rousseau's ideas are recontextualized. And, of course, the critical debate with Rousseau forms much of the basis of the *Vindication of the Rights of Woman* (1792). In both *Maria* and *Secresy*, theory and fictional method may be usefully and critically updated. And, as Wright has pointed out, *Secresy*, even more than *Maria*, illustrates the breakdown of both theoretical models and fictional tropes. The Wollstonecraftian and Fenwickian critique may be summed up as such: for social theory *and* the novel, the enjoined problem is to salvage brilliant but morally flawed and patriarchal material through de-systemization.

For Wright, the 'conflicts of genre' in *Secresy* provided by differing discourses ultimately highlight a public–private conflict best seen through the lens of Wittgensteinian private language theory. It is worth quoting Wright at some length:

> 'Genres', as Jacques Derrida notes, 'are not to be mixed', as they 'play the role of order's principle'. Instead [Fenwick] grafts them together to articulate the complex cultural topography in which the various genres do not mingle, but collide to mark separations in cultural perspective and the principles of order with which they are commensurate. In *Secresy*, generic naming tends to mark an artificiality, a literary derivativeness that diverts the character who follows it from the proper course.... For Fenwick's characters, literary genres often offer a means by which the incomprehensible and the alien can be differentiated from the cultural codes that they accept and so securely bounded.... Fenwick thus puts a different spin on a pattern which Bourdieu analyzes; genre does not only create a sense of place, but is used to put people in their place.... By foregrounding the literariness of another's cultural perspective, Fenwick's characters imply not complete cultural integrity but a rift between nature and (artificial) culture that misdirects the individual, or produces a mask that conceals the proper self.... But the mixture of voices in her novel means that each classifier's perspective is coded as literary: no one voice stands above the rest, secure from critique, contradiction, or generic classification.[30]

Wright's formulation is without doubt the most sophisticated critical representation of *Secresy*'s genre concerns. It is certainly true for Fenwick that generic convention and derivation is associated with artificiality, and that each character is potentially and self-consciously associated with one novelistic convention or another, and, certainly, coded as literary. For this reason, though, I'm not certain that the characters, though they express constant concern about truth and transparency, are outfitted with 'proper selves' entirely distinct from their generic placement. I believe that the novel's primary shifts in consciousness do not so much mark generic *distinction*; rather – and this is

82   *Jonathan Sadow*

where I differ from Wright and other critics – the novel's shifts in register primarily rely on the credulous or incredulous reactions, from both readers and characters, to plot elements from romance. As for Wollstonecraft, 'sentimental' and 'Gothic' characters, alongside their narrative modes, exist as either hackneyed or useful conventions. What accounts for the novel's 'strangeness' is the uncertain nature of the didactic parody of romance that it contains, as well as the existence of conflicting and changing figures. In other words, *Secresy* is a blatantly didactic novel with an oddly unclear message, and a romance parody with an ambiguous relationship to romance.

What, ultimately, is the effect of *Secresy*'s none-too-subtle nods to genre convention? Terry Castle, again, describes these elements as 'kitsch'.[31] However, the novel is quite a bit more conscious of its deployment of plot elements than this term implies. The isolated, wandering Sibella is the object of traditional romantic admiration that is, I think, both serious and comic. Her would-be suitor, Murden, writes to her,

> thinking of you, my Sibella, in my imagination seeing you, seeing your fawn, your wood, your oak, your black angry-looking rock, your solemn ruin, your clumps of yew trees, your white marble tomb. And these objects engrossed my whole attention.[32]

Stock elements are parodied throughout the novel: 'Gloomy Hall, or Gloomy Castle – some such name, I formerly gave that turret-crowned building' sarcastic libertine Lord Filmar comments later on.[33] Many of the scenes, however, rely on Sibella's and Caroline's didactic and incredulous responses. Sometimes, these responses are a reply to flaws in Rousseau's educational theories, but often they are simply rejections of dubious romantic notions. There are a number of moments where it is unclear if the novel is taking itself entirely seriously. When a mysterious alien spirit (who later turns out to be Sibella's suitor Arthur Murden in disguise) appears to tell Sibella: 'Fair virgin, weep not!... Here, Mildew, Mischief, and Mischance cannot harm you.... I was the hallowed tenant of yon ruined mansion; once, an inhabitant of earth.... Stay', cried he. 'Do you doubt my supernatural mission?'[34] Sibella replies: 'I do not deem you worthy of enquiry ... for you came with pretences of falsehood and guile, and those are coverings that virtue ever scorns'.[35] The alliterative 'Mildew, Mischief, and Mischance' does indeed, at least briefly, remove Murden from the realm of the serious. Sibella's responses to novelistic excess are a rationalist rejection of the same kind of logic with which she uses to reject tyrannical claims of power. In a typical remark, she tells her uncle:

> I would not offend you, but I must expostulate ... [you have] No right to the exercise of an unjust power over me!... I have looked on every side, and I find it is your caprice, and no principle of reason in you, that forbids our union.[36]

Although Sibella and Caroline function as moral observers and resistors, it is also the case that the novel seems mostly comfortable walking a line between the sublime and the slightly satirical. Whether or not this produces a 'good' or even coherent novel is murky, and it is a good question as to whether some of the satirical elements are intentionally or unintentionally funny – though, of course, the novel is ostensibly concerned with outcomes. Much as in the non-comic *Maria*, *Secresy* purposefully draws attention to the ludicrous convention with the intent of destabilizing the reader's unreflective relationship to encountering a romantic, sublime, or sentimental element. The perplexing part of the novel is not, therefore, its minor oddities, but that it is so consistently didactic a novel that does not, finally, present an obviously coherent point of view; a libertine figure may sometimes nod to Laclos, sometimes to Richardson. This, I think, is the reason that criticism usually finds *Secresy* to be either incoherent or philosophically complex.

Whether or not *Secresy* presents a coherent social allegory is debatable; more to the point, it *does* consistently and simultaneously question and deploy romance convention. Sibella and Murden die tragic deaths in stock fashion, but neither death seems particularly justified from the point of view of Caroline's reformist polemics, nor do her recriminations produce any obvious conclusions about the ostensible topics of the novel: education, reason, virtue, and the moral dangers to each that lie with a hidden or self-deceptive identity. Therein lies its basic innovation (or failure): *Secresy* presents a constantly shifting relationship between the reader and its own didacticism. As an epistolary novel without an accompanying editor, collector, or story of origination, it leaves the reader at sea with regard to its ultimate ethical authority. And yet, it *begins* in a conventional fashion, with Caroline presented as a seemingly virtuous mentor to her correspondent, Sibella. As one progresses through the text, however, one's own ethical position becomes murkier and murkier. One is led to identify with Caroline's point of view; however, Caroline's judgement seems impaired by the end of the novel even while her moral authority seems – at least, on a structural level – to remain intact. Nevertheless, she increasingly seems to be playing a kind of fictional role herself. Late in the novel, she writes: 'I have heard myself called pedantic, inflexible, opinionated; I have been told, by some gentler people, that I am severe, misjudging, giving to those little foibles almost inseparable from human nature the name of vice, and this may be true'.[37] This moment is not exactly 'satirical', and it is followed by Caroline's serious takedown of Murden's flaws and his reliance on false sentiment ('your imagination teems with the rhapsodies of passion! – I hear your high-wrought declamation, the dictates of a fevered fancy'[38]). Still, it is a moment when the novel both recognizes and problematizes Caroline as a voice of moral authority. And the same might be said for the didactic critique of sentiment; Caroline's and *Secresy*'s limitations as an instructional voice are consciously bound together. At the end of the novel, Caroline is placed alongside Valmont and Filmar as culpable authorities in the death of Sibella and Murden. That, too,

84   Jonathan Sadow

is part of the 'lesson' of *Secresy*; our own discernment of Caroline's worth and drawbacks may be necessary.

Everything about the novel, in fact, tends to self-consciously fracture conventional expectations about didactic texts, and a straightforward lesson is therefore not to be had. The introduction of a libertine letter-writer late in the novel who, though 'villainous', is more entertaining and knowledgeable than previous moral authorities blurs the issue even further, allowing the reader's own arbitrating position to be corrupted. Filmar is another stock character – knowing and comic, as libertines are – but his overwhelming presence in the second half of the novel is in no way justified in an ethical text that should be dominated by Caroline. If Filmar is meant, like Lovelace, to be a readerly temptation to be ultimately resisted, he does not seem to be a villainous enough presence to create the proper opprobrium. Rather, he is Lovelace 'lite' and reformable, but not so initially vicious as to make that reform particularly 'didactic': 'The plot thickens, and I am more of [Caroline] Montgomery's sort than I believed I was'.[39] Filmar increasingly takes on the language of narrative machinery ('The scene is almost prepared to shift'[40]), but this only serves to give the reader a sense that he is more puppet than puppet-master. Libertine figures are well-known arbiters of plots and plotting, but a libertine character who is so obviously a shadow of others can only produce a shadow of menace.

All of this continuously unsettles the reader while simultaneously appealing to her moral judgement. That unsettling quality, I would argue, is partially a product of the novel's own didactic anxieties – it is, after all, a novel about female education that spends much of its time wrestling with Rousseau's *Émile*. It does not seem to have made up its mind about the virtues of a single, particular, educational mode. Similarly, it seems mixed on whether emotional sublimity ought to be parodied, avoided, or embraced. Sibella is often perceived as a figure of sublimity, as when Caroline first encounters her:

> it was again before me as a wild ruin tottering on the projecting point of a rock. Silence, solitude, the twilight, the objects filled my mind with a species of melancholy. Fancy had become more predominant than judgment.... I beheld a female form, cloathed in white, seated at the foot of a large oak. Her hair, unrestrained by either hat or cap, entirely shaded her face as she bowed her head to look on a little fawn, who in the attitude of confidence and affection was laying across her lap.
>
> The names of Wood Nymph, Dryad, and Hymadriad, with a confused number of images, arose in my memory; and I was on the point of reverently retreating, but a moment's pause prevented the romance of the scene from thus imposing on my reason.[41]

Many of the novel's encounters with sublimity are couched in a similar fashion. On the one hand, as Hornbuckle has noted, this early depiction of

Sibella is a 'real' aestheticized moment that begins Caroline's relationship with Sibella as a kind of alter-ego or self-projection. On the other, as Hornbuckle also observes, it is difficult to tell whether or not we are to take this scene 'seriously' or whether it is a form of Burkean satire.[42] The romance/reason conflict itself is also lightly mocked shortly thereafter, as Sibella's uncle proposes that she 'take again the attitude I saw you in when I entered the wood. There child; keep that posture a short time, your figure improves the scene'.[43] Various critics have rightly pointed out that *Secresy*'s polemics insist that emotion, particularly women's emotions, are consistent with reason. Still, it is hard to argue against the idea that the novel constantly presents and simultaneously undermines moments of emotion or sublimity. Sibella may be rational, but she *is* wandering through the woods at midnight with her fawn, Nina, who *does* later follow Murden into a rocky tomb. This kind of modulation of course appears in Radcliffe in some fashion, but *Secresy*'s relationship to the sublime is more self-conscious and equivocal than *The Romance of the Forest*'s. That, however, is primarily because the Radcliffian novel's own didacticism is taken for granted; the appearance of the sublime (at least in its gloomy form) is generally associated with the dangers of a romantic sensibility. It is precisely because the sublime encounter has already become a cliché that it may be lightly deployed with ambiguous effect. For Wollstonecraft, the methodology is the exposition of the trope; for Fenwick, the method is to play out the trope's narrative in a self-conscious, deadpan fashion.

Finally, *Secresy* is a novel about education that appears uncertain of its own ability to educate. Or, at least, it seems unwilling to entirely stand up for a systemic model even as it debunks others. Caroline opens by criticizing Sibella's uncle for educating her in seclusion, and the novel is serious about this critique ('a system as opposite to the general practice of mankind, and which I am inclined to think is not as perfect as you are willing to suppose'). Yet, Sibella possesses an intellect despite her flawed educational model:

> But how comes it to pass ... that when your uncle had the means of gratifying his darling wish in educating two children, and one of them a female, to whom according to his creed, nothing should be granted beyond what the instinct of appetite demands, how comes it, I say, that you possess the comprehensive powers of intellect? from what sources did you derive that eager desire of knowledge ... and how came you to be learned on subjects, which, in the education of females, are strictly with-held, to make room for trifling gaudy and useless accomplishments?[44]

Caroline spends a fair amount of time trying to parse the outcome of Valmont's educational experiment from its premise or value: Sibella possesses a superior character despite or due to her upbringing. Caroline often comes up with equivocal answers: 'The contrivance was worthless;

86   *Jonathan Sadow*

but the performance was admirable'.[45] That is one reason why I think that the novel, for Fenwick and Wollstonecraft, ends up as an appropriate vehicle for social critique despite its potential dangers: Fenwick, at least, declines to produce any new systems or solutions. However, *Secresy*'s didactic value lies in the work of separating admirable performances from worthless contrivances in existing systems of both fiction and social theory. It is a cautious form of didactic writing and a cautious form of novelistic innovation.

The stock situations in *Secresy* play themselves out. Though the novel ultimately has an ambivalent relationship toward the romance elements it deploys, its ultimate 'didacticism' may lie in its scepticism toward systemization. Even as Sibella is 'punished', *Secresy* still functions as a novel that criticizes constricting conceptions of virtuous women – both Sibella and Caroline have their virtues and drawbacks. This ambivalence is, again, a quite self-aware part of its tentative project. Though Filmar, like libertines in Richardson and Laclos, is the primary locus of the self-conscious gesture, he is not alone. 'This is no spirit of your uncle's choosing.... No: it is one refined upon romance',[46] Caroline warns Sibella. Wright correctly points out that Caroline lacks irony, warning in letters about the dangers of letter-writing.[47] This does not mean that the *novel* lacks irony. In short, it is difficult to see the novel as unreflective about the sentimental course of its plot, and it is therefore a mistake to suggest that it is either a fictional or political dead end.[48] Reflective ambivalence is not despair. One might say that the novel is less notable for its proliferation of 'generic' variety and characterized (some critics would say paralysed) by its unwillingness to deploy them fully and unselfconsciously – that is, to 'real' effect. It is too concerned with its own status as a novel. Filmar opens the final volume:

> have I allowed you to wear out your astonishment at my ingenuity, address, and perseverance, and to exercise your imagination in following me and my bride from stage to stage of this admirably contrived journey? – Does the novelty of the adventure wear off?[49]

Perhaps it does, and perhaps that is the point; one of the secrets *Secresy* exposes is the tyranny of the sentimental machination. But Fenwick offers an addendum to *Maria*'s exposé, believing that an admirably contrived novel, one that is able to discern the falsehood and guile of a sentimental, sublime, or libertine plot, may still seek to discern what is and isn't worthy of inquiry within them. The novel, if not considered as a complete system, still affords some persuasive expostulations. The 'lesson', as Wollstonecraft writes of Rousseau – for didactic fiction, the novel at large, and its ability to educate readers about women's education or the dangers of letter-writing – may be to understand the excellent advice amidst the gross errors, and not be blinded by prevailing ideas about the novel's potential. Like *Maria*, *Secresy* connects sentimental and Gothic tropes with social and personal tyranny. Unlike *Maria*, *Secresy* may secretly see its own didacticism as simply another feature of sentimental romance – and, perhaps, rightly so.

Notes

1. See M. Rooney, 'Charlotte Smith and the Persistence of the Past', Chapter 1 of this volume, and H. Havens, Introduction to this volume, pp. 7, 34.
2. Havens, Introduction, p. 8.
3. See N. J. Watson, *Revolution and the Form of the British Novel 1790–1825* (Oxford: Clarendon Press, 1994), pp. 39–40 and J. Todd, *The Sign of Angelica: Women, Writing and Fiction, 1660–1800* (London: Virago Press, 1989), pp. 232–40.
4. E. Fenwick, *Secresy: or, The Ruin on the Rock*, ed. Isobel Grundy, 2nd edn (Peterborough, ON: Broadview Press, 1998), p. 26. Grundy also provides a useful overview of the personal friendship between the Fenwicks and Wollstonecraft and Godwin on pp. 10–11.
5. J. Golightly, *The Family, Marriage, and Radicalism in British Women's Novels of the 1790s* (Lewisburg, PA: Bucknell University Press, 2012), p. 94. See also M. Butler, *Jane Austen and the War of Ideas* (Oxford: Clarendon Press, 1975).
6. See E. M. Ledoux, 'Defiant Damsels: Gothic Space and Female Agency in *Emmeline, The Mysteries of Udolpho*, and *Secresy*', *Women's Writing*, 18:3 (2011), pp. 331–47.
7. Watson, *Revolution and the Form*, p. 41.
8. See I. Grundy, Introduction to *Secresy*, pp. 7–30.
9. T. Castle, 'Sublimely Bad', *London Review of Books*, 17:4 (23 February 1995), pp. 18–19.
10. See J. Wright, '"I Am Ill-Fitted": Conflicts of Genre in Eliza Fenwick's *Secresy*', in T. Rajan and J. Wright (eds), *Romanticism, History, and the Possibilities of Genre* (Cambridge: Cambridge University Press, 1998), pp. 149–75; and C. Bundock, 'The (Inoperative) Epistolary Community in Eliza Fenwick's *Secresy*', *European Romantic Review*, 20:5 (2009), pp. 709–20. Alternately, Meghan Burke sees the 'secret' of *Secresy* as embodied by Sibella's hidden and powerless pregnancy ('Making Mother Obsolete: Eliza Fenwick's *Secresy* and the Masculine Appropriation of Maternity', *Eighteenth-Century Fiction*, 21:3 (2009), pp. 357–84). For readings of *Secresy* that see the novel as primarily addressing marriage law and politics, see S. Emsley, 'Radical Marriage', *Eighteenth-Century Fiction*, 11:4 (1999), pp. 1–22; M. Cannon, 'Hygienic Motherhood: Domestic Medicine and Eliza Fenwick's *Secresy*', *Eighteenth-Century Fiction*, 20:4 (2008), pp. 535–61; and L. Mandell, 'Sacred Secrets: Romantic Biography, Romantic Reform', *Nineteenth-Century Prose*, 28:2 (2001), pp. 28–54. For a convincing analysis of *Secresy*'s relationship to imperialism, see M. Snow, 'Habits of Empire and Domination in Eliza Fenwick's *Secresy*', *Eighteenth-Century Fiction*, 14:2 (2002), pp. 159–75. For readings that investigate *Secresy*'s relationship to female sexuality, see A. Close, 'Into the Public: The Sexual Heroine in Eliza Fenwick's *Secresy* and Mary Robinson's *The Natural Daughter*', *Eighteenth-Century Fiction*, 17:1 (2004), pp. 35–52; R. Chatterjee, 'Sapphic Subjectivity and Gothic Desires in Eliza Fenwick's *Secresy*', *Gothic Studies*, 6:1 (2004), pp. 45–56; and N. P. Fisk, '"I Heard Her Murmurs": Decoding Narratives of Female Desire in *Jane Eyre* and *Secresy*', *Brontë Studies*, 33 (2008), pp. 218–23.

88 *Jonathan Sadow*

11. C. Hornbuckle, 'Framing Foiled Love Attempts in Eliza Fenwick's *Secresy* and Emily Bronte's *Wuthering Heights*', Conference paper at British Women's Writers Conference, University of Louisiana–Lafayette, 14 April 2005, p. 12 n.
12. Castle, 'Sublimely Bad', p. 18.
13. M. Wollstonecraft, *The Works of Mary Wollstonecraft*, ed. J. Todd and M. Butler, 7 vols (New York: New York University Press, 1989), vol. 1, p. 85.
14. Ibid., vol. 1, p. 26.
15. Ibid., vol. 7, p. 26.
16. Ibid., vol. 7, p. 252.
17. A. Chandler, 'The "Seeds of Order and Taste": Wollstonecraft, *The Analytical Review*, and Critical Idiom', *European Romantic Review*, 16:1 (2005), pp. 1–21, on p. 7.
18. Ibid., pp. 7–10.
19. Wollstonecraft, *Works*, vol. 7, pp. 484–85.
20. See Grundy, Introduction; Wright, 'Conflicts of Genre'; and Emsley, '"Radical Marriage"'. Notably, Fenwick's much later letters to Mary Hays suggest that Fenwick also shared Wollstonecraft's strong interest in the development of 'serious' fiction. She complains in 1812 about the poor quality of Minerva Press novels, praises Scott's novels in 1821, Cooper's in 1823, and lauds the 'high tone' of contemporary fiction in 1824 (E. Fenwick, *The Fate of the Fenwicks: Letters to Mary Hays*, ed. E. F. Wedd (London: Methuen & Co., 1927), pp. 120, 208, 229, 233).
21. W. Godwin, *Memoirs of the Author of A Vindication of the Rights of Women* (London, 1798), p. 187.
22. J. Douthwaite, *The Wild Girl, Natural Man, and the Monster* (Chicago, IL: University of Chicago Press, 2001), p. 188.
23. Wright, 'Conflicts of Genre', p. 153.
24. 'Review of *Secresy*', *British Critic: And Quarterly Theological Review*, 6 (1795), p. 545.
25. Watson, *Revolution and the Form*, p. 40.
26. Wright, 'Conflicts of Genre', p. 173 n.
27. Ibid., pp. 160–61.
28. Wollstonecraft, *Works*, vol. 7, p. 142.
29. Ibid.
30. Wright, 'Conflicts of Genre', pp. 153–54.
31. Castle, 'Sublimely Bad', p. 18.
32. Fenwick, *Secresy*, p. 89.
33. Ibid., p. 174.
34. Ibid., p. 101.
35. Ibid., p. 103.
36. Ibid., p. 123.
37. Ibid., p. 284.
38. Ibid., p. 285.
39. Ibid., p. 341.
40. Ibid., p. 222.
41. Ibid., p. 54.
42. Hornbuckle, 'Framing Foiled Love Attempts', p. 6.
43. Fenwick, *Secresy*, p. 78.
44. Ibid., p. 65.

45. Ibid., p. 140.
46. Ibid., p. 188.
47. Wright, 'Conflicts of Genre', p. 158.
48. Hornbuckle, 'Framing Foiled Love Attempts' makes a convincing case that *Secresy*'s narrative strategies may be seen as a precursor to *Wuthering Heights*. See Fisk, 'Decoding Narratives' for a similar argument relating *Secresy* to *Jane Eyre*.
49. Fenwick, *Secresy*, p. 235.

5 Mary Hays and the Didactic Novel in the 1790s

Ada Sharpe and Eleanor Ty

Mary Hays is best known in literary history as a radical or revolutionary author of the turbulent 1790s, a follower of Mary Wollstonecraft and her band of 'unsex'd females',[1] in the words of Richard Polwhele. Gary Kelly includes Hays in the group of radical 'English Jacobins' of the 1790s, whom he describes as 'intellectuals and miscellaneous writers of liberal social views … who, inspired by revolution abroad and political protest in Britain, gave a much sharper edge to fiction' by uniting philosophical theory with tropes borrowed from popular literary genres, such as the Gothic novel, the domestic romance and the novel of sensibility.[2] Hays's contributions to feminist thought during this period and, more specifically, her use of fiction as a vehicle for political reform, have been explored by many scholars in the field of women's writing of the late eighteenth century, establishing her as a central force in the deployment of the popular novel as a medium to 'represent, indeed, *mold* people's social and historical awareness, and hence their social behavior'.[3] Recent scholarship on Hays, largely focusing on her two novels – *Memoirs of Emma Courtney* (1796) and *The Victim of Prejudice* (1799) – has continued to emphasize her efforts to further the cause of women by arguing for her particular kind of 'scientifically-grounded materialist' feminism, her desire to go against the prevailing ideologies which limited the education of women and against those which linked female virtue mainly with chastity.[4]

Yet the philosophy and themes explored in Hays's fiction continue to be largely and, as Scott A. Nowka argues, far too narrowly defined in relation to the writings of William Godwin, Hays's correspondent and acquaintance until the late 1790s.[5] The notoriety of her autobiographically inspired *Emma Courtney* has, moreover, long supplied fodder for critical readings of Hays 'as a more outrageous version of Wollstonecraft', giving body to a distorted biographical image of the writer which has threatened to overshadow her unique contributions to British fiction.[6] This essay aims to refine our understanding of those contributions by exploring the relationship between Hays's use of fiction as a vehicle for instruction and political formation and the rise of religiously-informed, domestic didactic or 'corrective' fiction, predominantly authored by women, during the late eighteenth and early nineteenth centuries. We focus on Hays's representations of female trial and suffering, emotional experience, and social injustice in order to put seemingly

Mary Hays and the Didactic Novel in the 1790s 91

antithetical texts and genres in dialogue, identifying shared as well as distinct rhetorical terrain between what we refer to as Hays's 'Jacobin didacticism' and the didacticism elaborated in specifically 'moral-domestic' fiction, Anthony Mandal's generic heading for the body of religiously-informed, heroine-centred narratives which flourished after 1800.[7]

In this vein, our essay begins by interrogating the apparent contradiction between the late eighteenth- and early nineteenth-century didactic novel as a characteristically antirevolutionary or conservative genre and the profoundly revolutionary and reformist feminist project pursued by Hays in *Emma Courtney* and *The Victim of Prejudice*. We re-read Hays's novels of the 1790s to find connections as well as fissures between her ideas and those propounded by conservative writers of the period,[8] working from the assumption that Hays experiments with the novel as a platform for philosophical and ethical instruction, much as moral-domestic women novelists would do with critical and commercial success in their narratives of Christian trial, duty, self-regulation, and good works.[9] Hays's fiction is united with the moral-domestic in representing the development and preservation of the heroine's moral and intellectual autonomy as signal concerns and, moreover, in identifying the formation of the heroine as a stimulus to readerly reflection and self-examination. For Hays, the emphasis on self-examination and individual agency is grounded in her Dissenting religious beliefs and the Enlightenment conviction in the power of rational thought to create social change. Thus although Hays's fiction certainly differs from the moral novels and tales of such popular writers as Amelia Opie, Maria Edgeworth, and Mary Brunton, most notably in terms of political climate, reception, and narrative point of view, we suggest that *Emma Courtney* and *The Victim of Prejudice* share with this later generation of fiction the common aim to initiate readers into a particular reformist vision which grants value to women as rational, moral agents, and positions heroines as not only the victims but the decriers of patriarchal iniquity.

To this end, we identify and explore Hays's preeminent objectives and modes of instruction. Through her first-person narratives of trial and formation, Hays develops a didactic approach with the view of modelling critical self-examination and forming political consciousness in the reading subject and, in particular, the female reading subject.[10] Hays's didactic approach as a novelist is two-pronged, establishing the immediacy of the heroine's emotions and experience by adopting her limited point of view and hence fostering identification with the heroine's plight and, simultaneously, recasting dominant cultural narratives (namely those surrounding heterosexual romance, women's social 'usefulness', and the 'fallen' woman) through the heroine's struggles in the face of insuperable social, economic, and legal barriers, thus encouraging critical reflection on the ideals, mores, and institutions that shape actual women's lives in the immediate historical context.

Invoking the Jacobin novel's emphasis on the effect of circumstance and education on the growth of the individual, Hays places explicit focus on the psychology of the gendered subject, the embodiment of experience, and the relationship between reason and feeling in order to imagine a new model of 'revolutionary female subjectivity'.[11] Yet while her didactic purpose serves the imperatives of protest and reform, Hays joins Opie, Edgeworth, Brunton, and, indeed, many women writers of this period, in claiming fiction as the preferred platform to represent middle-class female subjectivity and imagine alternate models of British womanhood. Hays thus grants power to the novel as a vehicle for drawing attention to barriers to women's meaningful contribution to the affective, economic, and civic health of the community and, more broadly, as a means to forming subjectivity and consciousness in the reading public.

Raising the Mind, Warming the Heart, Enlarging Our Views: Hays's 'Jacobin Didacticism'

In her essay, 'Crossing from "Jacobin" to "Anti-Jacobin"', Miriam L. Wallace reminds us that the original use of the term 'Jacobin novel' referred to any 'British reformist projects associated with the French Revolution', particularly with 'dangerous desires for social and political reform'.[12] However, she notes that, even 'if the philosophical, literary, and public political' rise of 'English Jacobinism' precedes that of 'Anti-Jacobinism', 'the trajectory of influence and reaction is nevertheless not simply one of thesis and antithesis'. Instead, Wallace avers, 'the philosophical, political, and parodic novels most often designated as "anti-Jacobin" are nearly co-terminus with the "Jacobin" novel – emerging in complex conversation with continuing debates on reforming political and social institutions'.[13] One of the first scholars to note the connection between those female writers who were labelled 'Jacobin' and those who were later called 'Anti-Jacobin' was Mitzi Myers, who, in her oft-quoted essay 'Reform or Ruin', notes the similarities across 'a wide spectrum' of women writers of the 1790s, who 'vigorously attacked the deficiencies of fashionable training and values' and sought 'to endow woman's role with more competence, dignity, and consequence'.[14]

In order to read Mary Hays through the lens of the didactic and build on Myers's and Wallace's shared recognition of continuity as opposed to polarity in this genre, it is necessary to expand our understanding and definition of the didactic novel. Lisa Wood equates didacticism with antirevolutionary ideology in women's writing of this period, and describes the popular didactic novel as 'concerned less with literary effect than with conveying and enforcing a conformist moral message'.[15] In this line of argument, didacticism implies narrative and ideological cohesion; accordingly, Wood argues, 'writers of antirevolutionary didactic fiction strove toward a single meaning and complete closure'.[16]

Hays's two novels complicate this equation of the didactic with ideals of generic order and narrative closure and the enforcement of ideological conformity. Similarly preoccupied with the psychologically and politically transformative power of narrative, her texts are characterized by their dialogism and generic subversion, presenting ripe opportunity for contradictory readings.[17] In fact, as Wallace has argued, Jacobin fiction works to form political consciousness by eliciting contradictory readings and stimulating critical self-reflection in the reader by putting into 'question the very ideals' it 'attempt[s] to illustrate'.[18] In doing so,

> These novels consistently engage the reader as an active agent whose ability to read and interpret will impact the national and familial social order. In the process of reflective and active reading, they aim at nothing less than reconstituting the reader as a politically resistant subject.[19]

Hays, in her essay 'On Novel Writing' in the *Monthly Magazine* (1797), articulates just this view when she parses generic terms in order to capture what she sees as 'the business' of the novel in the present age:

> It is not necessary that ... we should be able to deduce from a novel, a formal, didactic moral; it is sufficient if it has a tendency to raise the mind by elevated sentiments, to warm the heart with generous reflections, to enlarge our views, or to increase our stock of useful knowledge.[20]

Rejecting the neoclassical ideal of an imposed ('formal') moral easily deduced from unrealistic models of 'chimerical perfection and visionary excellence' (she cites Richardson's *Clarissa* (1747–48) as an example), Hays nevertheless turns to elaborate that fiction can offer 'a more effectual lesson' in 'tracing the pernicious consequences of an erroneous judgment, a wrong step, an imprudent action, an indulged and intemperate affection, a bad habit, in a character in other respects amiable and virtuous'.[21] Here she outlines an alternate theory of didactic fiction that focuses on the function of narrative in exercising and developing critical thinking in the (female) reader by tracing human trial and error 'in real and probable situations'. In a departure from the 'delight' implied by neoclassical didacticism, Hays's novels depict the heroine amidst relentless trial and suffering, drawing her as the witnessing subject of injustice and prejudice, in order to propel the novel's 'engine of truth and reform'. Such portraits of what she describes as 'the noble mind blasted by the ravages of passion, or withered by the canker of prejudice ... afford an affecting and humiliating lesson of human frailty' for, Hays continues,

> they teach us to soften the asperity of censure, to appreciate the motives and actions of our fellow being with candour, to distrust ourselves, and to watch with diffidence lest we should ... be precipitated into folly, or betrayed into vice.[22]

In locating formative potential in the novel's 'tendency to raise the mind ... to warm the heart ... to enlarge our views', Hays, moreover, grants agency to the critical, if not resisting reader, adopting the Godwinian concept of 'tendency' to flesh out her theory of Jacobin didacticism. Hays's intention for both her novels published in the 1790s, as stated in her 'Advertisement to the Reader' in *The Victim of Prejudice*, was to 'inculcate an important lesson' about the 'errors of sensibility' or the 'pernicious consequences of indulged passion' in *Emma Courtney*, and to call into question the 'means' which are used to ensure the 'reputation for chastity in woman' in *The Victim of Prejudice*.[23] After the reception of *Emma Courtney*, Hays realized that her work could be misread and noted at the outset of her subsequent novel that she had been 'accused of recommending those excesses of which [she] laboured to paint the disastrous effects'.[24] The unintended consequence or misreading is what Godwin had described as the 'tendency' of a work, 'the actual effect it is calculated to produce upon the reader' which cannot be ascertained 'but by experiment'.[25] Gary Handwerk comments that what Godwin calls 'tendency' 'captures the proclivity towards resistance that makes readers – and good readers in particular – resist the "moral" of a given work and actually want to read it otherwise than the author intended'.[26]

As William Stafford points out, the morals of Hays's *Emma Courtney*, like those of Opie's *Adeline Mowbray* (1804), Thomas Holcroft's *Anna St. Ives* (1792), Charles Lloyd's *Edmund Oliver* (1798), and Elizabeth Hamilton's *Memoirs of Modern Philosophers* (1800), 'seem surprisingly similar at a surface level: self-control must override passion, true and false sensibility may be distinguished by their differing effect, and gender-specific dangers threaten women and men who are unable to make such distinctions'.[27] What is different about Hays's *Emma Courtney* is that its 'tendency' has been so powerful as to provoke a number of resistant readings and caricatures. Most notably, the character Bridgetina Botherim in Hamilton's *Modern Philosophers* presents a 'bitingly cruel' caricature of Hays.[28] Hays's technique of using the first-person narrative voice and using events and letters based on her own life have been the reasons for the success of *Emma Courtney* and the bane of her career as novelist. Most of the moral-domestic novels of the period are told from the perspective of an omniscient narrator, usually older and worldly-wise. These include, for example, Opie's *The Father and Daughter* (1801), Hamilton's *Modern Philosophers*, Edgeworth's *Belinda* (1801), and Brunton's *Self-Control* (1811). Or else, there is Jane West's eccentric fictional narrator Prudentia Homespun, who takes on the persona of 'an authoritative woman writer with a recipe for wholesome English fiction'.[29] As David Thame notes, West employs a 'double voiced strategy' by at once condemning the 'enormous public appetite for novels' and at the same time serving up 'elopements, seductions, aristocratic villainies, confinement for madness, and finally a heroine who stabs herself then falls convulsed and bleeding, at her wicked father's feet: in short, the usual ingredients of the circulating library novel, proven to satisfy public taste'.[30] Thus despite its reputation for enforced meaning,

Mary Hays and the Didactic Novel in the 1790s 95

moral-domestic fiction exhibits parallels with Hays's fiction in its openness to dialogic and contradictory readings, as Thame's reading of West's 'double voiced strategy' intimates.

Mode of Instruction I: Immediacy of Experience

In contrast to the 'disciplined' third-person narratives of the early nineteenth century, Hays's novels of the 1790s tend to revolve around the thoughts and feelings of one woman, one voice, creating the effect of constriction and limitation rather than omniscience and authority. Whereas Hays was interested in the 1790s in exploiting the immediacy of first-person narrative and the epistolary mode to foster criticism of 'the social system' for which 'the novel was supposed to condition' the reading subject, moral-domestic fiction sought to corral the excesses of Jacobin fiction within the generic bounds of what Nicola J. Watson has called 'the novel of social consensus'.[31] The omniscience of Brunton's cool, measured narrator in *Self-Control*, as well as those in *Discipline* (1814) and *Emmeline* (1819), for example, typify the narrative distance characteristic of the moral-domestic world. Thus while Hays's aim was to advocate for educational reform for women, and to caution women against excessive reliance on passion in the same way as other didactic novelists of the period, her method was highly personal rather than detached. We recognize this as a fundamental aspect of Hays's particular modes of instruction as a novelist. As Louise Joy summarizes, Hays '[capitalized] on the angles that the novel can reach through manipulation of point of view' and thus 'used fiction to rehabilitate the subjective component that falls out of accounts of emotions offered by non-fictional philosophy'.[32] This means evoking 'the voice of individual feeling as a form of legitimate protest',[33] attempting to fashion the politically conscious fictional, writing, and reading subject through the language of sensibility.

This focus on the personal links Hays's fiction to a form of life writing popular at the time. In her book about eighteenth-century actresses, Felicity Nussbaum says of their memoirs:

> Richardson's epistolary novel *Pamela* has in common with the biographies of actresses the morally inspired voyeurism, the urge to rectify behavior through interested surveillance characteristic of an age in which self-fashioning invited intrusion into private space. The invasion of interiority through print culture gave special impetus to pouncing on an unconventional woman's reputation.[34]

Like the memoirs of actresses and the fictional letters of Pamela which provided details of her master's attempts on her chastity, Hays's *Emma Courtney* provided her readers a glimpse into the author's own struggles with unrequited love. Though she was not a celebrity like the actresses of London theatres, by the mid 1790s she had already published an Oriental tale, an essay about public worship, and a didactic manual, *Letters and Essays, Moral and Miscellaneous*. She was becoming known in the circle of London literati of the time. In sharing her private letters and exposing her story to the public, she was turning her private experience of disappointment and rejection into a marketable commodity. What Nussbaum says of actresses applies to a certain degree to Hays:

> as agents of their own commodification[,] they signaled the emergence of a culture in which the 'self' – creating the effect of a private interior depth combined with a very real physical presence – produces itself as a fluid commodity to be advertised and exchanged.[35]

Nussbaum describes the way in which a talented actress could 'affect a persona' and create an 'illusion of interiority' by blending personal elements with genre expectations, resulting in what she calls the 'interiority effect'.[36]

In *Emma Courtney*, Hays uses elements of her life, namely her passion for the mathematician William Frend, and blends them with the conventions of Richardson's epistolary novel and the memoir to create a work that would sell, but one that would also question women's sexual passivity and the lack of intellectual and emotional outlets for single women. Emma repeatedly emphasizes the private and secret nature of her story. Initially, when she makes up her mind to communicate her feelings for Harley to the Godwinian figure, Mr Francis, she says, 'I took up my pen, and though I dared not betray the fatal secret concealed, as a sacred treasure, in the bottom of my heart, I yet gave a loose to, I endeavoured to paint, its sensations'.[37] Later, when she writes to Harley himself to tell him of her strong passion for him, she states,

> that could I hope to gain the interest in your heart, which I have so long and so earnestly sought – my confidence in your honour and integrity, my tenderness for you, added to the wish of contributing to your happiness ... would triumph, not over my principles ... but over my prudence.... This proposition, though not a violation of modesty, certainly involves in it very serious hazards – *It is, wholly, the triumph of affection!*[38]

Emma uses the clichés and exaggerated language of the sentimental novel, 'fatal secret', 'sacred treasure', 'confess', 'violation of modesty', 'triumph of affection', to create interest and sway not only the addressee of her letters, but also her novel's reader. Emma herself is conscious of the fact that she is entering into a hopeless situation. In one instance, she describes her growing affection for Augustus as imbibing 'in large draughts, the deceitful poison of hope'.[39] But with the exceptions of the interruptions of the older Emma at the beginning of both volumes – 'My friend, my son, it is for your benefit'[40] – there is no authorial voice to distance us from her. Hays's way of inculcating the need for self-control and self-regulation entails our voyeurism and surveillance of Emma's emotional excesses, the confession of her weaknesses, and her self-punishments.

In both her novels, Hays emphasizes the importance of perception in shaping subjectivity, especially in terms of female moral development and the regulation of desire. With *Emma Courtney* in particular, Hays thematises 'the powers of human mind'[41] and the limits of subjective perception through the extended metaphor of 'gradation'. In her essay 'On Novel Writing', Hays avers that, 'Gradations, almost imperceptible, of light and shade, must mingle in every true portrait of the human mind'.[42] Explaining her objective to '[trace] … the phenomenon of the human mind' as a novelist, Hays makes an analogous point in the preface to *Emma Courtney* when she asserts that 'light and shade are more powerfully contrasted in minds rising above the common level', a theory of individual psychology elaborated through the extremity and intensity of her heroine's emotional experiences.[43] Emma repeatedly draws on the metaphors of light and shade to express the ways in which her feelings colour and condition her experiences, suggesting the force of her mind in shaping the immediate scene. Following the death of her father and facing her entrance into the family circle at Morton Park, Emma desponds, for instance, as 'Those ardent feelings and lively expectations, with all the glowing landscapes which my mind had sketched of the varied pleasure of society, while in a measure secluded from its enjoyments, gradually melted into one deep, undistinguished shade'.[44] Here 'the glowing landscapes' of futurity disappear within the 'deep, undistinguished shade' of Emma's 'despondency' upon entering the world as an unprotected young woman of limited means.

This emphasis on the heroine's interlaced aesthetic and moral sensitivities recalls the powers of perception that Ann Radcliffe assigns to her Gothic heroines, such as Emily St. Aubert and Ellena Rosalba, who learn a great deal about themselves and the moral universe through their balanced observations of the natural world. Writing on modes of perception in late eighteenth-century fiction, Fiona Price has argued that Radcliffe 'proposes an alternative kind of gaze' in her fiction akin to the use of chiaroscuro in visual art, using the heroine's sensitivity to contrast and variety 'of light and shade' in the natural landscape as a metaphor for her development as a rational, disinterested viewer equipped with 'the ability to gauge the feelings of others and respond appropriately'. 'In Radcliffe's work', Price explains, 'the act of viewing landscape, with its patterns of light and darkness, form a metaphor for understanding the moral shades of the human character. Moreover, in a sensitive human being, examining the scenery cultivates self-control'.[45] Hays uses the metaphor of gradation in a similar way, yoking the language of aesthetics to the development of moral subjectivity in her portrait of Emma Courtney. Assisted by the first-person narrative point of view and the epistolary mode, Hays departs from Radcliffe, however, in using light and dark to evince the enclosure and immediacy of subjective experience – typified by Emma's description of the 'deep, undistinguished shade' of her mind – as opposed to elaborating the heroine's cultivation of disinterest and self-control as a spectator.

In particular, Hays employs the metaphor of gradation in order to cast doubt on Emma's ability to see beyond her own solipsistic world. As Vivien Jones has observed, 'One of the most interesting aspects of this novel ... is the uncertainty as to how to judge its heroine'.[46] Emma's accounts of her unrelenting passion for Harley, and in the face of his consistent unresponsiveness and evasion, produce a great deal of this uncertainty, suggesting the extent to which Emma is 'bound within the confines of [her] own subjectivity'.[47] 'Emma's destructive obsession with Harley', Jones writes, is 'presented as the inevitable consequence of a "superior" female mind which lacks, and therefore constructs, an ideal object' in her lover.[48] Significantly, the maternal narratives of Mrs Harley, paired with the portrait of Harley that hangs in the family home, feed this ideal. In a critical instance of misperception, Emma, enabled by the powers of her 'uncommon' mind, translates representation into reality, ideal into real; as one reviewer in the *Critical Review* summarized, this is 'not love at *first sight*, but even *before* first sight'.[49] The immediacy of Emma's desire 'presents an opportunity for the reader vicariously to experience' the heroine's emotions and hence witness the 'gradations' of human psychology at work.[50] In doing so, the novelist solicits the reader to recognize the ways in which perception colours experience, and desire and passion threaten to confuse real and ideal. The extended metaphor of gradation thus generates some degree of distance in what Watson regards as the novel's 'coercive' strategies of identification between reader and heroine,[51] engendering sympathy for Emma's suffering while simultaneously opening opportunity for critical reflection on her desire.

Edgeworth's *Belinda* and Brunton's *Self-Control* draw similar connections between perception, moral growth, and female desire, although their approaches find greater resonance with that of Radcliffe than that of Hays. Edgeworth and Brunton are first and foremost concerned with modelling 'correct' ways of seeing as the basis for the cultivation of rational self-control. In *Belinda*, Virginia St. Pierre incarnates the novel's warning against women's Rousseau-like isolation and ignorance when she confuses romance narrative and reality and falls in love with a 'fatal picture' of a man, a projection of her chivalric fantasies.[52] Brunton's Laura Montreville is much more self-aware than Virginia, and uses her artistic pursuits in painting and sketching to redirect her sexual desire into creative self-expression and commercial activity, even if all her male figures bear a striking resemblance to her lover, her 'only standard of manly beauty'.[53] Her gaze, however, is disciplined by artistic practice, affording distance from the force of her own romantic fantasies. Edgeworth and Brunton similarly set out to correct female characters' modes of perception in order to induct them into disciplined subject positions. In contrast with Hays's strategy in *Emma Courtney*, Edgeworth and Brunton's novels espouse a female gaze chiefly defined by distance, disinterest, and self-control in order to demonstrate the value of individual self-regulation as the basis for women's freedom from the dictates of desire and the constricting narratives of heterosexual romance.

Mode of Instruction II: Recasting Narratives

In both *Emma Courtney* and *The Victim of Prejudice*, Hays undertakes the feminist project of recasting the dominant narrative surrounding sexual difference in order to engage the reader in a process of critical reflection and debate on the mores, ideals, and prejudices upheld in contemporary British society.[54] Chiefly concerned with the position of middle-class women, Hays seeks to recast prevailing cultural narratives surrounding, namely, heterosexual romance and female desire, women's social 'usefulness' and economic roles, and the social and economic marginalization of the 'fallen' woman. Her fiction involves the (female) reader in the process of imaginatively testing the possibilities and limits of rational, socially engaged, and economically independent womanhood in 1790s Britain, bearing out Wallace's claim that, '[even] at their most didactic the Jacobin novels teach not just the correct modes of thought, but how to frame an argument and how to draw lessons from the events of novels and of everyday life'.[55]

One difference between Hays and other women writers of the 1790s and early 1800s is that Hays, like the second wave feminists of the 1960s, was advocating for the possibility of women's equality in the sexual realm and labour economy. Myers stresses that both More and Wollstonecraft 'challenged popular conduct book recommendations for feminine training and behavior' and instead envisioned a 'pattern of female domestic heroism'.[56] In her *Vindication of the Rights of Woman* (1792), Wollstonecraft complained that 'women, whose minds are not enlarged by cultivation, or the natural selfishness of sensibility expanded by reflection, are very unfit to manage a family'.[57] The end result is that Hays's novels share ground with a good deal of moral-domestic fiction in interrogating suitable socio-economic roles and, more specifically, forms of remunerated employment for women of the middling classes. Hays shares the belief that education will make women better companions, wives, and mothers. She also had hopes, however, that women who did not or could not marry could be trained to become economically independent. In an article entitled 'Improvements Suggested in Female Education' published in the *Monthly Magazine* (1797), Hays points to 'a variety of trades and professions, by their nature peculiarly appropriate to women, exercised ... at present entirely by men.... A woman enabled to support herself, and to acquire property by her industry', Hays maintains, 'would gain by regular occupation, and the healthful exertion of her faculties, more firmness of mind and greater vigour of body'.[58]

In *Emma Courtney*, the heroine laments that she was not trained for a profession and is forced to become dependent on her relations upon her father's death:

> Cruel prejudice! – I exclaimed – hapless woman! Why was I not educated for commerce, for a profession, for labour? Why have I been rendered feeble and delicate by bodily constraint, and fastidious by artificial refinement? Why are we bound, by the habits of society as with an adamantine chain?[59]

Here Emma articulates her wish to go outside and beyond the confines of the domestic and the philanthropic, the spheres of suitably feminine activity promoted by Hannah More and others. One should note, however, that Emma's (and Hays's) desire for work and 'honest independence' is delimited by concerns over preserving social caste; hence Emma sneers at 'the degradation of servitude', refusing to 'submit' to the corporeal labour performed by servants.[60] She equally refuses to pursue trade or take up work in the cottage industries of carding, spinning, and clothing production, areas of employment open to women by the late eighteenth century.[61] Emma conceives of a particularly specific definition of suitable labour for herself as a genteel woman while still aspiring to be a 'useful' economic and social agent. Mary Raymond, the heroine of Hays's second novel, is similarly committed to making herself 'useful' – for the sake of her own financial and moral independence as well as in the spirit of social improvement through economic activity – but she is far more open and, perhaps, more desperate than Emma, and performs a range of paid jobs, from botanical illustration to agricultural labour. This interest in embracing remunerated work (if oftentimes narrowly defined in its scope) as a facet of women's social usefulness is not unique to Hays but, as Myers argues, takes part in a broader and emergent cultural ideal, explored by writers across the ideological spectrum, that women could 'take responsibility for realizing their own potential' and 'become self-improved, albeit modest, mistresses of their own – and the nation's – destiny'.[62]

Emma's pursuit of economic and moral autonomy is intimately yoked to her desire for sexual autonomy. Rejecting marriage as a means to economic security, Emma believes that she will be able to survive in society based on her intellect and moral conviction: as she explains to Mr Montague when she rejects his offer of marriage, 'I would not marry any man, merely for an *establishment*, for whom I did not feel an affection'.[63] Emma desires a partner based on affective rather than economic bonds, aspiring to the 'companionate marriage' Lawrence Stone has identified as emerging in the eighteenth century.[64] Advocating for the heroine's right to choose a partner with whom she feels 'sympathy' and 'a union between mind and mind' in *Emma Courtney*,[65] Hays also set out to recast narratives surrounding sexual purity and virtue in *The Victim of Prejudice*. Hays's *Victim of Prejudice*

Mary Hays and the Didactic Novel in the 1790s 101

contains two stories: one, a conventional story of what Susan Staves calls the 'seduced maiden' narrative, and the other, a story of a rape victim trying to recover her subjectivity outside of the limits of sexual identity.

In *The Victim of Prejudice*, the story of Mary, the heroine's mother, follows that of the seduced maiden, who, as Staves notes, 'strenuously resists invitations to illicit intercourse, yielding only after a protracted siege and under otherwise extraordinary circumstances'.[66] Her story is appealing because the seduced maiden '[embodies] precisely those virtues the culture especially prized in young women: beauty, simplicity (or ignorance), trustfulness, and affectionateness'.[67] The formula of resistance, seduction, pathos, and penitence was popular in a number of works of the late eighteenth and nineteenth centuries, as Staves remarks.[68] In *The Victim of Prejudice*, the older Mary's story is recounted to the younger Mary within the narrative of her guardian, Mr Raymond's own account of youthful indiscretion. Like the seduced maidens Hannah in Elizabeth Inchbald's *Nature and Art* (1796) and Agnes in Opie's *The Father and Daughter*, the elder Mary in Hays's novel '[listens] to the insidious flatteries of a being, raised by fashion and fortune to a rank', her imagination and vanity falling prey to her seducer. Like them, Mary is too trusting, 'too weak for principle, credulous from inexperience, a stranger to the corrupt habits of society', and loses her heart and yields her chastity.[69] Her story is similar to the narratives of pursuit and (attempted) seduction found in many novels of this period, including *Self-Control*, but Hays's *Victim of Prejudice* was not received in the same spirit.

Unlike other seduced maiden novels, Hays places the blame of seduction and fall not just on the victimized woman but also on society. That is, her novel makes overt references to structural inequities and failures in institutions such as education, law, and the customs of British society. The elder Mary, having led a life of 'folly' and 'infamy' after her lover leaves her, is arrested for his murder. Awaiting her death, she writes that, '*Law* completes the triumph of injustice. The despotism of man rendered me weak, his vices betrayed me into shame, a barbarous policy stifled returning dignity, prejudice robbed me of the means of independence'.[70] Here she blames legal institutions, the lack of what we would call social services, as well as social prejudices for her downfall. In a departure from Hays's approach in *The Victim of Prejudice*, Opie's Agnes in *The Father and Daughter* is praised by the community for her 'life of self-denial, patience, fortitude and industry', the basis of her social reclamation and 'atonement' after her sexual 'fall'.[71] In this rewriting of the 'fallen' woman narrative, Opie puts the onus on the individual to rescue herself from destitution so that the twinned ideologies of industry and self-improvement overshadow the tale's tangent, if muted, criticisms of the institutions and values responsible for the heroine's social and economic marginalization. In a review of *The Victim of Prejudice* in 1799, the reviewer in *The Critical Review* praised the novel as 'a tale of considerable interest' for its many passages of 'warmth and vigour of pathos', yet objected to the heroine's invocation of the law as a source in injustice, noting that 'municipal institutions' and 'public benevolence' were there to provide asylum 'for those repentant victims who would wish to escape from vice to virtue'. The reviewer did not understand Hays's complaints about 'tyranny', which belong to '*philosophical* jargon'.[72] Despite this critical objection, the frequent unhappy endings for seduced maidens – death, loss of social status, or banishment – suggest that these social services were few and often stigmatized, and that Hays was justified in her complaints.

The younger Mary's story, then, is not a traditional tale of seduction but one of institutional and socially sanctioned violence against women, exacerbated by class and economic differences. Unlike her mother, the younger Mary never yields but is kidnapped and raped like Richardson's Clarissa. But whereas Clarissa takes refuge in meditation and looks forward to going to her [heavenly] 'father's house',[73] Mary never ceases to demand liberty and independence from the man who pursues and rapes her. With her background as a rational Dissenter, she does not place her hopes in heaven but appeals to the 'tribunal of [her] country' and to her reason. After the rape, she still boldly asserts: 'Think not, by feeble restraints to fetter the body when the mind is determined and free'.[74] Her assertion of her liberty is based on a rights discourse influenced by Enlightenment philosophy, not a biblical one, as she asks for 'liberty, the common *right* of a human being'.[75] By portraying a heroine who refuses to have her body read as unchaste or to consider herself a 'fallen' woman, Hays encourages eighteenth-century readers to value women as moral and intellectual beings endowed with natural rights rather than as sexual commodities. The circularity and repetitiveness of Mary's narrative, with its motif of confinement, refuses to instruct by delighting readers but instead implements a pedagogy of discomfort in order to recast the narrative of seduction and fall. Over and over, Mary is placed in situations of distress and anxiety so that we, as readers, are placed in positions of surveillance and spectatorship experiencing not pleasure but uneasiness.

While many didactic novelists represent their heroines enduring difficulties with exemplary humility and patience, Hays's claustrophobic novels of the 1790s reveal the limitations of female docility, demonstrate the practical impossibility for women in achieving economic and legal independence in late eighteenth-century British society, and insist upon the need for social reform. Adapting the novel's didactic potential to her own radical philosophical and political imperatives, Hays calls upon the reader as a sympathetic witness to the barriers and prejudices faced by her flawed if admirable middle-class heroines, inviting us to participate in the critical examination of self, society, and the cultural narratives which underpin the popular novel itself. In doing so, Hays claims the feminized genre of novel as a platform to develop and circulate a vision of social transformation that situates the condition and potential of women – as readers, reformers, and autonomous moral subjects – at its fore.

Notes

1. Richard Polwhele, *The Unsex'd Females: A Poem* (1798), introd. Gina Luria (New York: Garland, 1974), p. 7.
2. G. Kelly, *English Fiction of the Romantic Period 1789–1830* (London and New York: Longman, 1989), p. 26.
3. A. Gilroy and W. Verhoeven, 'The Romantic-era Novel: A Special Issue – Introduction', *Novel: A Forum on Fiction*, 34:2 (2001), pp. 147–62, on pp. 152–53.
4. S. A. Nowka, 'Materialism and Feminism in Mary Hays's *Memoirs of Emma Courtney*', *European Romantic Review*, 18:4 (2007), pp. 521–40, on p. 521; A. Sharma, 'A Different Voice: Mary Hays's *The Memoirs of Emma Courtney*', *Women's Writing*, 8:1 (2001), pp. 139–67, on p. 139; M. L. Brooks 'Mary Hays's *The Victim of Prejudice*: Chastity Renegotiated', *Women's Writing*, 15:1 (2008), pp. 13–31, on p. 13.
5. Nowka, 'Materialism and Feminism', p. 526.
6. T. Rajan, 'Autonarration and Genotext in Mary Hays' *Memoirs of Emma Courtney*', in T. Rajan and J. M. Wright (eds), *Romanticism, History, and the Possibilities of Genre: Reforming Literature 1789–1837* (Cambridge and New York: Cambridge University Press, 1998), pp. 213–39, on p. 214.
7. A. Mandal, *Jane Austen and the Popular Novel: The Determined Author* (Houndmills, UK and New York: Palgrave Macmillan, 2007), p. 95.
8. As noted by Claudia Johnson in relation to the British novel in the late eighteenth century, 'the code words of conservative and reformist polemicists were not at first antithetical, but in fact often share a common tradition' (*Jane Austen: Women, Politics, and the Novel* (Chicago, IL: University of Chicago Press, 1988), p. xxii).
9. Mandal, *Jane Austen and the Popular Novel*, pp. 94–95.
10. M. L. Wallace, *Revolutionary Subjects in the English 'Jacobin' Novel, 1790–1805* (Lewisburg, PA: Bucknell University Press, 2009), p. 14; K. Binhammer, 'The Persistence of Reading: Governing Female Novel-Reading in *Memoirs of Emma Courtney* and *Memoirs of Modern Philosophers*', *Eighteenth-Century Life*, 27:2 (2003), pp. 1–22, on p. 3.
11. N. J. Watson, *Revolution and the Form of the British Novel, 1790–1825* (Oxford and New York: Clarendon Press and Oxford University Press, 1994), p. 26.
12. M. L. Wallace, 'Crossing from "Jacobin" to "Anti-Jacobin": Rethinking the Terms of English Jacobinism', in P. Cass and L. H. Peer (eds), *Romantic Border Crossings* (Aldershot, UK and Burlington, VT: Ashgate, 2008), pp. 99–112, on pp. 99–100.
13. Ibid., p. 101.
14. Myers includes in this list Catherine Macaulay Graham, Mary Wollstonecraft, Mary Hays, Anne Frances Randall, Clara Reeve, Maria Edgeworth, Anna Laetitia Barbauld, Priscilla Wakefield, Mary Ann Radcliffe, Sarah Trimmer, Hannah More, and Jane West. M. Myers, 'Reform or Ruin: "A Revolution in Female Manners"', *Studies in Eighteenth-Century Culture*, 11 (1982), pp. 199–216, on p. 201.
15. L. Wood, *Modes of Discipline: Women, Conservatism, and the Novel after the French Revolution* (Lewisburg, PA: Bucknell University Press, 2003), p. 11.
16. Ibid., p. 16. Gilroy and Verhoeven make a similar point when they claim that in contrast to the 'generic and aesthetic' and hence 'moral and ideological promiscuity' of 'the revolutionary novel' – defined by its engagements with 'new

104   *Ada Sharpe and Eleanor Ty*

philosophy', sensibility and the Gothic – 'the Anti-Jacobin novel was much less inclined to experiment with narrative format' in order to establish its moral and ideological authority ('The Romantic-era Novel', pp. 153–54).

17. Wallace, *Revolutionary Subjects*, p. 21; Rajan, 'Autonarration and Genotext', p. 216.
18. Wallace, *Revolutionary Subjects*, p. 34.
19. Ibid., p. 21.
20. M. Hays, 'On Novel Writing', *Monthly Magazine*, 4 (1797), pp. 180–81, on p. 181.
21. Ibid.
22. Ibid.
23. M. Hays, *The Victim of Prejudice* (1799), 2nd edn, ed. E. Ty (Peterborough, ON: Broadview Press, 1998), p. 1.
24. Ibid.
25. W. Godwin, *The Enquirer: Reflections on Education, Manners and Literature, in a Series of Essays* (London, 1797), p. 136.
26. G. Handwerk, '"Awakening the Mind": William Godwin's *Enquirer*', in R. Maniquis and V. Myers (eds), *Godwinian Moments: From the Enlightenment to Romanticism* (Toronto, ON: University of Toronto Press, 2011), pp. 103–24, on p. 115.
27. W. Stafford, *English Feminists and Their Opponents in the 1790s: Unsex'd and Proper Females* (Manchester, UK: Manchester University Press, 2002), p. 106.
28. C. Grogan, *Politics and Genre in the Works of Elizabeth Hamilton, 1756–1816* (Farnham, UK and Burlington, VT: Ashgate, 2012), p. 60.
29. D. Thame, 'Cooking Up a Story: Jane West, Prudentia Homespun and the Consumption of Fiction', *Eighteenth-Century Fiction*, 16:2 (2004), pp. 217–42, on p. 226.
30. Ibid., p. 227.
31. Watson, *Revolution and Form*, p. 68.
32. L. Joy, 'Novel Feelings: Emma Courtney's Point of View', *European Romantic Review*, 21:2 (2010), pp. 221–24, on p. 221.
33. Watson, *Revolution and Form*, p. 39.
34. F. Nussbaum, *Rival Queens: Actresses, Performance, and the Eighteenth-Century British Theater* (Philadelphia, PA: University of Pennsylvania Press, 2010), p. 93.
35. Ibid., p. 65.
36. Ibid., p. 21.
37. M. Hays, *Memoirs of Emma Courtney*, ed. E. Ty (Oxford and New York: Oxford University Press, 2000), p. 84.
38. Ibid., p. 123.
39. Ibid., p. 75.
40. Ibid., p. 93.
41. Ibid., p. 3.
42. Hays, 'On Novel Writing', p. 180.
43. Hays, *Emma Courtney*, p. 4.
44. Ibid., p. 32.
45. F. Price, *Revolutions in Taste, 1773–1818: Women Writers and the Aesthetics of Romanticism* (Farnham, UK and Burlington, VT: Ashgate, 2009), pp. 86–87.
46. V. Jones, '"The Tyranny of the Passions": Feminism and Heterosexuality in the Fiction of Wollstonecraft and Hays', in S. Ledger, J. McDonagh, and J. Spencer

(eds), *Political Gender: Texts and Contexts* (Hertfordshire, UK: Harvester Wheatsheaf, 1994), pp. 173–88 on p. 173.

47. Joy, 'Novel Feelings', p. 232.
48. Jones, 'The Tyranny of the Passions', p. 183.
49. 'Review of *Memoirs of Emma Courtney*', *The Critical Review*, 19 (1797), pp. 109–11, on p. 109.
50. Joy, 'Novel Feelings', p. 225.
51. Watson, *Revolution and Form*, p. 45.
52. M. Edgeworth, *Belinda*, ed. K. Kirkpatrick (Oxford and New York: Oxford University Press, 2009), p. 468.
53. M. Brunton, *Self-Control: A Novel*, 2 vols, introd. G. Luria (New York and London: Garland, 1974), vol. 1, p. 112.
54. Wallace, *Revolutionary Subjects*, p. 31.
55. Ibid., p. 31.
56. Myers, 'Reform or Ruin', pp. 204–5.
57. M. Wollstonecraft, *A Vindication of the Rights of Woman*, in J. Todd and M. Butler (eds), *The Works of Mary Wollstonecraft*, 7 vols (London, Pickering & Chatto, 1989), vol. 5, pp. 63–266, on p. 135.
58. M. Hays, 'Improvements Suggested in Female Education', *Monthly Magazine*, 3 (1797), pp. 193–95, on p. 195.
59. Hays, *Emma Courtney*, p. 32.
60. Ibid., p. 163.
61. R. Porter, *English Society in the 18th Century* (1982) (London: Penguin, 1990), p. 316.
62. Myers, 'Reform or Ruin', p. 202.
63. Hays, *Emma Courtney*, p. 56.
64. L. Stone, *The Family, Sex, Marriage in England, 1500–1800* (New York: Harper's Torch Books, 1979), p. 218. In *Novel Relations: The Transformation of Kinship in English Literature and Culture 1748–1818* (New York: Cambridge University Press, 2004), Ruth Perry also emphasizes the growing importance of marriage, arguing that there was a 'significant shift in the basis of kinship disclosed by the fiction of the period' involving a 'movement from an axis of kinship based on consanguineal ties or blood lineage to an axis based on conjugal and affinal ties of the married couple' (p. 2).
65. Hays, *Emma Courtney*, p. 99.
66. S. Staves, 'British Seduced Maidens', *Eighteenth-Century Studies*, 14:2 (1980/81), pp. 109–34, on p. 115.
67. Ibid., p. 118.
68. Ibid., pp. 110–13.
69. Hays, *The Victim of Prejudice*, p. 63.
70. Ibid., pp. 68–69.
71. Amelia Opie, *The Father and Daughter with Dangers of Coquetry*, ed. Shelley King and John B. Pierce (Peterborough, ON: Broadview Press, 2003), p. 140.
72. 'Review of *The Victim of Prejudice*', *The Critical Review, or Annals of Literature*, 26 (1799), pp. 450–52, on p. 452.
73. S. Richardson, *Clarissa*, introd. J. Butt, 4 vols (London: Dent Everyman, 1976), vol. 4, p. 157.
74. Hays, *The Victim of Prejudice*, pp. 117–18.
75. Ibid., p. 118.

6 Lessons of Courtship

Hannah More's *Cœlebs in Search of a Wife*

Patricia Demers

Hannah More – poet, playwright, essayist, and tract writer – was destined to teach. From the precocious student of Latin and mathematics in Stapleton and the junior teacher at her sisters' Park Street school in Bristol to the lionized Evangelical reformer identified with Abolitionist and anti-Jacobin causes, she became recognized as 'the most influential female philanthropist of her day'[1] and one of its most financially successful women writers. Success and service went hand in hand: her will bequeathed 'the very substantial sum of £27,500' with most of the money directed 'to about 200 selected charities'.[2] Innate gifts and social conditions worked in tandem to shape and speed her career; she rose to prominence at a time particularly conducive to her talents and national loyalties, both of which were rooted in her confessional identity and deep commitment to political stability. More's renown coincided with the end of the Republic of Letters, an imagined, international, travelling scholarly congregation where discourse was often cross-gendered and multilingual and where, ironically, she would have felt at home. However, as Peter Burke explicates with his analyses of the geographies of knowledge in the late eighteenth century, there are two reasons for the end of this community of letters: 'specialization and nationalism',[3] involving the rise of a sense of identity defined against other disciplines and other nations. Such a shift from cosmopolitanism to nationalism signalled the closing of this kind of intellectual free trade and harmony. Specialization would likely have been less attractive to such a voracious, endlessly curious reader as More; however, the appeal of national and religiously inspired pride, especially in light of her opposition to revolution on the Continent, was ready-made.

Yet her career and acclaim were more than the product of generative circumstances. In the midst of shifting sociologies of knowledge, Hannah More was never swayed by novelty. Although she benefited from the tutelage of Johnson, Garrick, and others, she exulted in standing her own ground firmly, confidently, and alone. A loyal but not uncritical counter-revolutionary, an independent woman who was not shy about using her rhetorical skills to instruct elite and plebeian readers, and a reforming presence concerned as much with middle-class manners as with working-class literacy, More was ideally suited to shine and galvanize in such a cultural setting. She was devoted to 'the reclamation of reading, and education, for the conservative cause'.[4]

Her seriousness of faith, devotion to four-square Anglicanism, and zeal to convince all Britons – but especially British women – to affirm and embody these principles imbue the whole body of her writing. The desire to inculcate her own strict views meant that every genre in which she worked became a vehicle for instruction. Acutely aware of the ways gender codes affected and often warped the moral and intellectual lives of women, More was committed to 'an aggressive national movement to reform the social order'.[5] For her, religion invited and required reform; religion and reform constitute the regular metronomic rhythm of her work. This steadfastness pleased her like-minded admirers as surely as it armed her critics, who contended that More's ambit was narrow, her didacticism dry, and her understanding of narrative blinkered.

Despite her reprobation of novels as a 'complicated drug' and 'vehicles of wider mischief', her own novel, *Cœlebs in Search of a Wife* (1808), is a ground-breaking embodiment of her reforming principles.[6] Though this sixty-three-year-old novelist, 'the form's greatest foe',[7] lived for another quarter of a century, she did not repeat the experiment of novel writing. Her single foray is a fusion of religion and cultural ideology. In the journey of an authoritative bachelor narrator finding his ideal partner, 'the teleological courtship plot lends weight to the didactic message'.[8] It is not only a synthesis of her talents; it remains a gauge of her popular appeal. Garnering mixed reviews, her religious novel was a curious bestseller that went through twelve London editions in its first year and was subsequently translated into French and German. In fact, *Cœlebs* 'brought more profits even than [Sir Walter Scott's] *Waverley*'.[9] The enormous success of the novel, 'with its peculiar way of condemning the novel in novel form, demonstrated the popularity of More's continued attempts to clean up literary culture'.[10] Despite the novel's popularity and wide circulation of over 14,000 copies, its first reviewers were cautious and stinting; their observations note how the steady gravitational pull of religion slowed and stiffened the narrative. Although *The Christian Observer* considered the novel 'defective in variety', it expressed 'delight, admiration, and gratitude' for the author's 'consecration of such talents to the cause of truth'. The reviewer also argued for particular assessment of its hybrid form: 'if this work is censured merely as a novel, it will be blamed for being what it is not'.[11] *The Monthly Review* judged the novel's zeal in 'combating the fashionable modes of female education ... too spiritual to be adopted by man in his present social state'.[12] In *The Edinburgh Review*, trenchant critic Sydney Smith lamented its 'dry, didactic form' and perpetual call for 'religious thoughts and religious conversation in every thing'.[13] For *The London Review*, the novel consisted of lengthy assertions rather than genuine arguments. Though praising the combination of 'the *utile cum dulci*', *The British Critic* objected to its 'Calvinistic notion of an original and innate evil propensity in human nature'.[14]

In current scholarly discourse, the prominence of religion in a novel ostensibly concerned with the choice of 'a suitably moral partner'[15] can be

108 Patricia Demers

discomfiting and perplexing. More's close-to-perfect fictional figures lead Mark Canuel to comment on the absence of any 'discernible characters'.[16] Yet commentary also directs attention to the novel's political and ideological resonance and its bold, at times dialogic, engagement with Evangelicalism. Andrew Heisel is forced to acknowledge More's 'narrowed' characters, who 'almost in spite of themselves and their readers convey vital moral truth'.[17] Lisa Wood reads the novel as 'a manual for maximizing the religious and antirevolutionary potential of the domestic circle' with the narrator representing 'an Evangelical form of domestic masculinity'.[18] While Anne Stott positions the rational and humane education which the novel promotes within the 'British Christian Enlightenment',[19] Kerry Sinanan goes as far as to label the 'Evangelical sincerity in *Cœlebs* ... more radical', since More's duty is 'a strategic means to engage with an imperfectible world' through characters whose 'striving to act out of a moral sense is *active*'.[20] Focusing on the role of conversation in this novel, Jon Mee credits More with a willingness to 'countenance "collision" in conversation when it comes in the defense of the truth of Christian values'.[21] But only in a few instances do such collisions effect real change or injury and result in repair or reform.

The dilemmas of terminology faced by More's contemporary reviewers and the polarized judgements of her novel by today's scholars all point to continuing questions about this text. Often read as a 'fictionalized conduct book' with aspects of a *roman à clef, Cœlebs in Search of a Wife*, related in the voice of a twenty-three-year-old bachelor, is a book of talk and little action.[22] The eponymous hero, whose given name is Charles, journeys from the north of England to visit the friend of his revered dead father. He passes through London on his route to Hampshire where at Stanley Grove he meets his predestined mate, Lucilla Stanley. Does the emphasis on conversation overpower More's narrative? Are her characters inertly, improbably good? Does her narrative demonstrate an understanding of human complexity? Is she able to represent anything beyond pasteboard passions? To take a cue from the reviewer in *The Christian Observer*, could More's novel be following an entirely different aesthetic principle than that of realistic fiction? This essay explores some possible answers by attending to and assessing the stability of More's moral compass throughout her career.

A salient feature of More's writing is her ability to bring religion and everyday urban and rural life into sharp, pragmatic focus. Though she never repeated the exercise, she turned to the novel as much more than a *jeu d'esprit* to pass the time during an illness. As her narrator explains, the novel aims 'to show how religion may be brought to mix with the concerns of ordinary life, without impairing its activity, lessening its cheerfulness, or diminishing its usefulness'.[23] The narrative, he alerts readers, will be as instrumental as it is theistic:

> Love itself appears in these pages not as an ungovernable impulse, but as a sentiment arising out of qualities calculated to inspire

Lessons of Courtship 109

attachment in persons under the dominion of reason and religion, brought together by the ordinary course of occurrences in a private family party.[24]

Despite being questioned and criticized by a variety of characters, the hegemony of reason and religion, so vital and so idiosyncratically construed in all More's writing, is never successfully subverted in the novel. Indeed this very firmness is the source of complaints about *Cœlebs*: its inaction, copiousness, and the prevalence of mere assertions rather than debates.

It involves considerable adjustment to speak of a sermon and a novel in the same breath, yet More actually delighted in such a coupling. Although reason and religion, as understood and practised by the main characters, underpin the whole work, this alliance could supply a way of understanding More's aesthetic, so removed from the expectations of a realist novel. Among the series of conversations comprising the narrative, Lucilla's father, a wealthy country gentleman, describes the sermon as a genre which combines erudition with faith:

> A sermon is a work which demands regularity of plan as well as a poem. It requires, too, something of the same unity, arrangement, divisions, and lucid order as a tragedy; something of the exordium, and the peroration which belong to the composition of the orator.[25]

Cœlebs challenges the reader to question traditional uses of learning with the feasibility of this unconventional combination. Since Mr Stanley acts as mouthpiece for the author herself, it is worth tracing the ways these exacting structural requirements of genres, in which More herself had experimented and won fame, connect her novel to her earlier body of work.

Writing for More is primarily a mode of instruction, whether in poetry, drama, essay, or tract, conveying either a female or a male voice of authority. From her ballads to her celebrations such as 'Sensibility' and 'The Bas Bleu', her poetics are always purposive, showing the way to reforms in action and temperament. In 'The Bleeding Rock' and 'Sir Eldred of the Bower', she concentrates as much on the remorse of the seducer Polydore and the passionate Sir Eldred as on the loves they have neglected or lost. Even though her heroines die, they fulfil a comparative design:

> Unlike the dames of modern days,
> Who *general* homage claim;
> Who court the *universal* gaze,
> And pant for *public* fame,
>
> *Then* beauty but on merit smil'd,
> Nor were her chaste smiles sold;
> No venal father gave his child
> For grandeur or for gold.[26]

110   *Patricia Demers*

Ironically, only when Sir Eldred has lost the 'peerless' Birtha does the narrator introduce this contrast with public 'dames'. Real beauty for More is quiet, unadorned, usually unnoticed, and never for sale. By apostrophizing 'Sweet SENSIBILITY' in the poem 'Sensibility', she stresses its 'unprompted moral' and 'instinctive kindness' which are guided by the prime motivator of religion: 'If RELIGION's bias rule the soul, / Then SENSIBILITY exalts the whole'.[27] Her praise of Mrs Vesey's assemblies in the poem 'The Bas Bleu' climaxes with the depiction of 'intellectual ore' and 'education's moral mint' being circulated productively in conversation, 'The noblest commerce of mankind, / Whose precious merchandize is MIND'.[28]

The privileging of religion and education, the salient feature of *Cœlebs*, is also on prominent display, even though their expression is in prose rather than verse. Religion informs all the discourse of More's spokespersons in the novel, including the Stanleys, the narrator, and the local clergyman, Dr Barlow. The talk often becomes uninterrupted disquisition, so much so that *The Christian Observer* quipped about 'sentences cut into lengths [and] delivered from a magazine'.[29] Engaged in the theological commerce More endorsed, Barlow explicates the intellectual and moral tenets which guide a true follower:

> Surely the followers of he [*sic*] who was 'despised and rejected of men' should not seek their highest gratification from the flattery and applause of men. The truth is ... that Christianity is a religion of the *heart*.... 'Let the same *mind* be in you which was also in Christ Jesus'.... In every other point it is still the spirit of the act, the temper of the mind, to which we are to look.[30]

In a narrative remarkable for its literary allusions, Mr Stanley later reinforces the claim that 'True religion is seated in the heart: that is the centre from which all the lines of right practice must diverge'.[31] Dr Barlow and Mr Stanley thus encapsulate More's own views of a Bible-centred, socially engaged, and loquacious Evangelicalism.

The novel rehearses More's judgements about favourite poets whose work accords with her Evangelical principles. In the Eden of Stanley Grove, talk often turns to the scenery of Cowper and Mason and, especially, the prelapsarian paradise of Milton, who occupies a towering pinnacle in More's estimate of poets. The incorporation of poetry through allusion, direct quotation, and criticism contributes to what Mr Stanley would call the regularity of plan of a sermon and, as it happens, of this novel. Not only do epigraphs from *Paradise Lost* introduce the two volumes of the novel, but Charles's narrative itself opens with extended praise of Eve as a model to be contrasted with acclaimed accomplished women. This apology for Eve supplies the 'novel's dialogue with a masculine epic language, from the top strata of literary languages'.[32] It also illustrates Charles's (and More's) rhetorical skills. Answering 'the ladies against the uncourtly bard', 'critics ... too apt to prejudge the cause' and 'the imaginary fair objector',[33] Charles's defence of Eve highlights her intellectual, cheerfully obedient and humble presence in Eden. 'Far from making Eve a mere domestic drudge', Milton, as Charles argues, 'restores her to all the dignity of equality', fashioning her as 'the inspirer of [Adam's] virtues' through the 'combination of intellectual worth and polished manners'.[34] Lucilla, More's reworked version of Eve, declares 'There is no female character in the whole compass of poetry in which I have ever taken so lively an interest'.[35] This interest, significantly, extends to both thoughtful and critical comments about Eve. Lucilla, herself such a dedicated and disciplined gardener that she is known as 'the little Repton of the valley', sees 'something wonderfully touching in [Eve's] remorse and affecting in her contrition', but judges her sorrow as misguided, arising mainly from 'being banished from her flowers'.[36]

The structure of the novel fulfils Mr Stanley's criterion of 'unity, arrangement, [and] divisions'.[37] The first twelve chapters detailing and then evaluating Charles's encounters with London matrons and their daughters serve as the prelude to his arrival in Hampshire. His critique of the London marriage market prepares the reader for the comparative excellence of Stanley Grove. Here, over thirty-six chapters, the bulk of the conversations, visits, and narrated experiences takes place, while Charles's attraction to Lucilla leads to his proposal of marriage, to which Mr Stanley consents. The final chapter returns Charles to the North, where he receives letters from the Stanleys in anticipation of the impending marriage. The key decisions and exchanges occur at Stanley Grove, which appropriately occupies the large centre of the novel.

More supplies Mr Stanley's additional ingredient, the 'lucid order' of tragedy, in her interlaced character portraits which serve as instructive vignettes, although not all end in misfortune. In her earlier work for the public stage More relied on borrowed plots to depict the downfall of her tragic heroines: Elwina succumbs to a pathologically jealous husband in *Percy* (1777); Attilia despairs and faints as her father sails away in *The Inflexible Captive* (1774); and Emmelina faces the rejection of the man she loves in *The Fatal Falsehood* (1779). In *Coelebs* the plots are condensed, the characterization is adroit, and the gallery of mothers with daughters on the marriage market and of marriages struggling for survival is clearly the product of More's astute observations of Georgian life. With some irony considering the punctilious source, Charles himself succinctly captures the value of dramatic conventions: 'The introduction of character dramatises what else would have been frigidly didactic'.[38] With vivid detail and the aphoristic terseness of a moral spectator, More sketches overinvested or neglectful mothers. Damning brush strokes introduce the quixotic despot Mrs Fentham: 'She is said not to love her daughters, who come too near her in age, and go too much beyond her in beauty to be forgiven; yet, like a consummate politician, she is ever labouring for their advancement'.[39] In contrast to such oblique dictatorship, the assaults of Lady Bab Lawless lure suitors by her disdain for decorum: 'A man could

112   *Patricia Demers*

never suspect that such gay and open assaults could have their foundation in design; and he gave her full credit for artless simplicity, at the very moment she was catching him in her toils'.[40] The supposedly pious Lady Denham, 'a dowager of fashion who had grown old with the trammels of dissipation', refuses a dinner invitation during Passion week in Lent, but indulges 'in the only pleasures which she thought compatible with the sanctity of the season, uncharitable gossip, and unbounded calumny'.[41] The aesthetic Lady Melbury, 'the acknowledged queen of beauty and of ton', who learns that her unpaid bills at the milliner's have led to the woman's ruin, had already been given money by her husband, 'three times for the purpose, which she had lost at faro'.[42] All lessons by negative example, the character portraits of the neglect, deceit, and sanctimony of these fashionable matrons tilt on the side of disastrous, embarrassing consequences. As the stories of these ambitious women unravel, we learn that Lady Fentham faces bankruptcy and disappearing friends and that Lady Denham uses the surprise of her daughter's elopement with a fortune-hunting singing master to justify her refusal to help Mrs Fentham. More not only connects these two exposés but underscores the moral blindness of each woman and their inability to assume personal responsibility:

> Poor Mrs. Fentham is more wounded by this total desertion of those whom she so sumptuously entertained, and so obsequiously flattered, than by her actual wants.
>   Lady Denham farther assigned the misery into which the elopement of her darling child with Signor Squallini had brought her, as an additional reason for withholding her kindness from Mrs. Fentham.[43]

The force of the adverbs intensifying Mrs Fentham's entertainments and flattery contrasts sharply with the practicality of 'actual wants', while Lady Denham's rationalizing of her refusal to help Mrs Fentham relies on the curious connection between 'misery' and a so-called 'darling child'. The narcissism of both women is on full display. Their flawed reasoning and especially the vengefulness of Lady Denham reveal the resistance of the self-satisfied, fashionable world to admit guilt, failure, or inadequacy. There is hope, however, for at least one of these matrons. Lady Melbury finds peace while visiting her aunt; initially disparaging the woman 'as a Methodist', she is led to value Aunt Jane as a companion, 'often read[ing] to [her] some rationally entertaining book, occasionally introducing religious reading and discourse, with a wisdom and moderation which increased the effect of both'.[44]

On the marriage front, with the obvious exceptions of the Stanleys and Charles's deceased parents, several unions are on shaky ground, often because of the wife's venality or vulgar perspectives. The striving of lower middle-class women to emulate fashionable matrons provides another series of negative examples, in which the uncultivated and uneducated assume domestic supremacy. The 'humble, pious, diligent' curate Mr Jackson, who marries a poor tradesman's daughter, is continually reproached by his wife 'that though he may know the way to heaven, he does not know how to push his way in the world'.[45] The 'wretched education of Mrs Reynolds' causes her husband 'to submit his excellent judgment to her feeble mind'; this woman who insists that 'never being contradicted at all would make her children happy' also asserts that 'reading will spoil the girls' eyes, stooping to write will ruin their chests, and working will make them round-shouldered'.[46] These character portraits expose the liabilities and errors of the uncultivated female intelligence. But, once again, there is a narrative of hope and change. In at least one case a marriage is transformed due to the virtues of the wife. The prayers and endless patience of Mrs Carlton finally touch her carousing, neglectful husband, causing him to see that 'a religion which produced such admirable effects could not be so mischievous a principle as he had supposed'. In the place of alienating distance, a real exchange is now at work: 'While Mrs Carlton is advancing her husband's relish for books of piety, he is forming hers to polite literature'.[47] As with the openness of Lady Melbury to appreciate her aunt, the enjoyment the Carltons experience is based on mutual participation in diverse sorts of reading—both rational and religious for Lady Melbury and pious and polite for the Carltons.

The reunion of the Carltons and the reinvigoration of their marriage illustrate through dramatic incident the underlying rhetorical emphasis on the domestic woman. As Mitzi Myers has argued, More is concerned with inoculating 'everyday routine with aggressive virtue'.[48] Delivering both the exordium and the peroration of the orator, More's novel echoes the exhortations of her *Strictures on the Modern System of Female Education* (1799) repeatedly and through a range of speakers. The rhetoric of this two-volume bestselling essay becomes the benchmark for character judgement in *Cœlebs*. The narrator's announced interest in talking 'on the multitude of marriages in which the parties are "joined, not matched," and where the term *union* is a miserable misnomer' is the most direct echo of More's earlier description of a fashionable couple 'not *matched but joined*, [who] set out separately with their independent and individual pursuits'.[49] Charles is definitely searching for a match, and it is obvious from the start of his stay in Hampshire that Lucilla's merits exceed his expectations. Significantly, his praise is couched in contrasts between ornamental attraction and elaborate polish versus 'native graces':

> Lucilla Stanley is rather perfectly elegant than perfectly beautiful.... Her beauty is countenance; it is the stamp of mind intelligently imprinted on the face.... She enlivens without dazzling, and entertains without overpowering. Contented to please, she has no ambition to shine ... she has rather a playful gaiety than a pointed wit. Taste is indeed the predominating quality of her mind; and she may rather be said to be a nice judge of the genius of others than to be a genius herself.[50]

114 *Patricia Demers*

Most of the judgements about behaviour and accomplishments are pronounced or, more accurately, declaimed by men. Charles's contrastive method recalls the admonitions of *Strictures* about the cultivation of intellect:

> A lady studies, not that she may qualify herself to become an orator or a pleader; not that she may learn to debate, but to act. She is to read the best books, not so much to enable her to talk of them, as to bring the improvement which they furnish, to the rectification of her principles and the formation of her habits. The great uses of study to woman are to enable her to regulate her own mind, and to be instrumental to the good of others.[51]

Although the contrasts are palpable between More's authoritative advice and her own practice as a public voice who announced her extensive reading in print, the consistency uniting Charles's views and the strictures of his creator is equally remarkable. Yet Charles, whom Sydney Smith characterized as 'a mere clod or dolt',[52] rarely reaches or matches his creator's rhetorical power. This prosing bore comments on the lack of 'intellectual gaiety' in 'the musical and dancing ladies, and those who were most admired for modish attainments',[53] but he is confident in depicting his future partner, 'elegant, informed, enlightened,... pious, humble, candid, charitable', with negatives:

> she is *not* a professed beauty, she is *not* a professed genius, she is *not* a professed philosopher, she is *not* a professed wit, she is *not* a professed any thing; and I thank my stars she is *not* an artist![54]

The fear of the woman artist appears to have two sources: a suspicion of inadequate educational preparation and a loss of culturally approved control. More's principal spokespersons take pains to locate female virtue within a household setting. Just as in *Strictures* she directs women 'to see the world, as it were, from a little elevation in [their] own garden',[55] the reformed Mr Carlton allows that 'women in their course of action describe a smaller circle than men; but the perfection of a circle consists not in its dimensions but in its correctness'.[56] Charles underscores the domestic setting by rehearsing More's own views in her 'Preface to the Tragedies' (1801) about the temptation of the theatre in its easily diverted, inattentive audience who applaud 'a successful bad play'; by contrast, Charles asserts, with a gesture toward More's *Sacred Dramas* (1782), which were designed as private theatre to be read or enacted at home, 'an intellectual woman, like a well-written drama, will please at home without all these aids and adjuncts'.[57]

However, More also introduces a challenging misfit in the person of the 45-year-old neighbouring lady, Miss Sparkes. Through Charles's voice the reader learns of her 'pretension to odd and opposite qualities'.[58] In judging male behaviour and defying female decorum, she is a woman who does not fit the demure mould of Lucilla and whose wealth of practical information distinguishes her from the mindless boisterousness of the aptly named Miss Rattle. As the narrator concedes, Miss Sparkes is 'something of a scholar and a huntress, a politician and a farrier: she outrides Mr. Flam, and out-argues Mr. Tyrrel; excels in driving four-in-hand, and in canvassing at an election'. Never given a first name, Miss Sparkes conveys independence while spurning feminine accoutrements. The fact that '[i]n her adoption of any talent, or her exercise of any quality, it is always sufficient recommendation to her that it is not feminine'[59] makes Charles decidedly uneasy. In appearance and disposition she is a critical presence, exemplifying the occasional 'collision' in conversations More countenanced; she even dares to caution Mr Stanley about his chastising of his child's stretching of the truth, which he terms 'infant prevarication'.[60] Although the child did not tell 'an absolute falsehood', Mr Stanley deprives her 'of the honour of carrying food to the poor in the evening'; Miss Sparkes's concern, which she expresses in the imagery of a knowledgeable horsewoman, is for the child's spirit:

> Too tight a rein will check her generous ardour, and curb her genius. I would not subdue the independence of her mind, and make a tame, dull animal, of a creature, whose very faults give indications of a soaring nature.[61]

More appears to be experimenting, possibly internally debating, with a Wollstonecraftian temperament in this figure. In More's novel, Miss Sparkes fulfils a provocative role, distinct from that of the cross-dressing Harriot Freke in Maria Edgeworth's *Belinda* (1801). While Miss Sparkes is a challenging presence, Harriot Freke is actually sinister and transgressive; she promotes an adulterous relationship and attempts, unsuccessfully, to terrorize a servant through disguise. Although Mrs Freke mangles Wollstonecraft-like slogans about wanting 'a strong devil better than a weak angel', she is also revealed as a figure of ridicule in her insistence that 'when one has made up one's opinion, there is no use in reading'.[62] Edgeworth's heroine judges Harriot Freke's wit as 'like a noisy squib, the momentary terror of passengers'.[63] Freke's rash 'attempts to appropriate power and control in a predominantly masculine world' backfire;[64] they do not make her into a resistant heroine. Rather, Harriot Freke is 'a false female philosopher who appears to be a caricature of a caricature', whom Edgeworth used 'to lampoon the idea of Wollstonecraft that circulated in the culture'.[65] Hannah More's Miss Sparkes, with flashes of Wollstonecraftian rhetoric, is a tart and critical presence, but she is not malicious. In the Stanley household, dedicated to clear, black-and-white demarcations between truth and falsehood, Miss Sparkes boldly articulates a situational ethic:

> She allowed that absolute falsehood, and falsehood used for mischievous purposes, was really criminal, and yet there was a danger, on the other hand, of laying too severe restrictions on the freedom of

116   *Patricia Demers*

> speech;... that people might be guilty of as much deceit by suppressing
> their sentiments, if just, as by expressing such as were not quite cor-
> rect.... She thought, also, that there were occasions where a harmless
> falsehood might not only be pardonable but laudable.[66]

This character who knows 'technical jockey phrases' and 'all the terms of
the veterinary art' has no real precedent in *Strictures*.[67] Her contrast with
Lucilla is noteworthy and signals the narrative's abrupt return to its moral,
reforming high-mindedness:

> When Miss Stanley expressed some fear of her danger, and some dis-
> like of her coarseness, she burst into a loud laugh, and slapping her on
> the shoulder, asked her if it was not better to understand the properties
> and diseases of so noble an animal, than to waste her time in studying
> confectionary with old Goody Comfit, or in teaching the Catechism to
> little ragged beggar brats.[68]

The dismissiveness and sarcasm bleeding into Miss Sparkes's voice could indicate More's reduced interest in this *agent provocateur*. Did the single-minded
More recoil from her own experiment? Did she decide on a retreat through
a not-so-subtle discrediting of Miss Sparkes?

Yet even while Miss Sparkes's appearances diminish, More re-introduces
her to the Stanley household discussion of domestic economy four chapters
later. Although Lady Belfield and Henrietta Carlton are present during this
exchange and colour appropriately when praised, Miss Sparkes is the only
woman who speaks. It is a one-sided debate with Mr Stanley and his male
friends opining that 'the operation of good sense is requisite in making the necessary calculations for a great family in a hundred ways'.[69] Characterized by a
look of disinterest, more precisely, 'sovereign contempt', from the beginning of
this conversation, Miss Sparkes finally breaks her silence to deliver this salvo:

> All these plodding employments cramp the genius, degrade the intel-
> lect, depress the spirits, debase the taste, and clip the wings of imagi-
> nation. And this poor, cramped, degraded, stinted, depressed, debased
> creature is the very being whom men, men of reputed sense, too,
> commonly prefer to the mind of large dimensions, soaring fancy, and
> aspiring tastes.[70]

Predictably, the problem which Mr Stanley and his confrères perceive in
this statement is its granting a woman the opportunity to indulge in imagination, as he fears, 'to abandon herself to the dominion of this vagrant
faculty'.[71] Here is a resounding, if abbreviated, echo of *Strictures*, where
More inveighed against the dangers of unmonitored reading of works of the
imagination by women whose education consists 'in continually crowding
more sail than they can carry'. Works of the imagination, she warned,

Lessons of Courtship   117

excite a spirit of relaxation, by exhibiting scenes and suggesting ideas which soften the mind and set the fancy at work: they take off wholesome restraints, diminish sober-mindedness, impair the general powers of resistance, and at best feed habits of improper indulgence, and nourish a vain and visionary indolence, which lays the mind open to error and the heart to seduction.[72]

Guarding against indulgence, indolence, and error, the Stanley household is the centre of necessary vigilance, where unabated parental surveillance results in the exercise of accepted control and assured compliance. Such tightly managed serenity contrasts both with the anxiety of the modish Londoners and the fears released by Miss Sparkes's contrarianism. The Stanleys' Establishment-supporting tutelage distinguishes their family from the fates of the visiting sceptic Mr Tyrrel, who sees 'no use of learning in the clergy',[73] and the unrepentant *bon vivant* lifestyle of Mr Flam. His 'proud heart brought low', Tyrrel dies in agony, abhorring 'himself in dust and ashes'.[74] Flam, by contrast, sees no lesson by negative example in his friend's demise but remains 'harden[ed] against reproof'.[75] Even the complacent interlocutor Sir John Belfield benefits from his time at Stanley Grove; he not only solicits Stanley's advice about 'a course of reading' but admits to his host 'that there is nothing in your sentiments but what a man of sense may approve, nothing but what, if he be really a man of sense, he will without scruple adopt'.[76] Yet there are discrepancies in this idealized household economy. Lucilla's siblings are models of obedience and tractability, however fantastical or anomalous their behaviour may seem. Observant of her father's celebration of 'the renouncing [of] baby books' that are 'read too much and too long', eight-year-old Kate announces on her birthday giving up 'all [her] little story books' just as a year earlier she 'gave up all [her] gilt books, with pictures'.[77] Kate Stanley is actually an anomaly, 'giving up her gilt books ... just as the majority of children were beginning to enjoy them'.[78] As Matthew Grenby comments,

> nor would most children formally and suddenly renounce them; rather they gradually advanced away from children's literature, like Miss Sprightly in one of Fenn's 1780s school stories, who has left *Goody Two-Shoes* and Barbauld's *Lessons for Children* ... and now prefers ... the works of Hester Chapone, Elizabeth Carter and Catherine Talbot.[79]

Mr Stanley, ever the patriarch and the pedagogue, is nevertheless convinced of the correctness of this brusque renunciation of baby books and gilt books. He even compares his direction of the children to gardening:

> I am a gardener, you know, and accustomed to study the genius of the soil before I plant. Most of my daughters, like the daughters of other men, have some one talent, or at least a propensity.... This propensity I endeavour to find out, and to cultivate.[80]

118   *Patricia Demers*

Accordingly, he puts a 'bridle' on his daughter Phoebe's 'superabundance of vivacity … by giving her a tincture of mathematics' and expresses satisfaction in the progress that has saved her from an alarmingly artistic fate. 'The girl, who if she had been fed on poetry and works of imagination, might have become a Miss Sparkes, now rather gives herself the airs of a calculator, and of a grave computist'.[81] The threat of Miss Sparkes, related to that of the female imagination, continues to haunt and stiffen the didacticism of Stanley Grove.

Characters who talk or who are talked about, in this talk-filled novel, are the chief vehicles of More's didacticism; they are primarily spokespeople for their creator or negative examples of conduct she deplored. Are they flesh-and-blood realities or merely cardboard conduits for More? Is the reader justified in expecting or demanding consistency in these figures? Consistency is the very feature that underscores the different aesthetic principle of this religious novel-as-sermon. For More's main characters it means that regularity and unity, the salient aspects Mr Stanley located in the sermon, also define and, yes, delimit their actions and expressions. More's novel does not inhabit a world of darkness with complex characters and unredeemed suffering; there is no suspicious melding of the erotic and the moral. Hers is a world of improving light, however controlled or blinkered its beams may appear, and however much it might minimize the success and broad appeal of her undertaking. Yet her characterization does offer wide diversity. At least two characters, both significantly women, are consistent *and* contrastive: Lucilla Stanley and Miss Sparkes. Unlike Phoebe, Lucilla does not risk becoming a grave computist. With her blushes, anxious dunking of cream in the sugar bowl when her expertise in Latin is revealed, and practical, generous management of time as a student, a gardener, and a dedicated older sister, she is the ideal Morean combination of seriousness, empathy and emotional truthfulness. She embodies More's ideology of 'religious domesticity'.[82] As for Miss Sparkes, though she alarms Lucilla, she is not a grotesque caricature. Strong-minded and independent, Miss Sparkes wants to give women wings or, in Wollstonecraftian terms, to snap their chains. Her very real and vocal presence within the text argues for a willingness on More's part to air the views of liberation as well as the cultural fears and objections Miss Sparkes generates. Lucilla possesses demure charm; but Charles, loquacious with the men at Stanley Grove and stiff and awkward with Lucilla, is simply a prig. Censorious and righteous, this sermonizer has no qualms pontificating about others. In visiting London before his journey south to Stanley Grove, when he is not indulging 'in all its safe sights,… its sober pleasures,… the best pictures,… the best museums,… the best speakers,… the best preachers',[83] he spends his time passing judgement on the active Christian faith, the ultimate criterion, of the women he has met:

> [W]hich of them would not have been startled had her Christianity been called in question? Yet how merely speculative was the religion of

even the most serious among them! How superficial, or inconsistent, or mistaken, or hollow, or hypocritical, or self-deceiving was that of all the others![84]

Upon his arrival in the Stanley household, he tends to provide the chorus of affirmation for his host (and future father-in-law) and Dr Barlow, who become the main speakers. The principal male speakers in the narrative are also, on occasion, credibly inconsistent. For instance, while Mr Stanley quotes liberally from approved poets (Milton, Akenside, Shakespeare, and Cowper), he is concerned about his daughter's unregulated enjoyment of poetry.

However recognizable as types or real people, More's characters exist in the curious hybrid she created, the didactic religious novel. Andrew Heisel concludes that More's depiction of 'passions subdued rather than gratified ... repeatedly requires [a] denial of the self'.[85]

Yet not only saintliness is on display in this novel which resembles a sermon in generic structures if not in condensed shape. More's gallery of backsliders, hypocrites, *à la mode* hostesses, and oblivious folk who refuse to face final things is actually an album of cultivated early nineteenth-century life. In echoing the dictates of *Strictures*, noteworthy for its 'ambivalent and problematic attitudes towards her own sex',[86] she was not shying away from or diluting her strong views. But she was also not indulging in an exercise doomed to damage her reputation among conservatives or fail to secure like-minded readers. That More remained, as Anne Stott has observed, 'clearly sceptical about the power of education to eradicate the fundamental traits of character' indicates her firm grip on reality.[87] Aware of the endurance of obduracy, fallibility, and recalcitrance, she also knew the unease which religious topics created in so-called polite society and the risk she was taking in this enterprise of programming a foreordained courtship. She persevered for two volumes, making *Cœlebs* a symptom of her career – daring to teach and preach about religion and reform, this time with the additive of a marriage. More may have predicted the phenomenal, short-lived, comet-like popularity of her undertaking, but such presumptions did not cause this cultural champion of aggressive female virtue to dilute her lesson or shorten the discourse.

Notes

1. F. K. Prochaska, *Women and Philanthropy in Nineteenth-Century England* (Oxford: Clarendon, 1980), p. 6.
2. A. Stott, *Hannah More: The First Victorian* (Oxford: Oxford University Press, 2003), p. 331.
3. P. Burke, *A Social History of Knowledge, Volume II: From the Encyclopédie to Wikipedia* (Cambridge: Polity Press, 2012), p. 198.
4. M. O. Grenby, *The Anti-Jacobin Novel: British Conservatism and the French Revolution* (Cambridge: Cambridge University Press, 2001), p. 15.

120   *Patricia Demers*

5. K. Gilmartin, *Writing Against Revolution: Literary Conservatism in Britain 1790–1832* (Cambridge: Cambridge University Press, 2007), p. 59. See also C. Grogan, Chapter 9 of this volume, p. 161.

6. H. More, *Strictures on the Modern System of Female Education*, in *The Works of Hannah More*, 11 vols (London: T. Cadell, 1830), vol. 5, p. 22.

7. Grenby, *The Anti-Jacobin Novel*, p. 24.

8. L. Wood, *Modes of Discipline: Women, Conservatism, and the Novel after the French Revolution* (Lewisburg, PA: Bucknell University Press, 2003), p. 90.

9. A. H. Jones, *Ideas and Innovations: Best Sellers of Jane Austen's Age* (New York: AMS Press, 1986), p. 11.

10. K. Andrews, *Ann Yearsley and Hannah More, Patronage and Poetry: The Story of a Literary Relationship* (London: Pickering & Chatto, 2013), p. 120.

11. 'Review of *Cœlebs in Search of a Wife*', *The Christian Observer* (February 1809), pp. 109–21, on p. 121.

12. 'Review of *Cœlebs in Search of a Wife*', *The Monthly Review*, 60 (February 1809), pp. 128–36, on p. 129.

13. S. Smith, 'Review of *Cœlebs in Search of a Wife*', *The Edinburgh Review*, 14 (April 1809), pp. 145–51, on p. 146.

14. 'Review of *Cœlebs in Search of a Wife*', *The British Critic*, 33 (May 1809), pp. 481–94, on p. 482. The praise is for the combination of the useful and the delightful.

15. M. Scheuermann, *In Praise of Poverty: Hannah More Counters Thomas Paine and the Radical Threat* (Lexington, KY: University of Kentucky Press, 2002), p. 14.

16. M. Canuel, *The Shadow of Death: Literature, Romanticism, and the Subject of Punishment* (Princeton, NJ: Princeton University Press, 2007), p. 54.

17. A. Heisel, 'Hannah More's Art of Reduction', *Eighteenth-Century Fiction*, 25:3 (2013), pp. 557–88, on p. 558.

18. Wood, *Modes of Discipline*, pp. 125, 126.

19. A. Stott, 'Evangelicalism and Enlightenment: The Educational Agenda of Hannah More', in M. Hilton and J. Shefrin (eds), *Educating the Child in Enlightenment Britain* (Farnham, UK: Ashgate, 2009), pp. 41–55, on p. 54.

20. K. Sinanan, 'Too Good to Be True? Hannah More, Authenticity, Sincerity and Evangelical Abolitionism', in T. Milnes and K. Sinanan (eds), *Romanticism, Sincerity and Authenticity* (Basingstoke, UK: Palgrave Macmillan, 2010), pp. 137–61, on pp. 157, 158.

21. J. Mee, *Conversable Worlds: Literature, Contention, and Community 1762 to 1830* (Oxford: Oxford University Press, 2011), p. 217.

22. Stott, 'Evangelicalism and Enlightenment', p. 50.

23. H. More, *Cœlebs in Search of a Wife*, ed. P. Demers (Peterborough, ON: Broadview Press, 2007), p. 39.

24. Ibid., pp. 38–39.

25. Ibid., p. 171.

26. More, 'Sir Eldred of the Bower', *Works*, vol. 1, pp. 379–80.

27. More, 'Sensibility', *Works*, vol. 1, p. 176.

28. More, 'The Bas Bleu', *Works*, vol. 1, p. 301.

29. 'Review of *Cœlebs*', *The Christian Observer*, p. 121.

30. More, *Cœlebs*, p. 160.

31. Ibid., p. 195.

32. E. Snook, 'Eve and More: The Citations of *Paradise Lost* in Hannah More's *Cœlebs in Search of a Wife*', *English Studies in Canada*, 26:2 (2000), pp. 127–54, on p. 142.
33. More, *Cœlebs*, pp. 42, 43, 45.
34. Ibid., pp. 45, 43, 45.
35. Ibid., pp. 341–42.
36. Ibid., pp. 140, 341.
37. Ibid., p. 171.
38. Ibid., p. 284.
39. Ibid., p. 88.
40. Ibid., pp. 91–92.
41. Ibid., p. 93.
42. Ibid., pp. 107, 112.
43. Ibid., p. 360.
44. Ibid., pp. 387, 388.
45. Ibid., p. 131.
46. Ibid., pp. 207, 206.
47. Ibid., p. 153.
48. M. Myers, 'Reform or Ruin: "A Revolution in Female Manners"', *Studies in Eighteenth-Century Culture*, 15 (1986), pp. 199–216, on p. 209.
49. More, *Cœlebs*, p. 99; *Strictures*, *Works*, vol. 5, p. 334.
50. More, *Cœlebs*, pp. 121–22.
51. More, *Strictures*, *Works*, vol. 5, p. 216.
52. Smith, 'Review of *Cœlebs*', p. 146.
53. More, *Cœlebs*, p. 125.
54. Ibid., p. 144.
55. More, *Strictures*, *Works*, vol. 5, p. 234.
56. More, *Cœlebs*, p. 293.
57. Ibid., p. 279.
58. Ibid., p. 255.
59. Ibid.
60. Ibid., p. 257.
61. Ibid., p. 256.
62. M. Edgeworth, *Belinda* (London: Pandora Press, 1986), p. 206.
63. Ibid., p. 211.
64. E. Ty, 'Freke in Men's Clothes: Transgression and the Carnivalesque in Edgeworth's *Belinda*', in J. Munns (ed.), *The Clothes That Wear Us: Essays on Dressing and Transgressing in Eighteenth-Century Culture* (Newark DE: University of Delaware Press, 1999), pp. 157–76, on p. 169.
65. D. Weiss, 'The Extraordinary Ordinary Belinda: Maria Edgeworth's Female Philosopher', *Eighteenth-Century Fiction*, 19 (2007), pp. 441–61, on p. 446.
66. More, *Cœlebs*, p. 258.
67. Ibid., p. 260.
68. Ibid.
69. Ibid., p. 292.
70. Ibid., pp. 289, 296.
71. Ibid., p. 296.
72. More, *Strictures*, *Works*, vol. 5, pp. 136–37.
73. More, *Cœlebs*, p. 168.

74. Ibid., p. 376.
75. Ibid.
76. Ibid., p. 327.
77. Ibid., pp. 201, 202.
78. M. O. Grenby, *The Child Reader, 1700–1840* (Cambridge: Cambridge University Press, 2011), p. 51.
79. Ibid.
80. More, *Cœlebs*, p. 319.
81. Ibid., p. 320.
82. Wood, *Modes of Discipline*, p. 122.
83. More, *Cœlebs*, p. 99.
84. Ibid, p. 113.
85. Heisel, 'Hannah More's Art of Reduction', pp. 573, 572.
86. Andrews, *Ann Yearsley and Hannah More*, p. 1.
87. Stott, 'Evangelicalism and Enlightenment', p. 50.

7 Maria Edgeworth's *Moral Tales* and the Problem of Youth Rebellion in a Revolutionary Age

Andrew O'Malley

Maria Edgeworth composed most of the stories in her *Moral Tales for Young People* (1802) in the particularly tumultuous period between 1795 and 1799, with the companion stories of youthful rebellion 'Forester' and 'Angelina; or, L'Amie Inconnue' most likely penned in 1797 and 1798 respectively.[1] Memories of the Terror in France were of course still very fresh in the minds of most, and an Irish uprising was arriving fast on its heels. As Mitzi Myers points out, Edgeworth's experience of these events was both immediate and personal:

> [she] lived through all the cataclysmic events which mark the beginning of 'modern' history and witnessed many of them at first hand. She saw revolutionary Paris, fled for her life when the French invaded Ireland in 1798, and lived amid Irish upheaval.[2]

Given the intense historical circumstances in which these tales were written, it seems striking that Edgeworth's two stories about young people defying both the authority of their guardians and the accepted social structures of the day do not, as Cliona Ó Gallchoir remarks, deal explicitly 'with the political controversy of the 1790s'.[3] While stories of 'idealistic young adults' reacting against social convention remain a staple of young adult (YA) fiction to this day,[4] it is worth noting that such tales addressed to youthful readers were rare in the period,[5] and that they would necessarily have had quite pointed political implications in the contemporary post-revolutionary climate. Despite an apparent unwillingness to make direct connections between youthful rebellion and the revolutionary climate, Edgeworth clearly felt that this particular historical juncture demanded a literary response geared to a category of young people – no longer strictly children, nor properly matured into adulthood – whose passions had taken on a new and dangerous aspect in the period.

As Matthew Grenby has shown, a surprising relative silence on the specific subject of the French Revolution extends across the literature for young readers produced in the 1790s and early 1800s. Making this silence even more odd is the fact that many prominent figures in both the production and distribution of children's literature were also 'leading British "Jacobins"'.[6]

124 *Andrew O'Malley*

Of course, the fact that children's books very rarely mention the defining historical event of the age did not prevent writers on the anti-Jacobin side from censuring the dangerously seditious leanings of both fiction and pedagogical theory. Sarah Trimmer, who 'sometimes saw Jacobinism when none was there',[7] regularly identified dangerous ideas in books for the young, while William Barrow, in his *Essay on Education* (1802) worried that what he called the 'present fashionable system of education',[8] with its encouragement to children to become, in a sense, their own authorities, 'would breed a race of Jacobins'.[9] Recent critics have also pointed out that children's books of the period often promoted the kinds of republican or at least meritocratic ideals that were increasingly clouded by suspicion in the reactionary 1790s.[10]

In his two separate studies on the subject (2003, 2011),[11] Grenby has offered several possible explanations for the reticence of children's authors on a subject that was at the very forefront of the popular imagination and the era's public discourse. The decision, with only a few exceptions, not to engage directly with current events and political debates suggests that even writers of a more Jacobin stripe 'studiously avoided politicising their work' when writing for children.[12] Grenby reads this avoidance as a 'retreat' from politics in the arena of children's literature,[13] motivated in part by emerging views on childhood's innocence in the period and a 'concern for [its] preservation' traceable to *Émile* (1762), in which Rousseau advocates isolating the child from the public sphere.[14] Grenby concludes that writers in the revolutionary and post-revolutionary periods were increasingly guided by the desire (one that persists to this day) to shelter children from 'adult' realities, which he attributes to 'the "Romantic" understanding of childhood, a state of natural innocence that should be protected from contamination by adult issues, which would certainly have included politics'.[15]

While I agree that most children's authors seem to have shared a sense that both the specific events and the revolutionary doctrines of the period were unsuitable for young readers, the 'Romantic' idealization of childhood innocence was not yet the dominant discourse it would later become in the nineteenth century. Indeed, the view that a child's deficient reason and mental incapacity barred him or her from grasping the complexities of the revolutionary moment seems to provide at least as likely a rationale for avoiding such difficult topics as does the desire to protect a putative innocence. Similarly, the view that held children as predisposed to disobedience and wickedness still retained considerable traction in the period and could also account for reservations about content in books that might nurture such tendencies in young readers. The assumption that the Revolution constituted a realm of experience and knowledge children could not grasp or should be shielded from did, however, coincide with an increased sense of childhood's difference in the period. Together, these developments fostered new ways of thinking about childhood and new strategies for writing for the young, which were both exemplified in the work of Maria Edgeworth.

Maria Edgeworth's Moral Tales   125

In his 'Preface' to his daughter's *Moral Tales*, Richard Lovell Edgeworth identifies as the book's imagined reader a different kind of child than she had addressed in earlier works of juvenile fiction: 'an attempt is made to provide for young people of a more advanced age a few Tales that shall neither dissipate the attention, nor inflame the imagination'.[16] He also hints that the tales recognize that young readers in this 'in-between' stage require special handling:

> stories suited to the early years of youth, and, at the same time, conformable to the complicate relations of modern society – fictions, that shall display examples of virtue, without initiating the young reader into the ways of vice – and narratives, written in a style level to his capacity, without tedious detail, or vulgar idiom![17]

The exigencies, then, of these particularly uncertain times demand an understanding of a new kind of childhood (what we would now call 'young adulthood' or 'adolescence'), one that is more 'complex' and aware of 'relations of modern society', as well as a type of fiction that can effectively manage young people presumably both prone to and capable of acting on the dangerous vices peculiar to the age.

Edgeworth seeks to help young readers navigate the dangerous waters of republican ideals and revolutionary sentiments to which they seem drawn in her companion tales about the young idealists 'Angelina' (her chosen name; Anne is her given name) and Forester. Both are narratives that chart, through the misadventures and eventual reform of their protagonists, a process of political and social maturation configured as 'outgrowing' the so-called 'New Philosophy' of the period. While the tales do not specifically address the Revolution, these events and the period's war of ideas act as what Perry Nodelman calls a 'shadow text' operating alongside the narratives. By this term, Nodelman implies the world of greater (i.e. 'adult') knowledge outside the children's book, which the book in its simplicity and lacunae acknowledges by avoiding it. Similarly, the narrator in Edgeworth's tales functions as the texts' 'hidden adult', whose guiding presence in both texts reflects the 'foundational situation' of writing for children: 'an adult knowing more writing for children because children know less and need to understand the implications of knowing less'.[18] The need for such an invisible, authorial textual presence became increasingly urgent at a time when structures of hierarchy – both social and familial – were under increased duress. The stories 'secure' the young reader both inside and outside the text – to borrow Jacqueline Rose's formulation[19] – through an often ironic narrative technique that identifies childishness in thought and action with revolutionary sentiment, while locating maturity in the acceptance of (in a slightly modified version, perhaps) 'things as they are'.

I do not mean to suggest by this a simplification of Edgeworth's politics to a merely reactionary anti-Jacobinism; she was a much more nuanced

126   *Andrew O'Malley*

and flexible political thinker than such an easy label allows for. As several critics have noted, Edgeworth's political sympathies are notoriously difficult to pin down. Remarking on Edgeworth's ability to elude easy identification with one camp or another, Myers sees her as partaking in both progressive and conservative positions: 'more than any other woman writer of her day, Maria Edgeworth managed to have things two ways, to keep her cake and enjoy it too'.[20] Ó Gallchoir, discussing the slightly earlier *Letters for Literary Ladies* (1795), regards Edgeworth's political slipperiness more as a compromise, perhaps brought on by the new political realities of the 1790s: 'The first edition of *Letters for Literary Ladies* exhibits an oscillation between a determined adherence to Enlightenment principles and concessions to post-Revolutionary (and specifically post-Burkean) anxieties'.[21]

'Angelina' in particular (although 'Forester' shares many similarities as well) bears more than a passing resemblance to the typically reactionary anti-Jacobin novels that proliferated in the period, as Gary Kelly's thumbnail sketch of the genre elucidates: 'a young woman or man enters the world, is taken in by the Jacobin villain, and is either destroyed in consequence or saved by a mentor or wise lover. The survivors learn to see things as they really are'.[22] Of course, in 'Angelina', the Jacobin villain is a female sentimental novelist, yet the narrative contours remain intact. Indeed, Edgeworth recognized that her stories would be considered alongside such notable anti-Jacobin works as Elizabeth Hamilton's *Memoirs of Modern Philosophers* (1800).[23] The completion and submission of the manuscript for *Moral Tales* actually predated the publication of Hamilton's novel, but Joseph Johnson was slow to publish it. This was a source of some concern to the Edgeworths, and letters written by Maria's stepmother Frances at the time exhibit 'anxiety that the public would assume Maria had borrowed the ideas in "Angelina" and "Forester" in particular from Elizabeth Hamilton'.[24] The main difference, of course, between Edgeworth's iterations of the genre and Hamilton's is that Edgeworth's deceived young people 'grow up' rather than die.

As with *Memoirs*, 'Angelina' and 'Forester' derive a good deal of their comic effect from their mockery of widely recognizable republican scapegoats. Forester takes the opportunity, for example, to expound on the evils of gratitude to his worthy cousin, Henry Campbell, who has just saved him from asphyxiating in the 'mephitic gas' of a brewer's vat: 'Gratitude shall never make me a *sycophant*'.[25] Forester's singular – and silly – rejection of natural gratitude here is quite likely meant to evoke and ridicule William Godwin's oft-cited and oft-attacked position in *Political Justice* (1793):

> Gratitude therefore, a principle which has so often been the theme of the moralist and the poet, is no part either of justice or virtue. By gratitude I understand a sentiment, which would lead me to prefer one man to another, from some other consideration than his superior usefulness or worth.[26]

Angelina's '*amie inconnue*', Araminta, is a monstrously 'mannish' and ludicrous figure reminiscent of Bridgetina, Hamilton's terribly ungenerous caricature of Mary Hays in *Memoirs*, and of the grotesque 'Republican Belle' figure from Isaac Cruikshank's satirical cartoons (Figure 7.1).[27]

Further, the language of both of Edgeworth's protagonists is seasoned to the point of absurdity with the various buzzwords of revolutionary discourse: 'energies', 'system', 'theory', 'prejudice', 'injustice', and 'slavery', to name but a few. Revolutionary ideas and discourse, and familiarity with their principal proponents, serve as the 'shadow text' here; they constitute the world of 'adult' knowledge beyond the grasp of the young reader, which the text hints at without engaging directly.

Figure 7.1 Isaac Cruikshank, 'A Republican Belle' (1794). From the Library of Congress, Washington, DC.

A disparaging view of revolutionary sympathies is also evident in 'Forester' in the figure of Tom Random, the would-be pamphleteer and irrational zealot who incites a mob riot, in which Forester is unfortunately swept up, with his intemperate rhetoric. His motivation, the narrator reveals, has less to do with righting social inequalities, than with exacting revenge on a confectioner (whose shop windows the mob smashes) who had denied Tom his daughter's hand: 'It was part of Random's new system of political justice, to revenge his own quarrels'.[28] The direct reference to Godwin's – for many notorious – treatise combined with the description of violent public disorder provide recognizable analogues to the recent, and highly complex, political turmoil without naming it directly.

Such revolutionary analogues are perhaps a little less evident in 'Angelina', in part at least because the most prominent reference point here is romance and sentimental fiction. The high-blown language and passionate heroines of the novel of sensibility, rather than the enthusiastic doctrines of the 'New Philosophy', provide here the faulty models that lead Anne Warwick (Angelina) astray. The language of sentiment, however, is often indistinguishable from that of revolution, a convergence anti-Jacobin writers were quick to use to discredit both, as Janet Todd contends: 'The *Anti-Jacobin Review*, the new organ of conservative opinion, worked to bind sensibility to radicalism, or "Jacobinism" as it insisted on calling any reformist view, and it blamed both for the unrest it feared was spreading in England'.[29] The threat sensibility was assumed to pose to the social order came from a few different quarters. In its promotion of what could perhaps be called an 'affectocracy', sensibility sought to displace the inherited aristocratic superiority imparted by 'breeding': 'By conservatives, sentimental doctrine was judged to be levelling since it evaluated a person not by achievement or breeding but by ability to feel'.[30] Moreover, Todd adds: 'Sensibility appeared to favor reform by its emphasis on life's victims, and to question, if not attack, the established hierarchies of birth and gender'.[31] While informed by affect more than Enlightenment reason, the novel of sensibility with which Angelina is so smitten posited reforms equally radical to those of Forester's 'New Philosophy'.

Edgeworth's disapproval of romance novels and their passionate heroines had likely less to do with a desire to protect traditional class hierarchy and privilege than with a discomfort with their seeming antipathy to the strong filial and communal bonds of affection she considered essential to a lasting social harmony.[32] Her sympathies can rightly be described as middle-class in that she was quite comfortable critiquing the hypocrisy and irresponsibility she saw in some quarters of the upper classes. In *Moral Tales*, this critique is directed at the figures of the status-obsessed Lady Catherine Mackenzie and her conniving, duplicitous son Archibald in 'Forester', and in that of Anne/Angelina's ineffectual guardian, the worldly socialite Lady Diana Chillingworth. Janet Todd notes, however, that 'as the eighteenth century closed, sensibility was viewed more and more as anti-community',[33]

Maria Edgeworth's Moral Tales   129

and this association would have tainted it most in Edgeworth's eye. The sentimental novel 'saw only subjective selfhood as authentic and natural and all social categories as irredeemably relative and conflicted'; as such, it participated in 'a cult of individualism' that Edgeworth would have found particularly at odds with her notions of cohesive social interdependence.[34]

Edgeworth emphasizes this concern for a mutually responsible socialization by avoiding what would have been, in an anti-Jacobin novel, the conventional punishment for a young woman who abandons her family to pursue the passions of her heart: loss of virtue, social disgrace, and typically death. This is of course the fate Julia suffers in *Memoirs of Modern Philosophers*. Although Anne/Angelina recklessly abandons her guardian to join her imagined soul mate Araminta, the text avoids virtually any suggestion of sexual impropriety,[35] allowing Angelina the possibility of returning 'innocent' (and so still in the role of child) to the appropriate protection of friends and family. Since elopement and unsanctioned marriage are not the issue, focus turns to the unnatural state of a young person placing herself outside the proper matrix of familial and social relationships. Araminta has persuaded Angelina to pursue a fundamentally anti-social impulse, one now typically associated with the adolescent subject: 'the privilege of thinking and acting for myself'.[36]

It is worth noting that Angelina's departure from the protection of her friends and her subsequent misadventures are in part excused by the death of her parents. She is by nature an amiable girl of strong abilities, but the unfortunate absence of parental authority is not adequately mitigated by her guardian Lady Chillingworth, who categorically fails to provide the guidance and friendship a young person at a particularly susceptible stage of life requires. More concerned with the theatre and the card table than her responsibilities to her dependent, Lady Chillingworth represents the unreformed, *ancien régime*-styled aristocracy, whose failure to meet its obligations is nearly as dangerous to the social fabric as the levelling enthusiasm of Jacobins. In effect, her failure drives the orphaned Angelina out of her proper sphere and into the wilds of the Welsh countryside. The isolated setting of Araminta's crude cottage – not quite the 'charming romantic' place of 'tranquil, elegant retirement' Angelina imagines[37] – only serves to underscore the unnatural breakdown of social and familial bonds by its remoteness from normal human contact.

The unnatural, in Edgeworth's view, independence and 'free thinking' Araminta and her remote retreat promise are, of course, central tenets of the 'New Philosophy' to which Forester is drawn as a young adult, and his story clearly identifies his passion for individual freedom as the principal flaw he needs to correct. Like Angelina, Forester is a young person with a noble heart and many commendable qualities, but he is an orphan as well. The absence of a stable domestic setting has impaired the sense of interdependence and filial obligation that produces the kinds of healthy familial and social bonds Edgeworth advocates. These are admirably displayed by the Campbells, the family with whom Forester is sent to live following his father's death, but had seemingly not formed part of Forester's own upbringing. Even when his father was alive, he seems to have provided Forester inadequate, or at least highly eccentric, mentorship: '[he] had paid some attention to his education, but [he] had some singularities of opinion, which probably influenced him in all his conduct towards his children'.[38] The result is a wholly unnatural aversion to social life in any form: 'His love of independence was carried to such an extreme, that he was inclined to prefer the life of Robinson Crusoe in his desert island to that of any individual in cultivated society'.[39] Indeed, we find Forester on more than one occasion rejecting – often quite sulkily – the pleasures of polite company in favour of a quiet corner to read his beloved Defoe.

Forester's devotion to *Robinson Crusoe* (1719) resonates, in a late eighteenth- and early nineteenth-century context, in ways that might seem surprisingly unfavourable to modern readers. Since the Victorian period Crusoe has been almost universally celebrated as the ideal of the 'self-made man', the embodiment of muscular Christianity and the indomitable British spirit: in short, as an exemplary figure particularly well-suited to inculcating a range of noble virtues in young readers (especially boys).[40] In the late eighteenth and early nineteenth centuries, however, opinion on the book and its famous protagonist was somewhat less unanimously approving, especially among educational writers concerned that it may foment in young men wanderlust and filial disobedience.[41] Edgeworth herself expressed strong reservations about *Robinson Crusoe* in *Practical Education* (1798), where she suggests Defoe's book could inflame 'the incipient passions of avarice and ambition'.[42] While these are not exactly the defects manifesting themselves in Forester's character, they stem from the same individualism that creates a disregard for one's responsibilities to others. Forester's misguided reverence for Crusoe-like independence and his desire to be above and detached from the petty ceremonies and rituals of polite society prevent him from accepting the obligations and enjoying the benefits attached to the title of gentleman. In the terms the tale sets out, his excessive individualism jeopardizes his natural and necessary maturation into this role.

The difference in outcome between Hamilton's seduced and fallen Julia and Edgeworth's redeemed and successfully reintegrated Angelina and Forester has, of course, a great deal to do with the young audience for whom Edgeworth is writing. Her tales are primarily pedagogical, concerned more with the improvement of youth than with the punishment of vice or folly. Both tales chronicle a type of error – dalliance with radical ideas – construed as youthful and naive, but allow the young protagonists, with the help of rational mentors (Lady Frances in 'Angelina', Dr Campbell and his son Henry in 'Forester'), the opportunity to correct their errors in judgement and behaviour and so to mature into a more realistic and stable social awareness. The notion that children learn more effectively by example rather than precept had become generally accepted by late eighteenth-century writers for children.[43] The turn away from precept and toward experience would have been seen as perhaps more necessary in a work for young adults even less inclined than younger children to accept the direct dictates of authority. In their general contours, these tales are a typical application of the 'supervisory' method of education promoted by John Locke in *Some Thoughts Concerning Education* (1693) and adopted in countless children's books in the eighteenth century.[44] Edgeworth herself, in her most famous children's story, 'The Purple Jar', employed the model in which a child is given the space to commit and learn from errors by a mentor who remains at a remove, does not interfere, but helps reconfirm the requisite lesson at the end. Indeed, a version of this supervision appears in the *Moral Tales* as well; Forester, after he flees the Campbells' home to pursue his liberty, is still under the watchful eye of Dr Campbell: 'I have had my eye upon him ever since he left this house. I have traced him from place to place'.[45] Likewise, Angelina's misadventures through Bristol are shadowed by Lady Frances, who steps in to save Angelina and return her home before her reputation suffers irreparable damage. In the aftermath of the French Revolution and Irish uprising, and with young adults rather than small children involved, however, the stakes of youthful error and disobedience become much higher.

Contributing greatly to these raised stakes were the increased attention to and shifting status of the young adult. The figure of the 'rebellious youth' is now such a commonplace in Western cultures that commercial youth culture and young adult fiction have largely organized themselves around this topos. The *de facto* association of adolescence or young adulthood with either social maladroitness or (an often violent and passionate) rejection of and conflict with authority is by no means a historical given. As historians of childhood and youth have shown, a period of late childhood in which the transition to adulthood occurs has itself only recently been recognized as a stage of life in its own right.[46] The late eighteenth century, however, saw adolescence gain 'growing value and purpose. Massive state investment in its successful production promised to reproduce national power and advance civilization'.[47] Two of the key models for understanding youth as the time before mature, stable adulthood emerge from this period: Rousseau's *Émile*, with its 'call for development toward rational maturity' and the German *Sturm und Drang* writers' 'characterization of youth as a period of passionate, impulsive desire to be weathered and overcome'. Together, these would come to 'typify modern adolescence',[48] and would make late childhood an object of increasing concern.

Edgeworth's young people carried away by passionately held ideals, then, would already have been quite recognizable figures by the end of the eighteenth century; as Ó Gallchoir notes, her 'tale of youthful impetuosity ["Angelina"] is ... very clearly positioned in the philosophical and political context of the post-revolutionary 1790s, when idealism could be interpreted as dangerous sedition'.[49] The implied affinity between this period of life and

132 *Andrew O'Malley*

radical political views had also begun to crystallize at this time, and was in fact borne out by actual practice. Sergio Luzzatto has noted that many of the most active participants in the French Revolution were in their late adolescent years. He goes so far as to suggest that the Revolution can be understood partly in terms of a generational conflict: the 'Declaration of the Rights of Man' states 'in Article 28 that "one generation cannot subject future generations to its laws"'.[50] In a sense, the tension between the authority and tradition of older generations and the exuberance of youth is at the heart of the revolutionary project. The result, Luzzatto argues, was an increased political wariness over youth: 'the Revolution inaugurated a political rhetoric around young people that had lasting repercussions: that youth, in its liberality and exuberance, is a permanent danger to the political and social order'.[51] Nodelman asserts that children's literature 'exists only and always when adults believe that children need something special in what they read that child readers cannot provide for themselves and that adults must provide for them'.[52] In the wake of the French Revolution, Edgeworth was attuned to the shifting sensibility toward youth, and her *Moral Tales* can be seen as an effort to supply a new kind of 'need' in childhood. In 'Forester' and 'Angelina', she attempts to defuse freshly recognized dangers associated with the restive late stage of childhood with a literature that illustrates the pitfalls of radicalism and that encourages young readers toward a more sober maturity. The developing genre of children's literature, in which Edgeworth had already played an important, formative role, was well suited to the task.

According to Perry Nodelman, the key dynamic of children's literature – an adult writer supplying the perceived need or shortcoming of a child reader – has remained intact since Edgeworth's time, and has tended to express itself in certain shared structural and generic features. Chief among these has been the implied presence of a superior world of adult knowledge operating beyond the grasp of the implied child reader.[53] Children's literature, Nodelman argues, provides a simplified world for young readers while at the same time suggesting a more complex, 'adult' reality, the child's inability to comprehend which reinforces her dependence on the adult. Nodelman likens the effect to a subtle presence, which he dubs the 'hidden adult', ubiquitous in children's literature, and an expression of the fundamental imbalance of power that both motivates and shapes how, what, and why adults write for children. The eighteenth-century axiom that children's books must provide 'instruction with delight' is an early but enduring articulation of the dynamic Nodelman describes, 'a combination of the pleasurable and didactic that puts the pleasure in the service of the didactic ... by disguising the didactic in the mask of allowing the pleasurable'.[54] The didactic function – the adult presence, how the adult wants the child to be – is more effective for being hidden.

One way of disguising the didactic is to integrate it into the narration, which in children's literature has typically been in the third person, and

Maria Edgeworth's Moral Tales   133

which Nodelman argues has the effect of highlighting the difference in perspectives and knowledge between the child focalizer[55] and the (adult) narrative voice. The child reader is meant to identify or at least see something of themselves in the perspective of the young protagonist, to recognize a similarity between her understanding and that of the child in the book. At the same time, however, child readers are made aware of the limitations of the focalized character and, by extension, of their own limitations, by an adult-voiced narrator who can comment on and evaluate the attitudes and actions of the protagonist. As Nodelman suggests, third-person narration in children's literature is purposeful in that it provides

> a sense that there is a second point of view, that of the narrator. These texts [his representative six works of children's fiction] all seem to offer hints that the focalized child character is not seeing everything there is to see or possibly not understanding events in the various ways they might be understood. The narrator seems to see more and know more.[56]

In many works for children (*Alice's Adventures in Wonderland*, for example), this difference produces an ironic effect; '[t]he narrator knows more and apparently uses the knowledge to undercut the validity of the child protagonist's innocence'.[57] It is this ironic distance – between the naive perspective of the young protagonist and the knowing perspective of the narrator – that lends 'Angelina' and 'Forester' much of their humour, but that also enables their pedagogical goals. In both tales, the wiser, more mature narrative voice reveals the irrationality and impracticality of the 'New Philosophy' that informs the perspectives and directs the choices the young protagonists make and that represents the political perspective with which both characters must harmonize in order to achieve maturity.

In 'Forester', the ironic narrative voice renders the young hero's views unreasonable by drawing attention to their difference from those of a sensible and authoritative narrator who clearly understands better what is acceptable and 'normal'. Forester's dislike of formality and the rituals of polite society move him to ride in a lowly carrier to his new home at Dr Campbell's, rather than the stage coach in which he is expected. He arrives in such a dishevelled state that the Campbells' footman (comically) mistakes him for a vagabond rather than a young gentleman. Despite this awkward introduction, the narrator informs us that Forester remains pleased with his entrance, 'congratulat[ing] himself upon his freedom from prejudice'.[58] His principles are made to appear similarly absurd when Forester joins the Campbells at table for the first time:

> A table covered with a clean table-cloth – dishes in nice order – plates, knives, and forks laid at regular distances, appeared to our young Diogenes absurd superfluities, and he was ready to exclaim, 'How many

134 *Andrew O'Malley*

things I do not want!' Sitting down to dinner, eating, drinking, and behaving like other people, appeared to him difficult and disagreeable ceremonies.[59]

Forester's resistance to what he sees as irrational 'custom' is shown by the narrator to be a rejection of normal socialization and agreeable, civil behaviour, and so of the 'hail' of maturity; the narrator's perspective on Forester's views serves for the implied child reader as an adult voice that points out childishness.

After suffering a painful embarrassment at a ball hosted by the Campbells, Forester decides to reject fully the trappings of polite society; he leaves the protection of Dr Campbell's home and sets out to make his way alone and on his own terms. What follows are a series of ill-fated forays into menial labour; while Forester applies himself admirably at his various occupations, each effort is attended by some misadventure that highlights how unsuited he is, as a young gentleman of parts, to the lower stations of life. First, enchanted by bucolic notions of working the land, he takes a position assisting a gardener, and lives with him and his family in their rough cottage. The son, Colin, takes an immediate and aggressive dislike to the philosophical newcomer, and 'Forester now, to his great surprise, discovered that hatred could exist in a cottage'.[60] Forester's naivety appears at this stage merely harmless inexperience, with the narrator's irony suitably gentle. This ignorance of 'things as they really are', however, takes on greater political import when, while working at a printer's shop, Forester takes up with the young radical Tom Random, who asserts 'that "this great globe, and all that it inhabits," must inevitably be doomed to destruction, unless certain ideas of his own, in the government of the world, were immediately adopted by universal acclamation'.[61] Here childish self-absorption and ignorance of the 'real world' of politics have substantial consequences, as Forester's imprisonment following the riot Tom instigates soon demonstrates.

Confirming that the ironic narrative voice should be understood as that of parental or at least adult authority is its uncanny similarity to the voice of Forester's guardian, Dr Campbell, when he addresses his young charge. After his humiliation at the ball, Forester writes an impassioned farewell, instructing his guardian what to do with the belongings he leaves behind, including a letter to Flora Campbell, the doctor's daughter and the object of Forester's budding, but unacknowledged affections. In his reply, Dr Campbell employs a gentle mockery that highlights his greater knowledge and experience:

> I shall not break open the lock of your trunk (of which I hope you will some time, when your mind is less exalted, find the key) nor shall I stir in the difficult case of Flora's legacy. When next you write your will, let me, for the sake of your executor, advise you to be more precise in your directions, for what can be done, if you order him to give and burn the same thing in the same sentence?[62]

Like the narrative voice, Dr Campbell's letter wryly observes the logical and practical shortcomings of the protagonist's outlook and plans, while hinting at how the passionate enthusiasm and sense of injustice with which Forester has been so powerfully animated can produce only mental confusion.

Anne Warwick/Angelina's errors in judgement and faulty understanding, acquired from romance stories and novels of sensibility, are likewise subjected to the gentle ridicule of a more mature and sensible narrator. Anne leaves a letter on her desk (the romantic elopement convention), to be discovered after she departs on her quest for happiness with Araminta, about which the narrator remarks: 'Under all the emphatic words, according to the custom of some letter-writers, were drawn emphatic lines'.[63] The affective intensities of a not-yet-fully-rational youth are viewed in a droll light by the knowing adult, but this also serves to mark them for young readers as errors in need of correction. As with Forester, Angelina's inability to reconcile the world she wishes for with the world as it is acts as an indication of her naivety. When she arrives in Cardiff, she is ecstatic to encounter a Welsh harper – that bardic staple of romantic convention – but is quickly and inevitably disappointed with the prosaic reality of a man trying to make a living by entertaining the patrons of a public house:

> Angelina cast upon him a look of contempt. – 'He no way fills my idea of a bard – an ancient and immortal bard! – He has no soul, fingers without a soul! No "master's hand," or "prophet's fire!" – No "deep sorrows;" – No "sable garb of woe!" No loose beard or hoary hair, "streaming like a meteor to the troubled air!" – No "haggard eyes" – Heigho!'[64]

Expressing anger and dissatisfaction at an object when it does not conform to the child's wishes and expectations was identified by many eighteenth-century pedagogical theorists as one of the hallmarks of the child's deficient reasoning. Angelina's irrational response to the harper who is not what she imagines is indicative of immaturity, and her breathless jumble of quoted fragments underscores the confused state of her thinking. Her unrealistic and romance-inflamed expectations disconnect her from reality, with the consequence that her behaviour appears as madness: the harper, notes the narrator, 'began to think, by the young lady's looks and manner, that she was not in her right understanding'.[65]

When Angelina discovers the cottage only to find her Araminta has left for Bristol, she sends her a desperate note with a servant boy, who of course fails to deliver it. The romantic convention of the messenger flying urgently to deliver the critical message is, as the narrator notes, hardly a practical mode of communicating:

> The post seems to be the last expedient, which a heroine ever thinks of, for the conveyance of her letters; so that if we were to judge from the annals of romance, we should infallibly conclude, there was no such thing as a post office in England.[66]

136   *Andrew O'Malley*

On their face, such ironic narratorial asides merely point out in a humorous way the distance between the conventions of fiction and 'real life'. In the context of a pedagogical literature for young readers, however, they help readers recognize the difference between two worlds of knowledge: one predicated on fancy and desire, the other based in actual experience; one swept up in enthusiasm and passion, the other grounded in practical realities; one child-like in its naive expectations, the other mature in its understanding.

These stories and, as Nodelman suggests, much of the children's literature of the past two centuries, employ a dual-voiced strategy to make the child aware of the limitations and deficiencies of her own perspective while directing her toward the more mature perspective she would do well to adopt. The earliest text Nodelman discusses in his analysis is Edgeworth's 'The Purple Jar', mentioned above as an example of the 'supervisory' mode of pedagogy favoured in the period and adapted for the young adult reader of *Moral Tales*.[67] This story also shares with the later *Moral Tales* similar techniques for addressing its child readership. The function of the hidden adult in this text is, in part, to bring the child – young Rosamond – around to the superior perspective of the adult voice, in this case that of the narrator as well as that of her mother. By the end of the story, when Rosamond sees that her jar is not actually purple but only holds purple (foul-smelling, no less) water and must acknowledge that choosing much needed new shoes over a useless but pretty jar would have been the better decision, she announces, 'I hope I shall be wiser another time'.[68] Her proclamation 'removes the opposition and dissipates the sense of double perspective, as Rosamond moves away from her own previous perception and adopts that of the second voice'.[69] In other words, the second voice – the narrative voice of the 'hidden adult' in 'Forester' and 'Angelina' – represents the perspective with which the young protagonists must, and do, align themselves in order to move successfully toward maturity. Dr Campbell, who echoes the narrator's voice as we have seen above, and whose rationally-informed model of moderate reform mirrors Edgeworth's own politics, had predicted this trajectory for Forester from the day the young philosopher left his home: 'I am convinced, that the solidity of his character, and the happiness of his whole life, will depend upon the impression, that is now made upon his mind by *realities*. He will see society as it is'.[70] Dr Campbell's mention of the 'impression' Forester's experiences will make evokes Locke's *tabula rasa* and confirms the childlike quality of Forester's mind and opinions. It also reinforces that his passionately-held political views are the fantasies of inexperience, which the process of maturation will correct and bring around to the more 'realistic' views the doctor himself holds.

The child protagonist's evolution from the naive politics of radical egalitarianism and independence to the combination of traditional social structures and rational, moderate reform of aristocratic abuses that Edgeworth herself favours is configured as maturation: a process both necessary and desirable for the young person. It is also echoed in the plots by the physical

Maria Edgeworth's Moral Tales   137

return 'home' of the errant protagonists, who by the end of their tales both reconcile themselves to the adult/parental authority they had earlier rejected. In both tales, the protagonists assume their places in the protective circle of friends and family relations that is the appropriate environment for young people who are still not yet prepared for the independence and responsibility of adulthood. Nodelman's observation on the generic structure of children's literature featuring fantasy or secondary worlds is equally applicable here: 'The point at which ... children accept the certainty of the assertion – adopt the knowledge commonly accepted by most adults as true – is the point at which their fantasy worlds of desire must and do end'.[71] The radical utopianism promised by both the 'New Philosophy' and the novel of sensibility is, the *Moral Tales* aims to demonstrate, just such a fantasy world: a projection of childish desires for things that cannot be, which must yield to the solidity of a more adult political and social reality.

Notes

1. For details of the composition history of this book, see C. Ó Gallchoir, 'Introductory Note to *Moral Tales*', in *The Novels and Selected Works of Maria Edgeworth*, ed. E. Eger and C. Ó Gallchoir, vol. 10 (London: Pickering and Chatto, 2003), pp. vii–xxiii, on pp. xiii–xiv.
2. M. Myers, 'The Erotics of Pedagogy: Historical Intervention, Literary Representation, the "Gift of Education," and the Agency of Children', *Children's Literature*, 23 (1995), pp. 1–30, on p. 2.
3. Ó Gallchoir, 'Introductory Note', p. xvii. Ó Gallchoir does, however, concede that Angelina's (and I would add Forester's) 'ideals' are "located in the specific and politicised context of post-revolutionary culture" (p. xviii). The only direct reference to events in France in either tale is a passing mention by the milliner in 'Angelina'; she comments that 'Valenciennes' lace 'can scarce be had real, for love or money, since the French Revorlution [sic]' (M. Edgeworth, *Moral Tales for Young People; in Three Volumes*, 2nd edn (London: J. Johnson, 1806), vol. 2, p. 187). I have elected to use this edition due to its digital availability on Google Books.
4. Ó Gallchoir, 'Introductory Note', p. xiv.
5. Myers was one of the first and only scholars to consider these tales specifically as YA fiction, rather than simply and generally children's literature. She describes *Moral Tales* as 'an early example of fiction self-consciously tailored for a teen audience' ('Quixotes, Orphans, and Subjectivity: Maria Edgeworth's Georgian Heroinism and the (En)Gendering of Young Adult Fiction', *The Lion and the Unicorn*, 13:1 (1989), pp. 21–40, on p. 21), and remarks further that '[t]he *Moral Tales* were among the first fictional ventures designed to appeal to a teenage audience's reading interests and psychic needs' ('Daddy's Girl as Motherless Child: Maria Edgeworth and Maternal Romance; an Essay in Reassessment', in D. Spender (ed.), *Living by the Pen: Early British Women Writers* (New York: Teachers College Press, 1992), pp. 137–59, on p. 146).
6. M. O. Grenby, 'Politicizing the Nursery: British Children's Literature and the French Revolution', *The Lion and the Unicorn*, 27:1 (2003), pp. 1–26, on p. 2.

138 *Andrew O'Malley*

7. Ibid., p. 6.
8. W. Barrow, *An Essay on Education*, 2 vols (London: F. and C. Rivington, 1802), p. 320. 'Fashionable' is Barrow's preferred pejorative for modern educational thought and systems, and he uses it throughout his *Essay*.
9. M. O. Grenby, '"Very Naughty Doctrines": Children, Children's Literature, Politics and the French Revolution Crisis', in A. D. Cousins, D. Napton, and S. Russo (eds), *The French Revolution and the British Novel in the Romantic Period* (New York: Peter Lang, 2011), pp. 15–35, on p. 23.
10. See, for example, M. Levy, 'The Radical Education of *Evenings at Home*', *Eighteenth-Century Fiction*, 19:2 (2006), pp. 123–50. Grenby observes that the distinctly meritocratic, even anti-aristocratic, story 'The Basket Weaver' remained a mainstay in children's books throughout the revolutionary and post-revolutionary periods ('Politicizing the Nursery', pp. 18–19).
11. Grenby, 'Politicizing the Nursery' and 'Very Naughty Doctrines'.
12. Grenby, 'Very Naughty Doctrines', p. 24.
13. Ibid., p. 16.
14. Ibid., p. 25.
15. Grenby, 'Politicizing the Nursery', p. 8.
16. Edgeworth, *Moral Tales*, vol. 1, p. vi.
17. Ibid., vol. 1, p. v.
18. P. Nodelman, *The Hidden Adult: Defining Children's Literature* (Baltimore, MD: Johns Hopkins University Press, 2008), p. 22.
19. See J. Rose, *The Case of Peter Pan; or, The Impossibility of Children's Fiction*, 2nd edn (Philadelphia, PA: University of Pennsylvania Press, 1993), p. 2: 'If children's fiction builds an image of the child inside the book, it does so in order to secure the child who is outside the book, the one who does not come so easily within its grasp'.
20. Myers, 'Daddy's Girl', p. 139. See also H. Havens, Chapter 8 of this volume, pp. 147–48.
21. C. Ó Gallchoir, 'Gender, Nation and Revolution: Maria Edgeworth and Stéphanie-Félicité de Genlis', in E. Eger, C. Grant, C. Ó Gallchoir and P. Warburton (eds), *Women, Writing and the Public Sphere, 1700–1830* (Cambridge: Cambridge University Press, 2001), pp. 200–216, on p. 206. For Ó Gallchoir, Edgeworth's 'concessions' amount almost to a capitulation of the Enlightenment enthusiasm she earlier shared with her father than the kind of free choice from the political banquet Myers imagines. Edgeworth's 'Answer' to 'Letter to a Gentleman' is striking, Ó Gallchoir suggests, for how thoroughly it 'appears to validate conservative and reactionary fears':

> In the second paragraph, the enlightened father admits that he is 'sensible that we have no right to try new experiments and fanciful theories at the expence [sic] of our fellow creatures'. Edgeworth here allows the terms 'experiment' and 'theory' to remain under the cloud of their revolutionary connotations, more or less conceding defeat for rationalism.
>
> (p. 208)

22. G. Kelly, *English Fiction of the Romantic Period, 1789–1830* (London and New York: Longman, 1989), p. 63.
23. R. Carnell and A. T. Hale describe the political view articulated in 'Angelina' as 'anti-Jacobin but not entirely reactionary', and suggest the tale offers

Maria Edgeworth's Moral Tales 139

'a non-patriarchal anti-Jacobinism that nevertheless redeems the sympathy and sentiment (and potential protofeminism) of the initial intellectual underpinnings of both the American and French revolutions' ('Romantic Transports: Tabitha Tenney's Female Quixotism in Transatlantic Context', *Early American Literature*, 46:3 (2011), pp. 517–39, on pp. 526, 528). *Memoirs*, however, according to M. L. Wallace, was a definitive example of the anti-Jacobin novel; it 'receive[d] an entirely laudatory review from *The Anti-Jacobin*' and was 'read in its own time as unambiguously anti-Jacobin' (*Revolutionary Subjects in the English 'Jacobin' Novel, 1790–1805* (Lewisburg, PA: Bucknell University Press, 2009), p. 223).

24. Ó Gallchoir, 'Introductory Note', p. xiv.

25. Edgeworth, *Moral Tales*, vol. 1, p. 40.

26. W. Godwin, *Enquiry Concerning Political Justice and Its Influence on Morals and Happiness*, ed. F. E. L. Priestley, 3 vols (Toronto, ON: University of Toronto Press, 1969), vol. 1, p. 129. Edgeworth manages to get in a fairly subtle barb at the spiritual father of the Revolution, Rousseau, as well, by using a passage from *Émile* to mock Angelina's sense of being misunderstood by 'the world': 'Tais toi Jean Jacques, on ne te comprend pas' (Edgeworth, *Moral Tales*, vol. 2, p. 160). The sentence appears in French-language editions of *Émile*; see, for example, Jean-Jacques Rousseau. *Émile, ou De L'Education*, 2 vols (London, 1780), vol. 1, p. 223.

27. There are a number of specific points of similarity between Edgeworth's *Moral Tales* and Hamilton's *Memoirs*; for example, Forester favours the 'african simplicity' of the Hottentots over 'european etiquette' (Edgeworth, *Moral Tales*, vol. 1, p. 5), a preference discussed by Hamilton's modern philosophers to great comic effect. See Elizabeth Hamilton, *Memoirs of Modern Philosophers* (Peterborough, ON: Broadview Press, 2000), pp. 141–45.

28. Edgeworth, *Moral Tales*, vol. 1, p. 119.

29. J. Todd, *Sensibility: An Introduction* (London and New York: Methuen & Co., 1986), p. 130.

30. Ibid., p. 132.

31. Ibid., pp. 132–33.

32. In this sense, Edgeworth is perhaps better aligned with the Bluestockings and their programme of what Kelly describes as 'local social amelioration and reform, in and from the domestic sphere' than with conservative, post-revolutionary anti-Jacobinism (G. Kelly, 'Bluestocking Feminism', in Eger *et al.* (eds), *Women, Writing and the Public Sphere*, pp. 163–81, on p. 176).

33. Todd, *Sensibility*, p. 136.

34. Kelly, *English Fiction*, p. 43. A mistrust of the kind of individualism espoused by the sentimental novel was by no means unique to Edgeworth, but widespread in the period: 'During the 1790s the attacks on the excesses of sensibility became more pointedly directed at its subversive and individualistic tendencies' (C. Jones, *Radical Sensibility: Literature and Ideas in the 1790s* (London and New York: Routledge, 1993), p. 3).

35. The only clear insinuation of sexual immodesty in the story comes from the milliner, who seems to assume the unchaperoned Angelina must be a young woman of ill-repute: '"Do you please to want any thing else, ma'am?" said Mrs. Puffit, in a saucy tone, "Rouge, perhaps?"' (Edgeworth, *Moral Tales*, vol. 2, p. 192).

36. Edgeworth, *Moral Tales*, vol. 2, p. 155.

140   *Andrew O'Malley*

37. Ibid., vol. 2, p. 159.
38. Ibid., vol. 1, p. 1.
39. Ibid.
40. There have been, of course, some notable exceptions to this widespread approval, including Karl Marx, James Joyce, and more recently postcolonial authors and scholars.
41. Sarah Trimmer, for example, voiced grave concerns on this score in her review of *Robinson Crusoe* for her *Guardian of Education*. See Chapter 1, 'Performing Crusoe and Becoming Crusoes: The Pedagogical Uses of *Robinson Crusoe* in the Eighteenth and Nineteenth Centuries' in A. O'Malley, *Children's Literature, Popular Culture, and* Robinson Crusoe (Houndmills, UK: Palgrave, 2012), for a lengthier discussion of the mixed pedagogical opinion on Defoe's novel in the period.
42. M. Edgeworth and R. L. Edgeworth, *Practical Education*, 2 vols (London, 1798), vol. 1, p. 338.
43. See, for example, A. L. Barbauld, 'On Education', in *The Works of Anna Laetitia Barbauld*, 2 vols (London: Longman, Hurst, *et al.*, 1825). Barbauld likens 'set discourses' for the instruction of the young to 'a discourse from the pulpit, which you have reason to think merely professional' (vol. 2, p. 312).
44. For a discussion of Locke's 'supervisory education', see R. A. Barney, *Plots of Enlightenment: Education and the Novel in Eighteenth-Century England* (Stanford, CA: Stanford University Press, 1999).
45. Edgeworth, *Moral Tales*, vol. 1, p. 168.
46. Joseph Kett and others point to Stanley Hall's *Adolescence* (1904) as the first fully articulated formalization of the teenage years as an identifiable stage. The now seemingly self-evident view of the adolescent years, that it is, for example, 'an awkward and vulnerable stage of life', Kett claims was new to the mid-nineteenth century. Before this, people more commonly 'associated puberty with rising power and energy' (*Rites of Passage: Adolescence in America, 1790 to the Present* (New York: Basic Books, 1977), p. 17).
47. D. Romesburg, 'Making Adolescence More or Less Modern', in P. S. Fass (ed.), *The Routledge History of Childhood in the West* (New York: Routledge, 2013), pp. 229–48, on p. 230.
48. Ibid., p. 233.
49. Ó Gallchoir, 'Introductory Note', p. xviii.
50. S. Luzzatto, 'Young Rebels and Revolutionaries, 1789–1917', in Giovanni Levi and Jean-Claude Schmitt (eds), Carol Volk (trans), *A History of Young People. Vol. 2: Stormy Evolution to Modern Times* (Cambridge, MA: The Belknap Press, 1997), pp. 174–231, on p. 179.
51. Ibid.
52. Nodelman, *Hidden Adult*, p. 248.
53. This feature characterizes young adult literature as well, which Nodelman includes with only some reservation under the rubric of 'children's literature' (*Hidden Adult*, p. 6).
54. Nodelman, *Hidden Adult*, p. 36.
55. In narratology, 'focalization' refers to the presentation of events through the subjective perspective of a character. The 'focalizer' is the character from whose perspective events are seen and interpreted.
56. Nodelman, *Hidden Adult*, p. 20.

Maria Edgeworth's Moral Tales   141

57. Ibid., p. 22.
58. Edgeworth, *Moral Tales*, vol. 1, p. 2.
59. Ibid., vol. 1, p. 4.
60. Ibid., vol. 1, p. 80.
61. Ibid., vol. 1, p. 111.
62. Ibid., vol. 1, p. 70.
63. Ibid., vol. 2, p. 159.
64. Ibid., vol. 2, p. 163.
65. Ibid.
66. Ibid., vol. 2, p. 175.
67. Nodelman begins with 'The Purple Jar' as it is one of the more famous examples of children's fiction from the early days of the genre. There has been considerable debate over the 'origins' of children's literature and examples from many historical periods – medieval, classical, ancient Sumerian – have been pointed out by various scholars. The late eighteenth century can, however, be regarded as the starting point of a dedicated text industry for children with its own specialized narrative and bibliographic conventions.
68. Cited in Nodelman, *Hidden Adult*, p. 20.
69. Nodelman, *Hidden Adult*, p. 20.
70. Edgeworth, *Moral Tales*, vol. 1, p. 73.
71. Nodelman, *Hidden Adult*, p. 40.

8 Maria Edgeworth's Revisions to Nationalism and Didacticism in *Patronage*

Hilary Havens

A few years after the publication of her magnum opus, *Patronage* (1814), Maria Edgeworth wrote a letter, probably to her friend Dr Henry Holland, admitting the novel's principal shortcoming:

> The sad & irremediable fault of *Patronage* is that the moral *saute aux yeux* at every turn in every corner, in every page, in every line beginning middle & end the poor reader meets it & curses the useless light – Useless because too glaring – especially for tender eyes – I will do better next time & take for my motto
> 'Our story has a moral – and no doubt
> You all have wit enough to find it out'.[1]

The longest and most didactic of Edgeworth's novels, *Patronage* has long repelled potential readers.[2] Edgeworth acknowledges its inescapable morality in her letter, which hints at the nature of many of her later radical revisions to the novel. A few of her reviewers did respond positively to the novel's heavy-handed moralizing. The reviewer from *The Gentleman's Magazine* notes that Edgeworth's moral purpose 'is here happily illustrated, and strongly enforced'.[3] John Ward, in the *Quarterly Review*, gives Edgeworth's morality its due praise: 'It is of that sort which is most calculated to do real practical good'. But Ward's compliment is immediately succeeded by his criticism of Edgeworth's 'too little disguised' didacticism, a charge that Edgeworth echoes in her letter to Holland. For Ward, the novel's moral, which warns against patronage and celebrates independence, is 'presented to us in a thousand ways, and to which all the events are too plainly and unartificially made to bend, tires us by constant repetition, and diffuses an air of uniformity, approaching to dulness, over the whole work'.[4]

Ward's focus on 'repetition', 'uniformity', and 'dulness' in *Patronage* ignores the ambitious reformist aims of this 'darkly serious' novel.[5] The novel contains a brutal attack on patronage, for which it is heavily criticized in *The Critical Review*. That reviewer also condemns Edgeworth's negative portrayal of political careerists, especially Lord Oldborough, one of the central figures of the novel who is a good, clever man, but only ever at peace once he has retired to the country, far from the corrupting realm of politics.[6] Sydney Smith, in the *Edinburgh Review*, finds fault with Edgeworth's vilification and ostracism of daughters of divorced parents.[7] The

Quarterly Review and *The Critical Review* both deem the novel 'inferior' to Edgeworth's other productions.[8] Yet *Patronage*'s oppressive didacticism, especially in its treatment of male professionalization and female courtship behaviour, is directly linked to British preoccupations with national identity and prevailing prejudices against the French. The tangled nature of didacticism and nationalism within the text is reflected in its hybrid generic origins; Edgeworth's later revisions to the novel remove some of her awkward didactic and patriotic episodes and also attenuate her generic innovations.

The roots of *Patronage* are unsurprisingly located in the conduct book genre: it is Edgeworth's expansion of her father's oral bedtime stories about the 'Freeman' family,[9] which becomes the Percy family in *Patronage*. The independently-minded Percys are contrasted with the Falconers, who court the wealthy and titled for support and advancement. The trajectory of both families is driven mostly by the progress of their children both professionally and in marriage. By the end of the novel, the Percy sons become celebrated in their respective fields and the Percy daughters marry splendidly, while the Falconer children have proportionately spectacular failures. *Patronage* can also be read as Edgeworth's novelization of *Professional Education* (1809), an educational and professional tract that she had written with her father, Richard Lovell Edgeworth.[10] *Professional Education* is the second of two educational works that the Edgeworths wrote together, the first of which was their more popular *Practical Education* (1798), which gives a plan for a child's education from birth to young adulthood. While *Practical Education* credits both Edgeworths on the title page, *Professional Education* labels only Richard as the author, even though his daughter completed the bulk of the work. Maria Edgeworth intentionally omitted her name since she feared that advice on the masculine professions from a female author would not be well received.[11] The main theme of *Professional Education* is presented early in the text: 'prudent parents would decide as early as possible what the professions of their children are to be, and would trust securely to the power of education'.[12] Though the Edgeworths' belief that professional education should be inculcated from birth is radical and extreme, their book does make useful observations on the various professions and inspires the main thesis of *Patronage*: 'Advancement should be the certain consequence of knowledge and merit'.[13] *Patronage* is the fictionalized proof for this contention, and it expands the focus of *Professional Education* to include women.[14]

The resonances between the two works hint that *Patronage* complicates traditional generic descriptions. As her biographer Marilyn Butler observes, Edgeworth was 'anxious ... not to write mere novels'.[15] Michael Gamer has argued for a new generic understanding of Edgeworth, overturning earlier 'realist' interpretations of her texts:

> While the pedagogical bent of Edgeworth's fiction ultimately might be traced to French moral tales of the mid-eighteenth century, both her didacticism and her 'fondness for facts' also participate within a literary and generic tradition closer to home and more contemporary to herself.

144 *Hilary Havens*

Gamer classifies Edgeworth's texts as 'factual fiction' or 'romances of real life'.[16] This hybrid realist-didactic genre, which is a helpful description of Edgeworth's fictions, does not quite account for her nationalist strain, especially in *Patronage*. Edgeworth's nationalism was, according to Harriet Guest, part of a larger nineteenth-century trend in which

> some women of liberal education could assume that it was their right and duty to have opinions about what happened in the world; they did not see their exclusion from participation in the public life of the nation as natural; indeed, in some senses they did not think of themselves as excluded at all.[17]

Edgeworth's *Patronage*, which consistently undercuts the French and completely (though not blindly) celebrates the British, is her great contribution to political debates of the mid-1810s.[18] This is, perhaps, one of the primary causes of her reviewers' dismay. *Patronage* is no mere novel of manners:[19] its heavy-handed didacticism targets the assumed reader's staunch nationalism. Gary Kelly puts it best in his characterization of the novel as 'a major vehicle for Romantic nationalism in Europe and elsewhere ... Edgeworth may be said to have invented it'.[20] I contend, then, that Edgeworth's excessive use of didacticism and nationalism are inextricably linked and, furthermore, that while her revisions to the 1825 edition of *Patronage* address and dismantle the cloying didacticism that annoyed her reviewers, they also silenced the novel's most strident depictions of nationalism, by then unnecessary after the end of the war with France, and altered the novel's generic identity.

Patronage (1814)

British nationalism and its complement, anti-French sentiment, seep in at every turn within the early editions of *Patronage* and within *Professional Education*. In the latter, the Edgeworths decry the state of education in France after the civil war. Originally, French 'plans of public instruction and of national education' were 'full of eloquence and ability', but all was destroyed in the French Revolution: 'Men of sense or virtue, however they deplored this destruction, had no possible means of preventing it; they had no power; their only safety was in remaining unknown, during the reign of terror ... and for years afterwards'.[21] The Edgeworths firmly place the blame for the inadequate French educational system on the Reign of Terror and the subsequent and continuing political instability, but French radicalism is not the Edgeworths' only target. Interspersed throughout the text are brief, nearly imperceptible criticisms of French customs, for instance, their differing tastes regarding eloquence: 'The French would be *revolted* by what excites our admiration'.[22] French practices throughout *Professional Education* are continually placed in opposition to correct, English conduct.

This French–English dichotomy re-emerges in *Patronage* and is exemplified by Edgeworth's characterization of the Clay brothers, 'English Clay' and 'French Clay', given in the epistolary voice of Alfred Percy, one of the members of Edgeworth's revised 'Freeman' family. Reviewers strongly praised Edgeworth's depiction of the Clay pair; John Ward remarked that 'The characters of the two Clays are excellent. English Clay we think rather the best'.[23] English Clay, 'a cold, reserved, proud, dull looking man,... is a grave man of pleasure – his first care being to provide for his exclusively personal gratifications.... His next care is, that he be not cheated in what he is to pay'.[24] Edgeworth's comic tone surfaces in her paradoxical epithet of English Clay as a 'grave man of pleasure', selfishly indulgent, yet notoriously stingy with others. He is not, however, portrayed in a solely critical light. Some of his vices are partially redeemed by his excessive nationalism. While Alfred is initially cynical about the origin of English Clay's nationalistic feelings – 'Every thing about him is English; but I don't know whether this arises from love of his country, or contempt of his brother' – he does grudgingly concede that he 'would fight for old England, for it is his country, and he is English Clay', even though his love of country is dwarfed by his 'feeling for his horses, and his mother, and his coachman'.[25] Even though English Clay is a caricature, whose patriotism is somewhat qualified, he is still part of the novel's overarching nationalistic message.

His brother French Clay, on the other hand, 'is a travelled coxcomb', who 'is continually railing at our English want of *savoir vivre*, yet is himself an example of the ill-breeding which he reprobates'. Like English Clay, French Clay has contradictory qualities – 'His manners have neither the cordiality of an Englishman, nor the polish of a foreigner'– but French Clay's are far more objectionable. The generally tolerant Alfred is repelled by French Clay's affected 'Frenchness': 'But I am afraid I cannot speak of this man with impartiality, for I cannot bear to see an Englishman apeing a Frenchman. – The imitation is always so awkward, so ridiculous, so contemptible'.[26] The most damning criticism of French culture in *Patronage* could very well be that it is the single cause of French Clay's loss of patriotism:

> Public virtue, as well as private, he thinks it a fine air to disdain, – and patriotism and love of our country he calls prejudices, of which a philosopher ought to divest himself. – Some charitable people say, that he is not so unfeeling as he seems to be, and that above half his vices arise from affectation, and from a mistaken ambition to be, what he thinks perfectly French.[27]

The only concession that Alfred will give French Clay is that his vice is not wholly innate; the worst of it, his abandonment of 'patriotism and love of our country', is owing solely to his adoption of French culture and behaviour. Even the benevolent Mrs Hungerford implicitly condemns French Clay for his 'Frenchness' by placing him in contrast to the faultless hero, Count Albert Altenberg: 'He is an Englishman only by birth, and a Frenchman only by affectation. – Count Altenberg, on the contrary, a foreigner by birth, has all the tastes and principles that make him worthy to be an Englishman'.[28] Englishness is aligned with virtue, while the foreign, and especially the French, is undesirable; yet the two Clay brothers, who both embody numerous vices, complicate this simple dichotomy and exemplify the complexity of Edgeworth's characterizations.

The German hero, Count Altenberg, is the focal point of Edgeworth's nationalistic and didactic aims. Cliona Ó Gallchoir argues that Altenberg is the novel's political and nationalistic centre; his 'function in *Patronage* seems to be to awaken some of the English characters to a clearer recognition of patriotism and public virtue'.[29] Yet Altenberg is not exactly a foreigner. It is true that he is a German nobleman and eventually becomes Prime Minister, but his best qualities are those linked to his Englishness. Mrs Hungerford's strongest compliment of Altenberg is that his 'tastes and principles ... make him worthy to be an Englishman' despite his foreignness; moreover, she reveals that Altenberg himself wishes to be an Englishman: 'if he had liberty of choice, he would prefer residing in England to living in any country in the world. – Indeed, he expressed that sentiment at parting from us yesterday'.[30] Altenberg moves ever closer to becoming an English national by marrying Caroline Percy, who possesses 'the noble simplicity of character, that was once the charm of Swisserland', 'the polish, the elegance, that was once the pride of France ... without that undefinable, untranslatable French love of *succès de société*, which substitutes a precarious, factitious, intoxicated existence in public', and the presumably English qualities of 'the safe self-approbation, the sober, the permanent happiness of domestic life'.[31] This description of Caroline cements her status in the novel as an ideal, not just of female behaviour, but of English pre-eminence. Yet, this English pre-eminence is complicated by the fact that Caroline encapsulates a sort of exemplary cosmopolitanism; like her husband, she combines the best features of multiple nations, here France and Switzerland.[32] Caroline has clear connections to Edgeworth herself, whose views of England and Ireland were highly influenced by the 'Enlightenment ideals of citizenship and of the public' that she was exposed to during her 1802–3 visit to France.[33] Furthermore, Caroline's transnational romance with Altenberg has been read as wish-fulfilment on Edgeworth's part, after her failed romance with the Swedish courtier Abraham Niclas Clewberg-Edelcrantz.[34]

Caroline's multi-national virtues are not enough, however, to save her from the barbs of contemporary reviewers. *The Gentleman's Magazine* considers her 'uninteresting.... like Richardson's model of perfection in man, Sir Charles Grandison, she is cold and correct'; she is 'far below the powers of the Edgeworth pen' according to *The Critical Review*; and Ward identifies her as 'one of those "faultless monsters" that would be so delightful in real life, where they unluckily never appear, and that are quite insupportable in a novel, where we continually meet with them', while Altenberg is found to be 'equally perfect, and equally tiresome'.[35] Perhaps the most cloying aspect of their union is that it precipitates Altenberg's return to and permanent residency in England, near the Percy family. Caroline's marriage to Altenberg initially dooms her to the bittersweet fate of passing most of her days abroad; however, after Altenberg's prince has been killed by a stray cannonball and the prince's successor colludes with the French enemy, 'Count Altenberg refused to act as minister under his successor'; since 'no means of serving or saving the country remained, he at once determined to quit it for ever. Resolved to live in a free country, already his own, half by birth, and wholly by inclination', he settles on his estate in England.[36] Altenberg's immigration to England, which he denominates 'a free country', is Edgeworth's strongest nationalist statement within *Patronage*.

Though Altenberg represents British ideals, he also serves as the figure best able to expose English political and institutional corruption. In their discussions of the various respectable careers in *Professional Education*, the Edgeworths are most contemptuous of statesmen. They go so far as to blame politicians for the current turmoil in Europe: 'The misfortunes that have befallen the countries of Europe must be attributed to the errours of their [politicians'] rules, to their want of judgment, their party struggles, or their want of integrity'.[37] It is telling, then, that none of Maria Edgeworth's model characters end the novel as statesmen.[38] Oldborough's work in politics makes him suspicious and ambitious, qualities which are smoothed away once he retires in the country, and Altenberg must resign his post as minister because he refuses to compromise his principles. On the battlefield, Altenberg also values his moral principles above his military duties: when poised to kill an enemy soldier, he sees 'that the officer's right arm was broken. The Count immediately stopped, took hold of the disabled officer's bridle, and led him off to a place of safety'.[39] Altenberg's strong integrity is confirmed in his first appearance in the novel, when he protests his loyal servant's impressment into the British navy upon his arrival in England. Altenberg's comments on British impressment are damning; he initially uses sentimental language to describe his servant's hard fate:

> a faithful domestic, an excellent man, torn from the midst of his family, dragged from *that castle his home*, put on board a king's ship, unused to hard labour, condemned to work like a galley slave, doomed to banishment, perhaps to death!

Altenberg broadens his example, likening British officers to 'African slave-merchant[s]' in his decisive critique of the English system: 'Good Heavens! In all this where is your English liberty? Where is English justice, and the spirit of your English law?'[40] This is a rare moment in *Patronage* when Edgeworth can use her didactic voice to argue for political change. Even though this censure can be construed as an integral part of true patriotism, Jacqueline Pearson notes that these radical statements critical of the British government were correspondingly revised in later editions: Edgeworth 'cut some words which had been especially objected to'.[41]

Except for this one brief moment, Edgeworth's frequent interspersed references to the English military and navy are entirely adulatory.[42] The prominence she gives to the military is undeniable: while Godfrey Percy and his friend Mr Henry are the subjects of many of the military scenes, the sons of the Percy family friend Mrs Hungerford appear briefly and solely in order to foster nationalistic pride. Mrs Hungerford's second son is only mentioned fleetingly in the novel through one of his letters written 'ten minutes after an action at sea with the French': 'Dear mother – English victorious – of course – for particulars see Gazette. – In the cockleshell I have – could do nothing worth mentioning – but am promised a ship soon – and hope for opportunity to show myself worthy to be your Son'. The letter she receives from her eldest son in the military is very similar: 'A letter also from my Colonel! – Thanks of commanding officer ... gallant conduct abroad ... leave of absence for three weeks ... and will be here to morrow!'[43] These short missives, though slightly differentiated, convey unalloyed patriotism. The diction used by the Hungerford sons, especially in phrases, such as 'to show myself worthy' and 'gallant conduct', is one of the most overt indications of Edgeworth's didactic nationalism. Edgeworth's commentary on English patriotism is not merely limited to the scenes involving the British armed forces and Count Altenberg. Through the use of negative examples, Edgeworth continues to employ her brand of didactic nationalism, most notably through the duplicitous French diplomat, Monsieur de Tourville, and many members of the Falconer family.

Monsieur de Tourville appears early in the first chapter, and his primary importance in the novel is as the custodian of the encrypted, treasonous packet that the Falconers find and use to insinuate themselves into Oldborough's patronage. De Tourville is marked by his selfishness; the events of *Patronage* are precipitated by the sinking of a Dutch ship, of which de Tourville is a passenger. When the Percys come to rescue the distressed travellers, de Tourville uses his position as political envoy to justify his attempts to get passage in the Percy's first rescue boat, which is already full of people. Instead of allowing de Tourville into the boat, which he probably would have overturned, Mr Percy, an adherent of utilitarian principles, lets de Tourville fall into the water,

> justly considering that the lives of the number he had under his protection, including his son's and his own, were not to be sacrificed for one man, whatever his name or office might be, especially when that man had persisted against all warning in his rash selfishness.[44]

This scene foreshadows de Tourville's traitorous intentions against Oldborough, which are similarly foiled by the Percys later in the novel. Even though he possesses French refinement – 'agreeable manners and conversational

Maria Edgeworth's Revisions to Nationalism   149

talents' – he is not able to seduce the more discerning Percys or Edgeworth's readers, who have been given didactic warnings of 'the duplicity and pitiful meanness of a character, which was always endeavouring to seem, instead of to be'.[45]

Once de Tourville loses the important packet and subsequently disappears from the narrative, it is up to Cunningham Falconer to take his place. Cunningham is appointed as Oldborough's private secretary in return for the possession and partial translation of the packet. Cunningham, who is 'cunning' but not clever, maintains his post by purchasing and passing off the work of Alfred Percy's brilliant friend, Mr Temple, as his own.[46] Cunningham's supposed merit leads to his promotion abroad, but once he is separated from his ghost writer, 'many mistakes, and much ignorance, had frequently appeared in his ... despatches'.[47] After Oldborough's 'first moment of surprise at the difference between the ineptitude of the Envoy, and the talents of the author of the pamphlet,... these mistakes, and this ignorance, had passed without animadversion'.[48] Oldborough's suspicions remain dormant until the arrival of Altenberg, who

> without design to injure Cunningham, had accidentally mentioned ... a private intrigue which Cunningham had been carrying on, to get himself appointed Envoy to the Court of Denmark, by the interest of the opposite party, in case of a change of ministry.[49]

Through Altenberg, Cunningham's treachery is ultimately discovered and punished; instead of becoming the new Danish ambassador, he is thrown into Danish prison for the debt he undertook to finance his treacherous intrigue. Cunningham's abandonment of his country is directly correlated to his professional and personal disgrace.

Cunningham's fate epitomizes one of the main reasons the Falconer family fails by the end of the novel: they betray their patriotic duties as English citizens. Nowhere is this more evident than in the Falconers' courtship of the Petcalf family, whose wealth springs from dubious Indian origins. India is not unequivocally the seat of nationalistic corruption in *Patronage*: the good Colonel Hungerford is sent to India on a British military mission, but this is countenanced by Edgeworth since his undertaking is patriotic. The Falconer connection to India begins once the most dim-witted Falconer son, John, is coerced by his father into marrying Miss Petcalf, daughter of a British general who has 'an Indian fortune to suit an Indian complexion',[50] which will assure him promotion in the military. Miss Petcalf's brother, Petcalf, is also the object of Mrs Falconer's scheming on behalf of her eldest daughter, Georgiana. Georgiana, engrossed with the exotic and foreign, is instead intent on performing a translation of Voltaire's play *Zaïre* (1732) and captivating Altenberg with her acting. She wants a Turkish dress for the play, and her mother agrees to give her money for the dress in exchange for her promise to marry Petcalf if no better offer appears.[51] Of course, this all

150 *Hilary Havens*

ends in disaster. The Falconer family is undone by Cunningham's plotting and Mrs Falconer's treasonous behaviour against Oldborough. Falconer reveals in a letter to Percy that his wife and daughter's scheming has been predictably unsuccessful – they 'have so *overmanaged* matters with respect to Petcalf' – and the once sought-after Georgiana must now go abroad to find a husband:

> she is fitting out for India. She is going to be sure in good company; but in my opinion the expense, (which Heaven knows I can ill afford), will be thrown away like all the rest, for Georgiana has been much worn by late hours, and though still young, has, I fear, lost her bloom, and looks rather old for India.[52]

Unsurprisingly, Georginia is exiled to India. After her exotic and expensive tastes have spoiled her and ruined her family, she is no longer worthy to remain in England (and marry a British husband). Even her emigration – like previous efforts of the Falconers – seems destined to miscarry since she has 'lost her bloom, and looks rather old for India'. Georgiana's only function now is as a didactic warning of the fate awaiting those who are disloyal to their British homeland.

Patronage (1825)

Edgeworth's unwieldy didacticism and English nationalism are two of the distinguishing features of *Patronage*, but a number of these scenes are minimized and sometimes excised in the 1825 edition, both in response to her critics and to the changing national climate. It was not the first time that Edgeworth radically revised one of her novels. Edgeworth's popular *Belinda* (1801) was criticized by the reviewers for several reasons; for one, the eponymous heroine was a jilt. Edgeworth systematically removed Belinda's flirtatious language towards and engagement to Mr Vincent, the creole suitor who would never become her husband. She also excised the interracial marriage between the black servant Juba and a white country girl Lucy for the 1810 third edition.[53] Edgeworth's revisions to *Patronage* were even more substantial: she planned to incorporate them into the third edition of 1815, but the 1825 first edition of her collected stories and novels is the first to include all of the changes.[54] Many of Edgeworth's modifications are redresses to 'the "parti nombreux" of physicians, surgeons, churchmen, lawyers, and politicians who were objecting to the manner in which she had treated their various professions'.[55] While a number of Edgeworth's changes to *Patronage*, like those to *Belinda*, were precipitated by the reviewers' remarks, they often are mitigations of her ever-present nationalism and didacticism.

Occasionally Edgeworth's revisions are bizarre; one of the most notable examples involves the episode in which Buckhurst Falconer saves a bishop from choking. According to the *Monthly Review*, that scene is 'disgusting, and unworthy the pen of this superior writer'.[56] In the first-edition text, after the bishop begins to choke on some food, 'Buckhurst Falconer ran for the bellows, and applying the muzzle directly to the prelate's ear, produced such a convulsion as expelled the pellet from the throat with a prodigious explosion, and sent it to a mighty distance'.[57] The 'bellows' is an 'instrument or machine constructed to furnish a strong blast of air', which has industrial and mechanical applications.[58] Edgeworth's diction in this scene – marked by words such as 'muzzle', 'convulsion', 'expelled', and 'prodigious explosion' – is correspondingly indelicate. Her later version is much more unoffending: 'Falconer, with more presence of mind than was shown by any other person, saved his patron's life. He blew with force in the bishop's ear, and thus produced such a salutary convulsion in the throat, as retrieved his lordship from the danger of suffocation'.[59] The origin of Buckhurst's blowing is not revealed; the word 'convulsion' remains, but it is mitigated by the addition of the adjective 'salutary'; and 'expelled' and 'prodigious explosion' are replaced with the inoffensive 'danger of suffocation'. Edgeworth also adds a footnote, alluding to Voltaire's *Zadig ou la Destinée* (1747), as a means of justifying the inclusion of this episode, which contradicted current medical research, in her revised text: 'The assertions against the possibility of the fact remind us of the physician in Zadig, who ... wrote a book to prove that Zadig should have gone blind, though he had actually recovered the use of his eye. – Zadig never read the book'.[60]

Edgeworth also addresses the reviewers' criticism of Caroline Percy as a 'faultless monster' by revising Caroline's interactions with Lord William. William, a British foil of Altenberg who is also in love with Caroline, garnered strong praise from Edgeworth's critics: 'It is a remarkably well drawn picture of a person labouring under that morbid shyness which is so common in England, so rare out of it'.[61] As with English Clay, William is another of Edgeworth's modest tributes to the stereotypical Englishman. He meets Caroline after she has fallen in love with Altenberg, but before Altenberg has expressed his mutual love; thinking that she is unattached, Lord William pursues her ardently, only to be gently, though decisively rejected. In the first edition of the novel, Caroline nearly disappears from the narration during their painful parting:

> 'Fear not – I shall not misinterpret – I know too well what love is. – Speak freely of my sentiments to Lady Jane, when I am gone – her friendship deserves it from me'. –
>
> He stopped – he was silent – they came within view of the servants – he walked quietly to the carriage – assisted her into it, pressed her hand –
>
> 'Farewell – for ever', he said in a low voice, and let it go.[62]

152   Hilary Havens

In her later revisions, Edgeworth makes two small additions to this scene:

> '. . .her friendship deserves it from me'.
> He stopped speaking. 'Stay', said Caroline. 'It may give your noble mind some ease to know that my heart was engaged before we ever met.'
> He was silent. It was the silence of deep feeling. They came within view of the servants – he walked quietly to the carriage – assisted her into it, pressed her hand – and said in a low voice, 'Farewell – for ever.'[63]

Caroline's admission that her heart is pre-engaged to a man who does not return her affections is a deviation from accepted social codes and a substantial blow to her status as a 'faultless monster', even though her actions seem justifiable here. Her decision to contravene social norms adds a tinge of realism to her character. Lord William's response, his 'deep feeling', explains his final gesture of farewell, which is more touching in the revised scene.

Edgeworth's more substantial revisions to *Patronage* are, primarily, tied to the pervasive intertwined themes of didacticism and nationalism. The most significant of these revisions relates to Percy's arrest for debt. Shortly before Percy's incarceration, Caroline and Altenberg marry, and Caroline shares a maudlin farewell with her family as she prepares to leave for Germany with her husband:

> Caroline, flushed crimson to the very temples one instant, and pale the next, commanded with the utmost effort her emotion.... [her] lips quivered with a vain attempt to speak – she could only embrace Rosamond repeatedly, and then her mother – in silence.[64]

Just as the Altenbergs are about to depart, Percy is seized for 'an enormous sum – the amount of the rents received by Mr Percy during the whole time he had been in possession of the estate', which the usurper Sir Robert Percy had before agreed to waive.[65] Percy prefers to be taken to prison rather than pay the unjust sum, and Altenberg, instead of continuing on his journey with Caroline, urges her to remain: 'Heaven forbid! that I should separate you at this moment from your father ... that I should exert the right which the name of husband gives me, to sever the ties of nature! – Stay with your father, dearest Caroline!'[66] Edgeworth's version of filial duty here is extreme; Altenberg's unselfish relinquishing of his spouse on his wedding night is preposterous, especially when Percy already has an able companion in his wife. The didactic lesson bleeds into the descriptions of Caroline's life with her father and mother in prison as they predictably become model prisoners. Once the Percys enter their prison rooms,

> Caroline began to arrange the little furniture they contained, in such a manner, as to make her father and mother as comfortable

as circumstances would admit. – They uttered no complaints. – The gaoler was not used to see people so mild and resigned.[67]

Claire Connolly affirms that this scene contains an important, but 'unnoticed' 'negotiation of national and cultural allegiance'.[68] Caroline's choice to stay with her parents is also a refusal to leave England for Germany and hence a strong affirmation of her British identity.

These scenes are completely transformed in the 1825 edition of *Patronage*. Caroline and Altenberg's marriage takes place, and Caroline goes to Germany with the Count. The maudlin leave-taking is not present, though a brief description of Rosamond's bittersweet feelings appears: 'It had passed with the rapidity of a dream: the hurry of joy, the congratulations – all, all was over; and in sad silence, Rosamond felt the reality of her loss'.[69] Percy is not arrested; he is merely notified by letter of Sir Robert's intentions to seize the 'mesne rents', a legal term for the rents he received while he lived in Percy Hall. He subsequently prepares to 'take the proper steps to bring the affair to trial, and … submit to the decision of the law, whatever that might be'.[70] This scene is not now a didactic episode, and very little else is mentioned, other than the discovery of the original deed to Percy Hall, before Percy goes to trial with Sir Robert to reclaim his family estate. One reason why Edgeworth revised the scene was that Percy's arrest was not legal; the trial regarding his supposed debt would have had to take place first.[71] Ward criticized Edgeworth's legal mistakes – 'as Miss Edgeworth was determined to introduce law, it would have been better to make it sound law'[72] – and Edgeworth also received a detailed letter from a lawyer called 'Lycurgus' with similar criticisms.[73] Butler believes that these reasons were enough to compel Edgeworth to revise the novel; yet in a letter of March 1814, written shortly after the novel's publication, Edgeworth indicates that she was planning to retain the Percy jail scenes despite their inaccuracies. She came to her decision after a brief discussion of the legal impossibilities of *Patronage*'s plot with her father's friend Judge Fox:

> After ¾ of an hours [sic] sitting and careful investigation it was determined to leave things exactly as they are – because as he says none but lawyers will see the errors & men of sense will allow in a work of fiction all that … in short cannot be altered without diminishing interest or *truth* of character.[74]

While the criticism Edgeworth received from authorities on legal matters may have partially motivated her decision to revise, too many other aspects of the scene, such as the sentimental leave-taking, are missing in the later edition for the revision to simply be for the purpose of increasing accuracy. Edgeworth's replacement of Caroline's trip to jail with her parents for her honeymoon with Altenberg was a stylistic decision that reflected not only

154   *Hilary Havens*

Edgeworth's turn against the didactic mode, but also the diminished nationalistic threat that was menacing Britain.[75]

The removal of the Percy prison sequence in the 1825 edition is linked to the excision of several other scenes that generally contain a distinctively nationalistic character. Even though Caroline remains in England in the first edition, we learn far more about the difficulties in Germany there than we do in the 1825 edition. Caroline and the Percys receive their news through British newspapers and Altenberg's contrasting dispatches:

> Count Altenberg had flattered himself by the last despatches from his Court, that the strong measures taken by the Prince would have prevented danger; but the French party had formed new intrigues, – they gained ground. – Every symptom threatened revolution – and, if the newspaper accounts were true, civil war, and foreign invasion, were inevitable.[76]

The French invasion is given in much greater detail, and the French military are demonized in the first edition: 'Their General boasted, that he would be within the gates of their city, and within the walls of their palace, before the ensuing month should be at an end'.[77] In Edgeworth's revision, the French 'foreign invasion' is not as important, though the threat of war remains: 'there was Caroline, in the midst of a country torn by civil war, and in the midst of all the horrors of revolution'.[78] The later version also excises much of Caroline's exemplary behaviour, despite her husband's danger and her own absence from England. In the first edition, we get a description of Caroline's angelic patience during her separation from her husband and residence with her parents in prison:

> Caroline prepared for the anxiety that must be more or less the lot of the wife of a man in Count Altenberg's public situation, bore it with fortitude, and however it preyed upon her mind, she never uttered any expression of impatience or complaint.... Never for an instant did she remit those daily, hourly, fond and grateful attentions, which convinced her father, that she did not repent the determination she had made.[79]

Again, these are cloying didactic scenes which confirm Caroline's status as a 'faultless monster' within the novel. They describe both her exemplary emotions and her untiring devotion to her parents, which confirm her role as a didactic model. Edgeworth's removal of these episodes, along with Caroline's original decision to accompany her father and mother to prison, addresses the concerns of her critics, but her reduction of the novel's didactic, and by extension nationalistic, aims leads to a greater degree of realism.

Scenes depicting Godfrey Percy, a Dutch captive of war in the later chapters of the novel, are also altered to similar effect in Edgeworth's 1825 edition. Both editions give a brief account of Godfrey's seizure: 'the transport, in which Major Percy's division of the regiment had embarked, had been separated from her convoy by a gale of wind in the night, and it was apprehended that she had been taken by the enemy.' In the 1825 edition, Godfrey's captivity is briefly confirmed: 'it was at last too clearly established and confirmed by official intelligence, that the transport was taken by a Dutch ship'.[80] The scene is dragged out in the first edition:

> Colonel Gascoigne with his division of the regiment arrived safely, and no doubt remained of the misfortune, which had happened to Godfrey.
> For some weeks they never heard more of his fate. – This suspense was dreadful. The Percys have often since declared, that of all they suffered at this period of their lives suspense was the evil, which they found the most difficult to endure. – And each individual of the family was held in anxious uncertainty, for a considerable length of time, on many points the most nearly interesting to their hearts. –
> Mr. Percy's son was a prisoner, he knew not in what circumstances.[81]

Edgeworth's diction, as she describes the suspense and anxiety felt by the Percy family, is overwrought and repetitive. The language Edgeworth uses here resembles that of her didactic scenes; Godfrey's capture, along with Altenberg's turmoil, double then as moralistic lessons, serving as a link between the pervasive nationalistic and didactic themes in *Patronage*. Godfrey's capture by the Dutch is no longer a centrepiece of the Percys' exemplary behaviour; instead the scene is presented briefly and without adornment, just as the Percys' response becomes correspondingly pragmatic.

The omissions of some of the most excessively didactic and nationalistic scenes in the later version of *Patronage* confirms the extent to which Edgeworth was guided by her reviewers. With her deletions, mostly of tiresome Percy-centric passages, the original 285,000 word length of *Patronage* shrunk roughly by 10 per cent to about 250,000.[82] Even though Edgeworth's changes were not consistently adopted until 1825, some of them appeared in the 1815 third edition, published when the Napoleonic threat was no longer as severe; Napoleon had been finally defeated at Waterloo on 18 June 1815, and the Second Treaty of Paris was signed. In addition to the negative reviews, the diminished threat to British nationalism is a cogent reason for many of Edgeworth's changes to *Patronage*. The fact that Edgeworth trimmed her flagrant moralism and patriotism signals not only their connectedness, but also the changing generic form of *Patronage* itself. Edgeworth's revisions, which lessened the exemplary qualities of many of her characters, as well as the novel's exaggerated nationalism, brought the novel closer to a work of literary realism. In 1825, Edgeworth's own brand of didactic nationalism was less in demand after the end of war with France; instead of looking backwards, her revisions anticipated the rise of the realist novel during the Victorian era.

Notes

1. The letter is quoted in M. Butler, *Maria Edgeworth: A Literary Biography* (Oxford: Clarendon Press, 1972), p. 440. It is undated, though Marilyn Butler believes it was written in 1817 and that the recipient is probably Dr Holland. The two last lines paraphrase the final lines in Edgeworth's *Belinda* (1801), which are in turn a paraphrase of two lines from the epilogue of John Gay's play, *The What D'Ye Call It* (1715).
2. Butler claims that '*Patronage* ... in places reads like a deliberate adaptation of the educational treatise for the popular-novel-reading public' (Butler, *Maria Edgeworth*, p. 330). Cliona Ó Gallchoir is harsher, agreeing that '*Patronage* is of Edgeworth's longer texts the one most open to the charge of a crippling didacticism' (*Maria Edgeworth: Women, Enlightenment and Nation* (Dublin: University College Dublin Press, 2005), p. 107).
3. *The Gentleman's Magazine*, 84:1 (1814), p. 265.
4. [J. Ward], *Quarterly Review*, 10 (1814), pp. 301–22, on pp. 307, 315.
5. M. Gamer, 'Maria Edgeworth and the Romance of Real Life', *NOVEL: A Forum on Fiction*, 34:2 (2001), pp. 232–66, on p. 234.
6. *The Critical Review: Or, Annals of Literature*, 5, ser. 4 (1814), pp. 39–48, 168–77, on pp. 171, 173.
7. [S. Smith], *The Edinburgh Review, or Critical Journal*, 22 (1814), pp. 416–34, on p. 433.
8. *Quarterly Review*, p. 308 and *Critical Review*, p. 176. Smith is less severe, '*Patronage*, if not amongst the best of her productions, is at least not unworthy of her name and genius' (*Edinburgh Review*, p. 420).
9. M. Butler, Introduction, in C. Carville and M. Butler (eds), *Patronage*, vol. 6 of *The Works of Maria Edgeworth* (London: Pickering & Chatto, 1999), pp. vii–xxx, on p. viii. See also J. Pearson, '"Arts of Appropriation": Language, Circulation, and Appropriation in the Work of Maria Edgeworth', *The Yearbook of English Studies*, 28 (1998), pp. 212–34, on p. 233.
10. See M. Woodworth, *Eighteenth-Century Women Writers and the Gentleman's Liberation Movement: Independence, War, Masculinity, and the Novel, 1778–1818* (Aldershot, UK and Burlington, VT: Ashgate, 2011), p. 163.
11. C. E. Colvin, 'Edgeworth, Richard Lovell (1744–1817)', *Oxford Dictionary of National Biography* (Oxford University Press, 2004); online edn, January 2008 at www.oxforddnb.com/view/article/8478 (accessed 21 August 2012).
12. R. L. Edgeworth [and M. Edgeworth], *Essays on Professional Education* (London: J. Johnson, 1809), pp. 2–3. See also Butler, *Maria Edgeworth*, p. 331.
13. Edgeworth, *Professional Education*, p. 52.
14. Jenny Davidson also notes this expansion: 'Unlike *Professional Education*, which treats exclusively the education of boys for the professions, *Patronage* juxtaposes arguments about professional education to a related set of arguments about the education of women' ('Professional Education and Female Accomplishments: Gender and Education in Maria Edgeworth's *Patronage*', *Eighteenth-Century Women*, 4 (2006), pp. 259–85, on p. 266).
15. Butler, *Maria Edgeworth*, p. 304.
16. Gamer, 'Maria Edgeworth and the Romance of Real Life', p. 235.
17. H. Guest, *Small Change: Women, Learning, Patriotism, 1750–1810* (Chicago, IL and London: University of Chicago Press, 2000), p. 14. See also T. Doerksen, Chapter 10 of this volume, p. 181.

Maria Edgeworth's Revisions to Nationalism 157

18. Claire Connolly similarly contends that

    By the time Edgeworth wrote *Patronage*, an influential intersection of discourses (to which she had herself contributed in the 1790s) had created the conditions in which the public roles of women as participants in the British state could be frankly debated. ('"A Big Book about England"? Public and Private Meanings in *Patronage*', in J. Belanger (ed.), *The Irish Novel in the Nineteenth Century: Facts and Fictions* (Dublin: Four Courts Press, 2005), pp. 63–79, on p. 66) See also Woodworth, *Eighteenth-Century Women Writers*, p. 172.

19. See J. E. Dunleavy, 'Maria Edgeworth and the Novel of Manners', in B. K. Bowers and B. Brothers (eds), *Reading and Writing Women's Lives: A Study of the Novel of Manners* (Rochester, NY: University of Rochester Press, 2010), pp. 49–65; J. Nash, 'Introduction: A Story to Tell', in J. Nash (ed.), *New Essays on Maria Edgeworth* (Aldershot, UK and Burlington, VT: Ashgate, 2006), pp. xiii–xvii; and J. Nash, *Servants and Paternalism in the Works of Maria Edgeworth and Elizabeth Gaskell* (Aldershot, UK and Burlington, VT: Ashgate, 2007).

20. G. Kelly, 'Romantic Fiction', in S. Curran (ed.), *The Cambridge Companion to British Romanticism*, 2nd edn (Cambridge: Cambridge University Press, 2010), pp. 187–208, on p. 199.

21. Edgeworth, *Professional Education*, p. 30.

22. Ibid., p. 392. W. J. McCormack discusses French–English educational and cultural dichotomies, which later appear in *Patronage* within the chief justice's remarks (W. J. McCormack, 'The Tedium of History: An Approach to Maria Edgeworth's *Patronage*', in C. Brady (ed.), *Ideology and the Historians: Papers Read Before the Irish Conference of Historians, Held at Trinity College, Dublin, 8–10 June 1989* (Dublin: Lilliput Press, 1991), pp. 77–98, on pp. 89–90).

23. *Quarterly Review*, p. 319.

24. M. Edgeworth, *Patronage*, ed. C. Carville and M. Butler, vols 6 and 7 of *The Works of Maria Edgeworth* (London: Pickering & Chatto, 1999), vol. 6, p. 252.

25. Ibid., vol. 6, p. 252.

26. Ibid., vol. 6, p. 251. Ó Gallchoir observes that, even though the trope of a 'frenchified Englishman' was common in Edgeworth's fictions, 'the "Frenchness" that French Clay seeks to imitate has a very particular sense of indifference to homeland that is not evident in Edgeworth's earlier work' (*Maria Edgeworth*, p. 115). Pearson also highlights Edgeworth's 'anti-French line' in *Patronage* ('"Arts of Appropriation"', p. 224).

27. Edgeworth, *Patronage*, vol. 6, p. 252.

28. Ibid., vol. 7, p. 64.

29. Ó Gallchoir, *Maria Edgeworth*, p. 104.

30. Edgeworth, *Patronage*, vol. 7, p. 64. These testimonies of Altenberg's Englishness belie Ó Gallchoir's claims that his primary function 'is to provide the perspective of an intelligent and sophisticated external observer, a "philosophical traveler", on aspects of English life, including customs, law, landscape and architecture' (*Maria Edgeworth*, p. 113).

31. Edgeworth, *Patronage*, vol. 7, p. 52.

32. Ó Gallchoir also reads this passage as a statement of 'English superiority', though 'what makes Caroline so special, in the eyes of Altenberg, the sophisticated foreigner, is that she combines a variety of qualities, typical of different nationalities' (*Maria Edgeworth*, p. 116).

33. Ó Gallchoir highlights the complicated nature of Edgeworth's nationalistic perspectives given her commitment to Ireland: 'Edgeworth makes use of references to France, to fashion and to aristocracy to develop a unique Enlightenment perspective that accommodates women but does not conform to the demands of post-revolutionary British nationalism' (*Maria Edgeworth*, p. 23). Even though the Edgeworths supported religious toleration and were benevolent landlords, they were strongly in favour of Ireland's parliamentary Union with England (Butler, *Maria Edgeworth*, pp. 181, 184).
34. See Butler, *Maria Edgeworth*, p. 218.
35. *Gentleman's Magazine*, p. 265; *Critical Review*, p. 168; *Quarterly Review*, p. 316.
36. Edgeworth, *Patronage*, vol. 7, p. 230.
37. Edgeworth, *Professional Education*, p. 359.
38. See p. 142 above and *Critical Review*, p. 173.
39. Edgeworth, *Patronage*, vol. 6, p. 213.
40. Ibid., vol. 6, p. 238–39.
41. Pearson, '"Arts of Appropriation"', p. 222. Ó Gallchoir observes that Edgeworth's inclusion of this impressment scene indicates that '*Patronage* contains criticism of some measures specific to the war period' (*Maria Edgeworth*, p. 109). Butler also mentions that such criticism in *Patronage* caused a 'mild furore in London' (*Maria Edgeworth*, p. 233). See also A. O'Malley, Chapter 7 of this volume, p. 126.
42. See Ó Gallchoir, *Maria Edgeworth*, p. 118. Ó Gallchoir argues that 'The plot of *Patronage* is … driven by its wartime setting', which is, moreover, inextricably tied to its didactic themes (p. 108).
43. Edgeworth, *Patronage*, vol. 6, p. 173, Edgeworth's ellipses.
44. Ibid., vol. 6, p. 9.
45. Ibid., vol. 6, p. 14.
46. Ibid., vol. 6, p. 95.
47. Ibid., vol. 6, p. 249.
48. Ibid., vol. 6, pp. 249–50.
49. Ibid., vol. 6, p. 250.
50. Ibid., vol. 6, p. 91.
51. Ibid., vol. 7, p. 28.
52. Ibid., vol. 7, p. 239–40.
53. See Butler, *Maria Edgeworth*, pp. 494–95.
54. Edgeworth, *Patronage*, vol. 6, p. 287.
55. Butler, *Maria Edgeworth*, p. 496.
56. *Monthly Review*, 74 (1814), pp. 109–10, on p. 110.
57. Edgeworth, *Patronage*, vol. 6, p. 96.
58. 'bellows, n.', *OED Online* (Oxford University Press) (June 2012), at http://oed.com/view/Entry/17473 (accessed 21 August 2012).
59. Edgeworth, *Patronage*, vol. 6, p. 293.
60. Ibid.
61. *Quarterly Review*, p. 321.
62. Edgeworth, *Patronage*, vol. 7, p. 138.
63. Ibid., vol. 7, p. 266.
64. Ibid., vol. 7, p. 207.
65. Ibid., vol. 7, p. 208.

66. Ibid.
67. Ibid., vol. 7, p. 209.
68. Connolly, "'A Big Book about England"', p. 78.
69. Edgeworth, *Patronage*, vol. 7, p. 268.
70. Ibid., vol. 7, p. 270.
71. See Butler, *Maria Edgeworth*, p. 497 and Butler, Introduction, p. viii.
72. *Quarterly Review*, p. 314.
73. Butler, *Maria Edgeworth*, p. 498.
74. Quoted in Butler, *Maria Edgeworth*, p. 497.
75. Butler agrees that Caroline's absence from the prison sequence is an improvement: 'while dramatically a great deal was lost by saving Mr Percy from prison, something was also gained by preventing Caroline from accompanying him there on her wedding day' (*Maria Edgeworth*, p. 499).
76. Edgeworth, *Patronage*, vol. 7, p. 211.
77. Ibid., vol. 7, p. 215.
78. Ibid., vol. 7, p. 269.
79. Ibid., vol. 7, pp. 215–16.
80. Ibid., vol. 7, p. 218.
81. Ibid.
82. Butler, *Maria Edgeworth*, p. 499.

9 Didacticism after Hannah More

Elizabeth Hamilton's *The Cottagers of Glenburnie*

Claire Grogan

It is not too much of an exaggeration to claim that any discussion of didactic literature written specifically for the poor at the turn of the nineteenth century starts (and often ends) with Hannah More's *Village Politics* (1793) and *Cheap Repository Tracts*. What I wish to consider in this chapter is how the popular writer Elizabeth Hamilton not only negotiated More's dominance but also developed her own unique type of didactic tale. But first we need to recall why there was such interest in didactic material. Concerns about the plight of Britain's poorest citizens prompted the publication of many works at the turn of the nineteenth century. Influential works such as Sarah Trimmer's *The Oeconomy of Charity, or, an Address to Ladies; Adapted to the Present State of Charitable Institutions in England* (1787), Thomas Robert Malthus's *An Essay on the Principle of Population* (1798), and Patrick Colquhoun's *A Treatise on Indigence: Exhibiting a General View of the National Resources of Productive Labour* (1806) address middle- and upper-class readers ('legislators', 'able men' or 'ladies') in order to propose changes and policies to 'ameliorate the condition of the poor'.[1] In such works the poor are spoken about but not spoken to. Traditionally, when the poor themselves were addressed, it was through tracts, chapbooks, and broadsides.[2] Tract writing has a long history in England, but the genre took on a particular style and political resonance during the tumultuous 1790s in large part because of Thomas Paine's *Rights of Man* (1791–92).[3] Paine directly addressed the working classes of Britain and encouraged a far broader readership to engage with topics such as the nation's history, governance, economics, and individual rights. In assuming his readers were intelligent, thinking individuals, though not necessarily educated, he fundamentally changed the language of political discourse.[4]

Such a radical change to the tone and content of a pamphlet stirred the government (under Pitt) to declare a state of 'literary warfare' during which writers were commissioned to produce government-approved reading material for the working classes, countering the dissemination of 'seditious', 'leveling', and 'Anti-Christian' ideas.[5] Central among the writers who responded to this call was Hannah More. Addressing what she described as the 'most vulgar class of readers', More wrote to promote 'loyalty, good morals, and attachment to church and state among the poor people', determined that 'such poison [as Paine's work] should not be doled out to the English without some corrective'.[6] Unlike Paine's work, which challenged readers to engage with political and philosophical concepts as intellectual equals, More's *Village Politics* was more in keeping with traditional didactic literature: the assumed reader was from a lower class and thus had a limited intellect and reading capability.[7] More's correspondence indicates her clarity of purpose: 'Vulgar and indecent books were always common … but speculative infidelity, brought down to the pockets and capacities of the poor, forms a new aera in our history'.[8] *Village Politics* exemplifies her professed goal of providing suitable reading material for what she perceived as a dangerously engaged working-class readership, but it fell well short of encouraging them to further studies.[9] She categorically rejected Paine's belief that the working class had any right to discuss politics or issues of governance and hence carefully chose the subject matter and tone of her tracts.[10] Her tone and content highlight how impertinent she found those poor who tried to disrupt the social order by appropriating the language, mannerisms, or subjects of their social superiors. The reader is left in no doubt regarding appropriate actions and behaviours. More described her relationship to her readers as a righteous seduction of an ignorant class of people: 'Alas! I know with whom I have to deal, and I hope I may thus allure these thoughtless creatures on to higher things'.[11]

The success of *Village Politics* prompted a second publishing venture since More, like the Government she supported, was firmly convinced that 'the shoots of 'Jacobinism' had their 'roots [in] popular culture'.[12] *Cheap Repository Tracts* was issued monthly between 1795 and 1797. The target was broadened from Paine's *Rights of Man* to include his irreligious *Age of Reason* (1794–95) and any other work promoting civic unrest or anti-Christian sentiment.[13] The tracts were advertised as providing 'Striking Conversations, Holy Lives, Happy Deaths, Providential Deliverances, Judgments on the Breakers of Commandments, Stories of Good and Wicked Apprentices, Hardened Sinners, Pious Servants &c'.[14] They were 'designed to supply such wholesome aliment as might give a new direction to [the public's] … taste, and abate their relish for … corrupt and inflammatory publication'.[15] More was the major contributor and compiler of this collaborative and explicitly didactic venture, which as Kevin Gilmartin has noted, worked with a 'predictability and crude directness' as part of an 'evangelical enterprise [to] … dictate and manage popular consciousness'.[16] Indeed, 'the fundamental aim of [More's] tract … [was] to use the medium of cheap print to make local orthodoxy available on a national scale'.[17] More's goals in designing and contributing to the *Cheap Repository Tracts* were threefold. Believing that 'the poor exist to be saved by the upper classes',[18] she wished to subdue and thus control the working classes; she wanted actively to improve the lot of the poor by instructing them in religious and social matters; and she wished to flood the market with suitable material to offset the impact of works such as Paine's *Rights of Man*.

162   *Claire Grogan*

More worked assiduously with her friends to promote the *Cheap Repository Tracts*, changing paper quality, size, and price to maintain sales. As Anne Stott explains in her engaging biography, initially 'tracts and ballads were sold at 1d. and 1/2d. respectively' with 'discounts for bulk orders', but when it became clear this was an untenable marketing venture, 'tracts' were 'published in annual collected volumes, priced 3s. 6d'.[19] Gilmartin further details how in 1796 More

> reorganized the Cheap Repository as a series of octavo (rather than duodecimo) tracts in two formats, distinguished by their paper quality and price structure. Profits from the more expensive version were used to subsidize the distribution of cheaper editions, reinforcing the different roles played by different sorts of readers, and suggesting as well the circular structure of a print economy of charitable provision.[20]

In this way More's tracts assuaged two distinct groups of readers. On the one hand, they were designed to 'teach' or remind the working-class readership of the benefits of the status quo by providing clear moral messages of social and religious acquiescence. On the other hand, they were intended to calm the middle and upper classes anxious about possible social foment. One group was meant to read the works, or be read to, while the other was meant to distribute and facilitate their reading.

Gilmartin traces the 'strategies of self-representation, through complex narrative interpolations of its own conditions of production, and through the careful orchestration and layering of implied audiences' in the *Cheap Repository Tracts*.[21] This was a process whereby real impoverished readers met fictional counterparts, where tales were referenced within other tales, or tales were physically packaged with advertisements of other tracts. This impressive self-promoting marketing machine attempted to create and sustain its own market and readership. The *Cheap Repository Tracts* were undeniably popular, though it is less clear how many of the poor actually read them.[22] While firm readership numbers remain elusive, the influence of More's work on the genre is indisputable. Though Paine's *Rights of Man* had far greater long-term impact, in the short term – considering his flight to revolutionary France in 1792, the guilty verdict at his trial back in London for sedition, the Reign of Terror in France, and mob actions overseas and at home – More's patronizing manner of addressing the poor on approved or 'safe' topics prevailed. Indeed, More's *Village Politics* and *Cheap Repository Tracts* provided a template for other writers, which confirms her great impact. Many publications imitated More, capitalizing on her work's format, content, and style to address a similar readership.[23] What I wish to consider for the remainder of the chapter is what More's dominance meant for a woman writer who penned a quite different type of didactic tale.

More's looming presence is evident when Elizabeth Hamilton published her own didactic tale, *The Cottagers of Glenburnie*, over a decade later in

Didacticism after Hannah More 163

1808. Hamilton acknowledges More's influence in her dedication in which she positions her work in relation to the *Cheap Repository Tracts*. She clearly anticipates that the publication of a didactic piece of literature in the early nineteenth century aimed at the poorer classes, despite her own standing as a commercially-successful writer, would necessarily prompt comparison with More's works. By 1808, Hamilton was the author of two fictional works, a historical biography, several popular educational treatises, and was the recipient of a royal pension.[24] Her *oeuvre* is marked by dramatic changes in genre and topic, but of interest here is what drew her to write a didactic tale. Though the subject matter was fashionable and thus marketable to the middle classes (as evidenced by the recent works of Malthus and Colquhoun), a text that addresses the poor themselves seems to have offered far less inducement to the publisher. Elizabeth Benger notes in her *Memoirs of The Late Mrs. Elizabeth Hamilton* that 'Glenburnie [was only] with some diffidence on the part of the publisher ... committed to the Press'.[25] Perhaps More's success had so cornered the market that no publisher could see the value of a competing work? Evidence indicates that Hamilton had to exert her full influence in order to overcome her publisher's reticence. But why was she so determined?

Critics have been all too willing to assume that if, as Hamilton herself asserts in her dedication, *The Cottagers of Glenburnie* was 'originally formed ... in form and size [to] resemble the tracts in the "Cheap Repository"', then it follows that Hamilton addresses the same readership about similar issues to achieve similar results. In fact, though Hamilton refers to More, she does so only to immediately draw attention to the differences between the two works ('Had I adhered to the plan'). While Hamilton might have begun with an imitation of More's tracts in mind, her final publication is far more ambitious both in its use of didacticism and its target audience. However, the temptation to align these works (though perhaps understandable) has proven almost irresistible: both authors were well-respected writers during the 1790s and early 1800s; both wrote educational treatises; both were critical of French revolutionary principles; and both were devoted Christians. Further, both shared an imperative to offer practical assistance to those in need within their local communities.[26] It is a small step to then place More and Hamilton in the same anti-Jacobin or anti-revolutionary political group that shared similar views on revolutionary ideas, female education, Christian faith, and a common agenda when it comes to addressing the poor.

But the myth of a homogeneous Conservative or anti-Jacobin camp has been appropriately debunked in the excellent studies by critics such as Gilmartin. We no longer group all conservatives indiscriminately together in opposition to the equally amorphous pro-revolutionary or English Jacobin camps.[27] Similarly, as Miriam Wallace and I have endeavoured to show, a challenge to the over-simplification of political positions is overdue.[28] How can such shifts help us separate the conservative politics of Hamilton from those of More? To be fair, it is not so long ago that any critical attention on

164   *Claire Grogan*

Romantic women writers was so welcome that drawing attention to differences seemed inappropriate. However, since More and Hamilton are now safely re-established as influential writers, a more nuanced examination of such pairings (through aspects such as historical moment, implied reader, and marketing strategies) is not only appropriate but apposite. This chapter will challenge the assumption Hamilton wrote the same kind of 'popular propaganda for the poor' as More.[29]

To start, the passage of time between 1795 and 1808 should alert us to the perils of unquestioningly assuming that More and Hamilton shared a political and religious didactic purpose. The social, political, and economic realities of 1808 were quite distinct from those More and her readers faced in the mid-1790s. Preoccupations and concerns, whether for the working-class or middle-class readership, were dramatically different from those in the early days of the French Revolution (Paine's 1791–92 *Rights of Man*), during the Reign of Terror (More's 1793 *Village Politics*), or during Napoleon Bonaparte's ascent to power in the mid-1790s (More's 1795–97 *Cheap Repository Tracts*). From the late 1790s Britain suffered repeated crop failures and ensuing food shortages, which exacerbated the pressures associated with increased industrialization and a shifting population as people relocated from rural to urban centres. Conflict with France was almost continual during this time, and possible invasion by the Napoleonic forces after 1803 was an ever-present threat. Residual public sympathy for revolutionary sentiment had largely abated. The English-Jacobin threat had been silenced through the various censorship legislation that was enacted by 1800, which saw most political writers and activists either incarcerated, transported, or subdued. Thus it seems reasonable to suggest that Hamilton was prompted to write *The Cottagers of Glenburnie* by something other than fear. She further distances her tale from More's political agenda by setting it in the summer of 1788. Placing it prior to the revolutionary upheaval of the 1790s suggests the work offers a peaceful alternative to the political, social, and economic turmoil of the French Revolution. It is also significant that, by placing her tale in 1788, Hamilton envisions alternative modes of didactic literature since Hannah More had yet to appear and dominate the genre. Hamilton's interest in the rural poor of Scotland suggests other factors at play than a fear of civic unrest or the kind of popular uprising that caused More so many sleepless nights in 1793. *The Cottagers of Glenburnie* presents an alternative way for Scotland to reform itself and emerge 'as a new, economically and commercially vibrant country'.[30]

That Hamilton self-consciously uses a 'humbler composition of dull prose', what she later calls a 'trifling production', to address a different readership than those already familiar with her work is indisputable. She writes to her friend and mentor Dr S—,

> You will see in the newspapers, that I have not been quite idle all winter; but were you to look into the little work which is now advertised,

Didacticism after Hannah More   165

> I am afraid you would think I have been employing myself to very little purpose. Had I thought it worthy of your perusal, I should have sent a copy; but in fact it is intended for a very different order of readers, and was written solely with a view to shame my good country folks into a greater degree of nicety with regard to cleanliness, and to awaken their attention to the source of corruption in the lower orders.[31]

Of interest is Hamilton's strategy in speaking to 'good country folks'. Despite her dedicatory comment that *The Cottagers of Glenburnie* 'was originally formed … to resemble the traits in Cheap Repository' and her diffidence at her friend seeing a work ostensibly intended for the working classes, Hamilton actually claims a far broader readership than More. This is evident when she immediately qualifies her statement in the dedication by noting,

> had I adhered to the plan on which those sketches were originally formed, and published them as separate pieces, in form and size resembling the tracts in the 'Cheap Repository', I should have had no apprehension concerning the justice of the sentence to be passed upon them; for then they would have had little chance of falling into other hands than those of the class of persons for whose use they were intended.[32]

Somewhere during composition, her narrative became more complicated – what began life as a tract ended up as a novel. More's work might have been the starting point, but Hamilton's finishing point offers a more complex and nuanced tale. Her concern that middle-class readers (whom she implies would not be critical of a simple tract) might not respond as favourably to *The Cottagers of Glenburnie* suggests that the poor are not the only intended readers of the work. Thus, while More implicated middle-class readers in her tracts through their roles as purchasers and distributors, Hamilton's work actually provides a series of plot lines that follow different social classes: the working-class MacClartys, the middle-class Stewarts, and the upper-class Longlands. These three social groupings are interconnected by marriage, by the labour market, by religious faith, and by community. The multiple readers implied in the work are evident both in Hamilton's deployment of language and her plot lines.

Hamilton addresses readers across classes and political groupings with a wider-reaching project in mind than just political quietude. As her sub-title, 'a tale for the farmer's inglenook' indicates, the work was specifically directed to the rural poor, but it was not limited to them. In her dedication she notes that there are 'others besides professed critics, concerning whose opinion of the propriety or tendency of this little work I confess myself to be most anxious, and those are the well-wishers to the improvement of their country'.[33] Her readership includes politicians who work towards national happiness and prosperity. Elsewhere she singles out such men: 'Too much

166 *Claire Grogan*

praise cannot be given to the man ... who ... should turn his attention and expence to objects of such national utility and importance, which have for their aim the well-being, happiness, and support of a whole neighbour-hood'.[34] These men are distinct from those 'war-contriving' politicians or those whom she feels too often 'neglect individual happiness', believing 'riches and happiness are synonymous'. Hamilton wishes to engage the attention of those who oppose the view of the general population as 'so many teeth in the wheels of a piece of machinery'; bound by a 'fraternal tie', they share her concern with each cog's 'moral capacities and feelings'. She strives for a more efficacious form of charity and addresses those who con-cur: 'by minds such as these, my motives will not be misinterpreted'. Such readers 'forget not that the pleasures of the heart, and of the understanding, as well as those of the senses, were intended by Providence to be in some degree enjoyed by all'.[35]

Hamilton's self-effacing claim to Dr S—, that 'this little work' is of no concern to readers like himself, is undermined by the dedication in which she describes herself as 'most anxious' that the 'well-wishers to the improve-ment of their country' approve of it. This links her less to the explicitly polit-ical agenda of More's *Tracts* and more to the longer-held tradition of what Gilmartin describes as the 'moral reform projects of the 1780s', perhaps another reason she set her work in 1788.[36] Unlike the conservative tracts of the 1790s, Gilmartin contends, these earlier groups were not

> particularly retrospective nor suspicious of change; instead, they were part of a 'patriotic, improving, moralizing' campaign of 'project-oriented association', which understood itself progressively, as 'help-ing to create the social and institutional framework within which a more virtuous society might henceforth take shape'.[37]

Hamilton had been actively involved with various social programmes in Edinburgh since settling there in 1804. Central amongst these was her establishment and financing of a House of Industry for indigent women. The House – which provided women of all ages with shelter and the oppor-tunity to learn the useful skills of spinning, lace manufactory, or even how to be a domestic servant – speaks to her commitment to provide practical, tangible help.[38]

Hamilton wrote *The Cottagers of Glenburnie* less to promote a conser-vative agenda of social improvement and control or to promote herself as a writer, but more out of a desire to be of practical use. But what was partic-ularly compelling about the state of the Scottish poor in 1808? Her general affection for, and fascination with, all things Scottish stemmed from her child-hood. Though born in Belfast, Ireland, she had been raised outside Stirling by her maternal aunt and uncle from the age of six. Her childhood 'years of unalloyed happiness', filled with her aunt's proud retelling of family history, made Hamilton partial to all things Scottish.[39] However, by 1808 she was

Didacticism after Hannah More 167

anxious that rural Scotland be as much a source of pride as Edinburgh. She worried that people's love of the Scottish cottager, based upon misplaced nostalgia and nationalism, actually preserved the rural areas as social backwaters. Though proud of Scotland and all things Scottish, she was determined to cast a more critical eye over her countrymen in the hopes of stirring them to greater action and self-improvement. Hamilton follows her friend the Irish writer Maria Edgeworth in promoting the modernization of her own part of Britain.[40] Like Edgeworth, Hamilton believes that a work of fiction may well accomplish more than the politician, the economist, or the polemicist.[41]

The more immediate stimulus for *The Cottagers of Glenburnie*, however, was a visit in 1807 to the country home of one of her Edinburgh acquaintances William Tytler.[42] Tytler, then professor of History at Edinburgh University, had an estate on the nearby Pentland Hills to which he regularly invited a coterie of friends.[43] His estate, Woodhouselee, was a model of rural reform and innovation. Following in his father's footsteps, Tytler had renovated the cottagers' dwellings and introduced reforms in land-owning, housing, dairying, and sanitation. Woodhouselee so impressed Hamilton that she was inspired to write a work 'to shame my good country folks' to improve themselves in a similar fashion.[44] She constructed a tale about a rural Scottish community that manages to dramatically improve itself and, in doing so, becomes a model for all her readers.

Hamilton intended *The Cottagers of Glenburnie* to reform the lower classes by showing them how to materially improve their lot and so claim a justifiable pride of place within Scotland.[45] For Hamilton the fear of social stagnation rather than collapse, a moral inertia amongst the Scottish peasantry, excuses middle-class innovation and reform in the fictional persona of Mrs Mason. Through Mrs Mason, Hamilton opens up possibilities for her readers (of all classes) rather than closing them down in favour of the social quietude More advocates in the *Cheap Repository Tracts*. More's greatest fear is that the poorer classes will become self-sufficient and assert themselves: 'Oh Lord, grant me that this people may never rise up in judgement against me, and that, with all the advantages of knowledge and education, I may not fall short of these poor ignorant creatures'.[46] That Hamilton is more ambitious about the improvements she believes she can instigate is evident in whom she addresses and how she addresses them. Unlike More, who described her *Village Politics* as being 'as vulgar as heart can wish' and aimed at the 'most vulgar class of readers', Hamilton seeks to improve rather than subdue.[47] She eschews 'the rigorous subordination of the lower orders' that the government prescribed.[48]

The result, *The Cottagers of Glenburnie*, is Hamilton's final, and arguably most commercially successful, novel. It was reputed to have been found on every cottager's shelf between Burns and the Bible. The tale is divided into eighteen chapters, each with a brief header to guide the reader. The epigraph on the title page from Thomas Gray's 'Elegy, Written in a Country

168   *Claire Grogan*

Churchyard' suggests a middle-class readership, though it valorises the situation of the working class:

> *Let not ambition mock their useful toil*
> *Their homely joys, and destiny obscure,*
> *Nor grandeur hear with a disdainful smile,*
> *The short and simple annals of the poor.*

Susan Egenolf suggests this offers an implicit challenge to Robert Burns's epigraphic use of Gray in his nostalgic depiction of the cottager in 'Cotter's Saturday Night'.[49] This might well be true, but Hamilton is also critiquing her own earlier sentimentalization of the Scottish cottager. Her hero, Henry Sydney, in *Memoirs of Modern Philosophers* (1800) quotes Burns's poem to describe a night spent sheltering with a cottager's family.[50] Eight years later in *The Cottagers of Glenburnie* any lingering nostalgia has been replaced by a biting realism.

The narrative presents the tale of the recently retired Mrs Betty Mason who, having 'a hankering to return to her native country', is travelling to the small Scottish village of Glenburnie where she hopes to 'be of use' to surviving relatives.[51] En route she visits with the Stewart family of Gowan-Brae, claiming an acquaintance with the now deceased mother, formerly Miss Osburne. In the opening five chapters, Mrs Mason relates her life story as servant, then governess, and finally as an independent woman, to the younger daughter Mary Stewart. It was as a kitchen maid that Mrs Mason, then young Betty, met Mary's mother Miss Osburne, who was a dependent in Mrs Jackson's home. Miss Osburne took notice of Betty's aptitude and honesty, taught her to read and discuss the scriptures, and generally prepared her for a productive life. The reader follows Mrs Mason's life in service with the noble Longland family, rising through the ranks until she is finally able to run the nursery and oversee the young lords' and ladies' education. She earned the family's undying love when she rescued her charges from a house fire, though the incident left her crippled. The recent inheritance of the Longland estate by the eldest son from Lord Longland's first marriage has thrown Mrs Mason, along with the rest of the family, out of her home. Unable, because of her health, to travel overseas with the Longland daughter and not wishing to be idle, Mrs Mason travels to Scotland to live with her last surviving relative. This relative 'married one of the small farmers in Glenburnie' and since she lives 'in a place where money is scarce [has] agreed to take her as a lodger'.[52] We learn that Mrs Mason is financially comfortable, having wisely invested her wages over the years: a hundred and fifty pounds which the 'lord's steward placed out for [her], at five per cent … in public funds', as well as an additional fifty pounds with a further twenty a year from the young mistress Lady Charlotte.[53] Born to a life of servitude but no longer a servant, Mrs Mason still wishes to be of use.

Didacticism after Hannah More 169

Chapter six brings Mrs Mason's travels up to the present visit with the Stewarts. From here the plot divides. One strand follows the Stewart family, the widower (who 'is the factor on the Longland estate') and his four children. The other plot follows Mrs Mason as she moves in with her cousin's family, the MacClartys, in Glenburnie. The two plots intersect whenever Mr Stewart and Mrs Mason either meet or correspond. Mr Stewart's daughters Mary and Bell exemplify contrasting methods of education and upbringing and extend Hamilton's didactic message to her middle-class reader who sees him or herself implicated in this plot line. After the mother's death, the elder daughter Bell, raised by indulgent grandparents, was sent to a boarding school (a 'nursery of folly and impertinence') where she 'learned nothing but vanity and idleness' and imbibed 'ridiculous notions ... about gentility'.[54] By the novel's opening, she is a wilful and petulant girl who enjoys little except fashion and novel-reading. Mr Stewart despairs of his truculent daughter, but is unable to resist her entreaties. When Bell asks for his permission to join Miss Flinders for a week's excursion to the Edinburgh races, he laments: 'had she been brought up with the rest of my family, under the watchful eye of their dear mother, she would never have been this forward and intractable'.[55]

> At length ... [Bell] carried her parent, as she generally did; for Mr Stewart, though he saw, and hourly felt, the consequences of his indulgence, wanted the firmness that was necessary to enforce obedience, and to guide the conduct of this forward and self-willed child.[56]

The Stewart family dynamic highlights the dangers of an inappropriate education and the lack of appropriate parental control. This plot line follows Bell's unsanctioned courtship with a 'gentleman' of the Flinders's party who transpires to be a shoemaker.

The second plot follows Mrs Mason to Glenburnie despite Mr Stewart and Mary's concerns about its suitability: 'what place can there be at Glenburnie fit for you to live in?' Mrs Mason's boundless energy for reform and improvement continues despite the appallingly filthy living conditions and the slovenly behaviour of her relative's children in Glenburnie. The MacClartys, who are generally of good spirit and heart, are totally undirected in their household management. As with Bell Stewart, the children mirror the problems of undirected parental affection, but it is now coupled with domestic disarray. Mrs Mason sets about reforming the family through example by teaching the daughters to perform household chores more efficiently. However, she meets with some resistance when she introduces her 'foreign ways'. Mr MacClarty attempts to mediate on several occasions: 'There's a great spice o'gude sense in what Mrs Mason has said though ... but its no easy for folk like us to be put out o' their ain gait'.[57] Undaunted, Mrs Mason counters that a ship-shape house keeps the family in line and through each family, the nation itself: thus domestic reform effects a national revolution. She is determined to reform the Scottish cottager into a figure of emulation rather than of disgust. Mrs Mason fails with the MacClartys since she is too late to effect lasting change: the daughter elopes; the son joins the army, then escapes, but is captured and transported; the father dies; and the mother persists in refusing to improve her household. Luckily the neighbours are far more sensible of the advantages offered by Mrs Mason and gradually adopt her system.

Along the way *The Cottagers of Glenburnie* teaches its readers how to manage a household, balance domestic finances, develop and practice Christian faith, establish a small rural school, and generally transform a neighbourhood – not through a political revolution, but through a moral and spiritual one. It is very much a practical handbook in which Hamilton demonstrates women's power to effect positive change. If, as Ian Duncan claims, 'Scotch novels and Scottish reviewers were the most brilliant constellations in a northern literary galaxy', then Hamilton's *The Cottagers of Glenburnie* was a shining star.[58] Throughout the novel, she disseminates her ideas of self-improvement in an entertaining medium to a larger readership. The belief that a novel offered 'a representation of national life that should exceed local, social, and political differences to enfold a greater reading public' played to Hamilton's need to connect and unify her reading public rather than stress difference and distance.[59] For this reason, the same problems beset her fictional aristocratic Longland family, the middle-class Stewart family, and the working-class MacClartys – namely an appropriate education for the children, the importance of filial obedience and respect, and a strong Christian faith. Wealth is shown to be no guarantee of good parenting or success in life.

When Hamilton details the failings of the cottagers she provides few salacious details. We are not in the company of Hector MacNeil's 'joyless moralistic verse tale of once virtuous peasants ruined by drink' or More's drunken, cursing, wanton, or gambling protagonists.[60] The single instance of drunkenness occurs when the eldest MacClarty son, Sandy, is forbidden from attending this year's fair because of his 'daffin' the previous year. His father moans 'Did na he gang last year, and came hame as drunk as a beast!'[61] Hamilton suggests his drunkenness is a result of his youthful naivety rather than a symptom of a propensity for alcohol amongst the working poor. She anticipates her middle-class reader will smile when Mr MacClarty offers his visitors 'whisky, to prevent ... the tea doing them any harm'.[62] Though tea drinking, as a clear signifier of middle- and upper-class gentility, was spreading as a popular beverage among the working classes, the Scottish cottager remains sceptical.[63] However, when Sandy disobeys his father and attends the fair a second time, things quickly deteriorate. On hearing that his son has been 'enticed ... wi' drink to enlist' and 'fight the French', Mr MacClarty sets off to try and secure his release. He is assaulted by highway robbers and succumbs to his injuries and poor care.[64] Sandy escapes from his barracks to attend his father on his deathbed where he bitterly repents his rash behaviour. Though Mrs Mason is able to get his death sentence for desertion transmuted to transportation, she cannot secure his release.

The Cottagers of Glenburnie appeared in May 1808, 'excit[ing] an extraordinary sensation in Edinburgh', and 'received an immediate and overwhelmingly positive reception'.[65] Hamilton's narrative instilled in her readers a sense of pride in the new Scotland. 'Equally remote from the distortion of caricature or the colouring of romance, the picture is full of life, and without seeking to dazzle the imagination, surprises the heart'.[66] Her encouragement that each reader should aspire to better realize his or her economic, intellectual, and spiritual potential rather than passively accept one's lot in life was central to its success. But management of the soul was as important to Hamilton as that of the house. As Benger notes, 'although Mrs. M'Clarty be a prominent personage, it is highly injurious to the real merit of Glenburnie to consider it merely as a lesson of good housewifery'. Hamilton practised in the 'Christian missionary rather than meditative tradition', which prescribed 'visible activism' with a 'strong emphasis on social reform'.[67] This required the constant reading and contemplation of the Bible. Hamilton believed that a continual engagement with and questioning of Scripture was necessary – not just the passive acceptance of another's readings or teachings.[68] Though Hamilton was not an evangelical Anglican, she shared that group's conviction that faith must manifest itself as a practical contribution towards improving the life of ordinary lay Christians. In consequence, the fictional Mrs Mason lives among the Scottish poor rather than just dispensing advice during brief charitable visits. Mrs Mason exemplifies the evangelical Anglican John Newton's teaching that 'religion does not consist in doing great things, for which few of us have frequent opportunities, but in doing the little necessary things of daily occurrence with a cheerful spirit, *as to the lord*'.[69] Mrs Mason models the golden rule of active compassion, which is neither sorrow nor pity for the object of concern, but rather participatory empathy. Such empathy reduces the egotistic element of charitable gestures in favour of true compassion. Mrs Mason experiences life's vicissitudes with the MacClartys first-hand rather than from a safe distance. She struggles with flea-infested beds, cottage walls 'blackened by mud', butter covered in hair, a dung heap leaning against the back door, and a stagnant 'squashy pool' at the front door step.[70] Life with the MacClartys is uncomfortable.

As with Hamilton's work for the Edinburgh House of Industry, real action is called for. Her work reveals a belief that she can have a positive impact on the cottager's life – spiritually and economically. Hamilton suggests ways to improve one's lot. She shows her readers how, instead of passively accepting the will of God, they should capitalize on the materials and abilities God has bestowed upon them, not for individual gain but to benefit their families, their communities, and their nation. As Egenolf argues in *The Art of Political Fiction*, industry and industrious habits are paramount.[71] Most importantly, this prescribed programme of reform does not require

172   *Claire Grogan*

her fictional counterpart Mrs Mason to remain a resident forever amongst the cottagers, since they themselves inculcate the habits of industry she has modelled, along with a renewed application of Christian faith. There is no sense that Mrs Mason has to maintain a monitorial presence; once the cottagers see the economic and social advantages accruing to them, they will continue with the various reforms themselves. External direction is a necessary stimulus, but ultimately the cottagers become autonomous. Because the new habits of cleanliness in housekeeping and in butter and cheese production produce immediate economic benefits, the cottagers are more quickly convinced of their efficacy. While more conservative tracts idealized the impoverished peasants who embraced their (often pitiful) lot, Hamilton encourages them to improve themselves materially – though not to aspire to climb the social ladder.[72] Accumulating wealth is not antithetical to spiritual well-being, but the ostentatious display of wealth for its own sake is. As Mrs Mason notes, the cottagers, though 'ill brought up [are] ... not ... deficient in understanding; and if I can once convince them of the advantage they will derive from listening to my advice, I may make a lasting impression on their minds'.[73] Since Mrs Mason engages with them as rational people, common sense prevails. When her new methods save time, labour, and make money, they are quickly adopted.[74]

Likewise, though the educational reforms Mrs Mason introduces at the village school appear 'foreign', the master, Mr Morison, who eventually replaces her, comes from within the community. Mr Morison, who fell on hard times when he 'trusted o'er far, to the honesty and discretion of a fause-hearted loon' in an attempt to 'raise [his] wife and bairns above their station', exemplifies Hamilton's belief in second chances.[75] Like Bell Stewart, he is chastised for his social ambitions, but not irrevocably. Hamilton suggests the tools for success lie close to hand. The book, like Mrs Mason herself, provides guidance for the cottagers to pursue their own programme of renewal and reform.

Another innovative move in *The Cottagers of Glenburnie* is the incorporation of Scottish dialect which, as Gary Kelly has noted, is 'central to the novel's cultural politics'.[76] Hamilton described herself as following in the footsteps of Burns, Ramsay, and MacNeill and went as far as to suggest 'that the study of Gude braid Scotch be made a part of polite education'.[77] This is quite distinct from More's *Village Politics* and *Cheap Repository Tracts*, in which she purports to convey the language and dialect of the working class, but actually presents an outsider's perspective and ideology through her mimicry. The use of dialect amongst her peasantry suggests 'a middle-class evangelical fantasy about the ways such language might be recuperated for respectable society'.[78] More's characters speak very much as a middle-class woman imagined the working classes engaged and spoke with each other. Hamilton aims for greater linguistic authenticity by incorporating Scotch dialect within her tale. This signals her nationalist sympathies and also recuperates the language for a broad readership. Though her characters' oft

Didacticism after Hannah More   173

repeated refusal to help – 'I canna be fash'd' – apparently became prover-
bial amongst English readers, Hamilton endeavours to transcribe a fuller
lexicon of true Scots into her tale. The servant Grizzy's lengthy and perceptive explanation for the errant son Sandy's defection from the army illustrates this:

> Why ye ken ... that Sandy was ay a wilf' lad; so it's no to be wondered
> at that whan he was ordered to stand this gait, and that gait, and had
> his hair tugged till it was ready to crack, and his neck made sair wi'
> standing ajee, he should tak it but unco ill. So he disobeyed orders;
> and than they lashed him, and his proud stomach cou'd na get o'er the
> disgrace; and than he ran aff, and hade himself three days in the muirs.
> On the fourt day he cam here; and than the sogers got haud o' him;
> and they took him awa' to be tried for a deserter.[79]

The *Scots Magazine* praised Hamilton for exhibiting 'perhaps the purest
colloquial Scots that ever appeared in print' and so enabling 'the language
and manners of our country, with all their imperfections ... to be handed
down to posterity in full purity'. The *Edinburgh Review* thought it 'a specimen of the purest and most characteristic Scotch which we have lately met
with in writing [though perhaps] only intelligible [to a] small number of
readers'. The difficulties English readers faced unless they took 'the trouble
thoroughly to familiarize themselves with our ancient and venerable dialect'
only made it more praise worthy.[80] There are, however, limits to Hamilton's inclusion of Scots. It is significant that Mrs Mason speaks English as
opposed to the Scots of her relatives. Her command of language places her
socially above her working-class relatives and thus aligns with the middle-
and upper-class plot lines. One exception to this class demarcation occurs in
Mr Stewart who, as befits his role, moves back and forth between English
and Scots depending upon company.

   Though Hamilton might share some of the concerns and views of her
conservative peers, most particularly Hannah More, she did not agree with
them about the best methods to address and topics to present to the working
poor. Their motivations for writing didactic works were quite dissimilar. If
the government's primary goal was to quell the working poor, Hamilton's
was to inspire them to greater things. Olivia Smith relates the perhaps apocryphal story in her *Politics of Language* of how a boisterous crowd near
Bath was dissuaded from rioting when 'a gentleman of fortune' distributed
More's ballad and induced the riotous colliers to join him in singing 'Half
a Loaf is Better than No Bread'.[81] The didactic content so calmed the lis-
teners that chaos was averted. I suggest Hamilton was far more ambitious
about her didactic intent. She did not write to convince the working classes
that social quietism and obedience were preferable (to accept one's lot in
life), but to change her readers' behaviours. She challenged them to embrace
change and so bring about domestic, spiritual, and national renewal.

174   *Claire Grogan*

There is no disputing the popularity of *The Cottagers of Glenburnie*, though it is harder to determine categorically the number and class of her readers. The work initially retailed at 7s. 6d., putting it well beyond the reach of many Scottish cottagers. To remedy this, the *Edinburgh Review* suggested Hamilton 'strike out all scenes in upper life' and 'print the remainder upon coarse paper at such a price as may enable the volume to find its way to the cottage library'.[82] While this would align Hamilton's tale more closely with conventional tracts, I believe it misses a fundamental purpose of Hamilton's work, which was to address the middle-class as well as the working-class reader. To avoid any possible segregation of her readership, Hamilton arranged for a cheaper edition of the work in its entirety to be printed. Benger describes in 1818 how the 'cheap edition is to be found in every village-library' and notes the ingenuity of 'Isabel Irvine (the attendant of Mrs. Hamilton's juvenile years) [who] put some money into her purse by lending her single copy for a penny each reader'.[83] A second and third edition of *The Cottagers of Glenburnie* appeared in late 1808 with printings of each in Belfast and Glasgow to meet demand. By 1815, a sixth edition was available and a seventh in 1822. Its longevity is attested to with the Chalmer's 'People's Edition' in 1837, new Scottish editions in 1858, 1873, 1885, and 1898, while overseas American editions appeared in 1808, 1812, 1834, 1845, 1865, a Dublin edition in 1841, and a German translation in 1827, entitled *Die Huttenbewohner von Glenburnie*.

Hamilton's call to action appears to have been well received. *The Cottagers of Glenburnie* is credited repeatedly through the nineteenth century with having galvanized its readers into action. Reportedly it helped fuel the rage in the early part of the century amongst the wealthy for visiting the cottagers to offer assistance and support.[84] Pamela Perkins, in her modern edition of *The Cottagers of Glenburnie*, quotes the novelist and travel writer Elizabeth Isabella Spence who attributes the improvement amongst the Scottish cottagers directly to Hamilton's work. Spence enthuses: 'how greatly are the lower class indebted to Mrs Hamilton, for the "Cottagers of Glenbervie [sic]" which has tended to effect such a happy change amongst that community of people, that must ensure not merely comfort, but health'. In a similar strain the Irish novelist Maria Edgeworth acknowledges the persuasive power of Hamilton's work when she anticipates that Mary Leadbeater's *Cottage Dialogues* (1811) will 'be for Ireland, what the *Cottagers of Glenburnie* are for Scotland.... [hoping] they will do as much good in this country as her's did in Scotland'.[85]

The *Edinburgh Review*, while not crediting *The Cottagers of Glenburnie* with single-handedly effecting a revolution in manners, felt it was part of a

> strong current of improvement that runs through Scotland, and a much smaller impulse than would once have been necessary, will now throw the peasantry within the sphere of its actions. Beside, our cottagers [unlike those elsewhere in Britain] are reading and reasoning

animals and are more likely perhaps to be moved from their old habits by hints and suggestions which they glean up from a book, than by the more officious and insulting interference of a living reformer.[86]

While it is impossible to determine how many cottagers actually read Hamilton's work, it clearly became a familiar cultural reference: it was cited in numerous works throughout the nineteenth century and even appeared in a caricature. Interestingly Hamilton's work spread without the use of the elaborate publishing strategies employed for More's *Cheap Repository Tracts*. *The Cottagers* appears to have captured the imagination of large numbers and spread by word of mouth – an early instance perhaps of going viral.

Her tale shows how the actions of a determined woman can change a small rural Scottish community in profound ways. Improving oneself domestically has national, as well as local consequences. It also speaks to her belief that the nation's problems can best be resolved by women whom she calls to action. I leave the last word to Hamilton, who expressed this sentiment in a letter of 8 June 1802:

> [I] turn to the bright side of mankind, which I really believe will turn out to be – woman!... the more I see and know of the world, I am the more convinced, that whenever our sex step over the pale of folly, (which, unhappily, is a *feat* that by far the greatest number never attempt,) they ascend the steeps of wisdom and virtue more readily than the other. They are less encumbered by the load of selfishness; and, if they carry enough of ballast to prevent being blown into the gulf of *sentiment*, they mount much higher than their stronger associates.[87]

Notes

1. S. Trimmer, *The Oeconomy of Charity, or, an Address to Ladies; Adapted to the Present State of Charitable Institutions in England* (London, 1787); T. R. Malthus, *An Essay on the Principle of Population* (London, 1798); P. Colquhoun, *A Treatise on Indigence* (London, 1806).
2. See A. Stott, *Hannah More: The First Victorian* (Oxford: Oxford University Press, 2003), pp. 171–73.
3. K. Gilmartin explains how tract writing 'was part of a tradition of Christian moral reform that went back to the late seventeenth century and culminated in the 1780s, before the French Revolution had its galvanizing impact upon British radicalism' ('"Study to be Quiet": Hannah More and the Invention of Conservative Culture in Britain', *English Literary History*, 70:2 (2003), pp. 493–540, on p. 503.
4. T. Paine, *Rights of Man* (1791–92), ed. C. Grogan (Peterborough, ON: Broadview Press, 2011), pp. 9–40.
5. See Introduction to Paine, *Rights of Man*, pp. 34–40. See also L. Peterson, 'From French Revolution to English Reform: Hannah More, Harriet Martineau, and the "Little Book"', *Nineteenth-Century Literature*, 60:4 (2006), pp. 409–50.

176 Claire Grogan

6. W. Roberts, *Memoirs of the Life and Correspondence of Mrs Hannah More*, 4 vols (London: R. B. Seeley and W. Burnside, 1839), vol. 2, pp. 67, 73, 378.

7. H. More, *Village Politics Addressed to All the Mechanics, Journeymen and Day Labourers in Great Britain, by Will Chip, a Country Carpenter* (London, 1793).

8. Roberts, *Memoirs of Hannah More*, vol. 2, p. 75.

9. As with her Sunday School programme, More prescribed a restricted curriculum: 'They learn of weekdays such coarse works as may fit them for servants. I allow of no writing' (M. More, *Mendip Annals*, ed. A. Roberts (London, 1859), p. 6).

10. In Roberts's *Memoirs of Hannah More*, we discover that she 'was obliged to reject three ... submissions' for the *Cheap Repository Tracts* 'because they had too much of politics, and another because there was too much of love' (vol. 2, p. 234).

11. Roberts, *Memoirs of Hannah More*, vol. 2, p. 427.

12. G. Kelly, 'Revolution, Reaction, and the Expropriation of Popular Culture: Hannah More's *Cheap Repository*', *Man and Nature*, 6 (1987), pp. 147–59.

13. Gilmartin, 'Study to be Quiet', p. 525.

14. Qtd in A. Stott, *Hannah More: The First Victorian* (Oxford: Oxford University Press, 2003), pp. 178–79.

15. H. More, *The Works of Hannah More Including Several Pieces Never Before Published*, 19 vols (London: T. Cadell Jr and W. Davies, 1818), vol. 5, pp. vii–viii.

16. Gilmartin, 'Study to be Quiet', p. 520. See also P. Demers, Chapter 6 of this volume, p. 107.

17. Gilmartin, 'Study to be Quiet', p. 529.

18. O. Smith, *Politics of Language* 1791–1819 (Oxford: Clarendon, 1984), p. 93.

19. See Stott, *Hannah More*, pp. 169–90, and also Gilmartin, 'Study to be Quiet', p. 511.

20. Gilmartin, 'Study to be Quiet', pp. 512–13.

21. Ibid., p. 511.

22. Her recent biographer Stott claims that by late 1797 'two million tracts and ballads [had been] printed and distributed' (*Hannah More*, p. 207). More boasts in a letter how the tracts were disseminated nationally and internationally, quoting her friend Bishop Porteus, who in January 1797 wrote:

> the sublime and immortal publication of the 'Cheap Repository' I hear of from every quarter of the globe. To the West Indies I have sent shiploads of them. They are read with avidity at Sierra Leone, and I hope our pious Scotch missionaries will introduce them into Asia.
>
> (Roberts, *Memoirs of Hannah More*, vol. 2, p. 4)

Porteus's claim supports theories that the upper classes purchased vast numbers of the tracts which they then distributed within their communities in an endeavour to maintain civic calm. See, for example, K. Gilmartin, *Writing Against Revolution: Literary Conservatism in Britain, 1790–1832* (Cambridge: Cambridge University Press, 2007), pp. 55–95; Stott, *Hannah More*, pp. 169–90.

23. See *Scotch Cheap Repository Tracts* (Edinburgh: Oliphant, Waugh & Innes, 1809) and *Cheap Repository Tracts Suited to the Present Times* (London: F. C. & J. Rivington, 1819).

24. Published works prior to 1808 include *Translations of the Letters of a Hindoo Rajah: Written Previous to, and During the Period of His Residence in England* (1796); *Memoirs of Modern Philosophers* (1800); *Letters on Education* (1801);

Didacticism after Hannah More 177

Memoirs of the Life of Agrippina: Wife of Germanicus (1804); and *Letters Addressed to the Daughter of a Nobleman, on the Formation of Religious and Moral Principle* (1806). Hamilton received a Royal Pension in 1804. See C. Grogan, *Politics and Genre in the Works of Elizabeth Hamilton, 1756–1816* (Farnham, UK: Ashgate, 2012), p. 123.

25. E. O. Benger, *Memoirs of the Late Mrs. Elizabeth Hamilton*, 2nd edn, 2 vols (London: Longman, Hurst, Rees, Orme, and Brown, 1819), vol. 1, p. 184.

26. Hannah More and her sisters worked in the south-west of England, while Hamilton directed her energies in Edinburgh, Scotland.

27. Gilmartin, *Writing Against Revolution*.

28. Grogan, *Politics and Genre*, pp. 1–26; M. Wallace, *Revolutionary Subjects in the English Jacobin Novel, 1790–1805* (Lewisburg, PA: Bucknell University Press, 2009), pp. 13–35.

29. R. Hole, *Pulpits, Politics, and Public Order in England, 1760–1832* (Cambridge: Cambridge University Press, 1989), p. vii.

30. Grogan, *Politics and Genre*, p. 139.

31. Benger, *Memoirs of Elizabeth Hamilton*, vol. 2, pp. 89–90.

32. E. Hamilton, *The Cottagers of Glenburnie and Other Educational Writings by Elizabeth Hamilton*, ed. P. Perkins (Glasgow: The Association for Scottish Literary Studies, 2010), p. 47.

33. Ibid., p. 48.

34. Benger, *Memoirs of Elizabeth Hamilton*, vol. 2, p. 267.

35. Hamilton, *The Cottagers of Glenburnie*, p. 49.

36. Gilmartin, 'Study to be Quiet', p. 503.

37. Ibid., pp. 503–4.

38. The managers provided inmates with letters of reference which enabled them to enter, or sometimes re-enter, the work force and so avoid prostitution or the poor house.

39. See Benger, *Memoirs of Elizabeth Hamilton*, vol. 1, p. 40.

40. M. Edgeworth, *Castle Rackrent* (London, 1800) and *Popular Tales* (London, 1804).

41. See also H. Havens, Chapter 8 of this volume, p. 144.

42. Alex Fraser Tytler, Lord Woodhouselee (1747–1813), professor of history at the University of Edinburgh, Judge Advocate of Scotland, Lord Court of Session.

43. For an account of Hamilton's visit, see A. Alison's *Memoir of the Life and Writings of the Honourable Alexander Fraser Tytler, Lord Woodhouselee* (Edinburgh: Neill, 1818), pp. 20–21.

44. Benger, *Memoirs of Elizabeth Hamilton*, vol. 2, pp. 89–90.

45. See Grogan, *Politics and Genre*, pp. 136–41.

46. More, *Mendip Annals*, p. 138.

47. Roberts, *Memoirs of Hannah More*, vol. 2, p. 378.

48. Gilmartin, 'Study to be Quiet', p. 508.

49. S. B. Egenolf, *The Art of Political Fiction in Hamilton, Edgeworth, and Owenson* (Farnham, UK: Ashgate, 2009), p. 149.

50. See E. Hamilton, *Memoirs of Modern Philosophers*, ed. C. Grogan (Peterborough, ON: Broadview Press, 2000), p. 116.

51. Hamilton, *The Cottagers of Glenburnie*, p. 123.

52. Ibid., p. 96.

53. Ibid., p. 94.

178 Claire Grogan

54. Ibid., p. 53.
55. Ibid., p. 99.
56. Ibid., p. 56.
57. Ibid., p. 134.
58. I. Duncan, *Scott's Shadow: The Novel in Romantic Edinburgh* (Princeton, NJ: Princeton University Press, 2007), p. 20.
59. Ibid., p. 31.
60. Hamilton, *The Cottagers of Glenburnie*, p. 5; see for example More's *Sinful Sally* (1793); *Betty Brown; the St Giles Orange Girl* (August 1796); *The History of Idle Jack* (March 1796); or the sequel *Jack Brown in Prison* (April 1796).
61. Hamilton, *The Cottagers of Glenburnie*, p. 130.
62. Ibid., p. 134.
63. See K. Olsen, *Daily Life in Eighteenth-Century England* (Westport, CT: Greenwood Press, 1999), p. 238.
64. Hamilton, *The Cottagers of Glenburnie*, pp. 138–45.
65. *Scots Magazine*, 70 (September 1808), pp. 678–79; Benger, *Memoirs of Elizabeth Hamilton*, vol. 1, p. 184.
66. Benger, *Memoirs of Elizabeth Hamilton*, vol. 1, pp. 185–86.
67. D. L. Jeffrey (ed.), *English Spirituality: In the Age of Wesley* (Grand Rapids, MI: William B. Erdmans Publishing, 1987), pp. 28–29, 37.
68. Benger's *Memoirs of Elizabeth Hamilton* contains several excerpts from Hamilton's spiritual journal in which she works through a close reading of chosen Biblical passages.
69. 'Letter from John Newton to Mr. and Mrs. Coffin, "On Serving God in the Ordinary Duties of Life"', qtd in Jeffrey, *English Spirituality*, p. 38.
70. Hamilton, *The Cottagers of Glenburnie*, pp. 105–27.
71. Egenolf, *Art of Political Fiction*, pp. 129–56.
72. Bell Stewart's ambitions to climb socially by marrying the ostensible gentleman Mr Flinders, come to naught when she discovers he is the son of an honest shoemaker (Hamilton, *The Cottagers of Glenburnie*, pp. 184–91).
73. Hamilton, *The Cottagers of Glenburnie*, p. 123.
74. Ibid., p. 156.
75. Ibid., p. 167.
76. G. Kelly, *Women, Writing, and Revolution: 1790–1827* (Oxford: Clarendon Press, 1993), p. 290. See also T. Doerksen, Chapter 10 of this volume, p. 181.
77. Benger, *Memoirs of Elizabeth Hamilton*, vol. 2, pp. 12–13.
78. Gilmartin, 'Study to be Quiet', p. 508.
79. Hamilton, *The Cottagers of Glenburnie*, pp. 160–61.
80. *Scots Magazine*, 70 (September 1808), pp. 678–82; *Edinburgh Review*, 12 (July 1808), pp. 402–3.
81. Roberts, *Memoirs of Hannah More*, vol. 2, p. 384.
82. *Edinburgh Review*, 12 (July 1808), pp. 402–3.
83. Benger, *Memoirs of Elizabeth Hamilton*, vol. 1, pp. 196–97; vol. 1, p. 184.
84. P. Perkins, Introduction to *The Cottagers of Glenburnie and Other Educational Writings by Elizabeth Hamilton*, ed. P. Perkins (Glasgow: Association for Scottish Literary Studies, 2010), pp. 1–5.
85. Ibid., p. 3.
86. *The Edinburgh Review*, 12 (July 1808), p. 410.
87. Benger, *Memoirs of Elizabeth Hamilton*, vol. 1, pp. 159–60.

10 A National *Bildungsroman*

Didacticism and National Identity in Mary Brunton's *Discipline* and Susan Edmonstone Ferrier's *Marriage*

Teri Doerksen

During the century following the Act of Union, the Act's influence could be felt in literary explorations of British national identity. This was particularly true in Scotland, which was always intimately aware of its political and cultural proximity to and interconnectedness with England. The 'union' had always been characterized by subtle tensions; the Acts of Union of 1707, passed by both the parliament of England and the parliament of Scotland, united the two countries into a single Kingdom of Great Britain, but as Daniel Defoe lamented in his 1713 pamphlet *Union and No Union*, the marriage of the two countries was not a love match: 'a Firmer Union of Policy with Less Union of Affection has hardly ever been known in the whole World'.[1] Defoe is speaking here out of bitterness that resistance to the union was growing rather than fading, and he was correct in his assessment that a sense of British national identity trailed far behind the legal status of the kingdom. In fact, more than a century of negotiation would follow. As Linda Colley argues, what existed after the Acts was

> much less a trinity of three self-contained and self-conscious nations than a patchwork in which uncertain areas of Welshness, Scottishness and Englishness were cut across by strong regional attachments and scored over again by loyalties to village, town, family and landscape.

What finally did unite them, in Colley's estimation, was not a sense of internal similarity but because

> circumstances impressed them with the belief that they were different from those beyond their shores.... Not so much consensus or homogeneity or centralization at home, as a strong sense of dissimilarity from those without proved to be the essential cement.[2]

By the end of the eighteenth century, a sense of what national identity might mean was beginning to take shape, although the shape it took was naturally distinct in the different regions of the 'united' kingdom, and it was complicated by many different factors.

180 *Teri Doerksen*

Literary representation was one of these factors. As Benedict Anderson has famously argued, the modern nation state can be defined loosely but very usefully as 'an imagined political community – and imagined as both inherently limited and sovereign'.[3] Anderson continues on to argue very persuasively that the imagined community develops by means of print-capitalism, which solidifies shared language use via widely disseminated print materials such that readers

> gradually became aware of the hundreds of thousands, even millions, of people in their particular language field, and at the same time that *only those* hundreds of thousands, or millions, so belonged. These fellow readers, to whom they were so connected through print, formed, in their secular, particular, visible invisibility, the embryo of the nationally imagined community.[4]

The literary public sphere of Scotland and England at the end of the eighteenth century and the beginning of the nineteenth, however, shows less a gradual progression toward a shared language and nationhood and more a complex series of negotiations regarding Scottish, English, and British identities that shift with political changes. As Evan Gottlieb recently argued, the beginning of the nineteenth century 'saw a significant growth of uncertainty regarding the question of national identity [in Scotland and England]. The increasing unease of Romantic writers reflects ... a growing recognition that the nation can never achieve full unity of identity'.[5]

Many critics focus their investigation on Scottish Regency writers, and particularly Sir Walter Scott, as they address print cultural exploration of national identity in the light of this growing unease. Gottlieb, for example, in his discussion of sympathy and economics, concludes with the argument that Scott ultimately is able to 'formulate a conception of Britishness founded on internal difference rather than sameness'.[6] Maureen M. Martin points to the 'marriage plot' of British national identity, reading Scott's *Redgauntlet* (1824) to investigate 'the submerging of Scottish nationality into a greater England as the inevitable outcome and defining moment of Scottish history – a teleology of union that is, in effect, a marriage plot'.[7] The Scottish Regency, though, afforded a multiplicity of voices contributing to the larger discourse of national identity. Exploring how national identity was constructed in light of different audiences has the potential to reveal other visions of how Scotland and England shared a common Britishness, and of how that Britishness affected individuals of both genders on both sides of the border. Two of Scott's contemporaries, Mary Brunton and Susan Ferrier, are being rediscovered for their didactic novels, novels that are noteworthy both for their multifaceted representations of gender and for their characterizations of both Scottish and English regional types. Careful reading of these novelists illuminates the inherently complex relationship between England and the 'regional' areas that together comprise Britain.

A *National* Bildungsroman   181

Both Mary Brunton and Susan Edmonstone Ferrier were distinguished by the distinctly Scottish context in which they embedded their novels. As Kathryn Kirkpatrick notes in her introduction to the Oxford edition of *Marriage*, 'The female novel of development might threaten to take minor characters to Scotland's Gretna Green for an unsanctioned marriage, but no English novelist cared to write about them once they got there or assumed they would stay'. Ferrier, she notes, negotiates a complex sense of national identity 'in representing Scotland as a viable setting for the female *Bildungsroman*, in intermarrying English and Scots characters, and in portraying Scots women as heroines'.[8] Brunton's novels engage similarly with the complexity of life on both sides of the border. In particular, Brunton's second novel, *Discipline*, published in 1814, and Ferrier's first novel *Marriage*, which appeared in 1818, both illuminate a British and Scottish, rather than one-sidedly English, perspective on gender, class, and national identity.

These Scottish novelists are positioned at the culmination of the late eighteenth-century rise in women's domestic and didactic novel writing; in their novels national, religious, and class identity are represented as mutually informing and occasionally conflated concepts. Without simplifying the relationship between the nations into the kind of inevitable 'marriage plot' submerging Scotland into England described by Martin, both Brunton and Ferrier use the discourse of didactic and domestic fiction to produce multivalent portraits of a British coming of age. In these novels the Romantic unease about Britishness becomes a kind of adolescent angst, eventually resolving into a union that unites elements of Englishness in the principle Scottish characters and vice versa, rather than simply marrying one to the other. In effect, Brunton's and Ferrier's works are constructing a national *Bildungsroman* – they are representing the coming of age of a single unified British nation, metaphorized through the uniting of the Scottish and the English into specific individual characters, which are then joined in marriage with one another. The novels accomplish this, amazingly, without losing a sense of the complexity of each nation's citizens and characters. The novels' inherent didacticism becomes a platform to reinterpret the Act of Union – the uniting of Scotland and England in these novels is a process under constant negotiation. *Discipline* and *Marriage* use and modify the familiar discourses of domestic and didactic fiction to illustrate the internal changes that must take place before Scotland and England can achieve a union of affection, and not merely of policy.

So who were Brunton and Ferrier? Mary Brunton was a well-respected Scottish novelist of the early nineteenth century who produced three religious didactic novels, *Self-Control* (1811), *Discipline* (1814), and *Emmeline with some other pieces* (1819). Although a recent biographer, Mary McKerrow, calls Brunton 'the forgotten Scottish novelist',[9] her novels were popular upon first publication and continued to appeal to Victorian readers into the middle of the century, appearing in several editions between 1832 and 1852, and recently her novels have inspired an upswing of critical attention. She was famously critiqued by Jane Austen, who read Brunton's first novel, *Self-Control*, and noted that it was 'an excellently-meant, elegantly-written work, without anything of Nature or Probability in it'.[10] Austen was not the only reader underwhelmed by the melodrama of *Self-Control*, which ends with the heroine's suspenseful and unlikely flight down a Canadian waterfall tied to a canoe, but others appreciated the moral impetus of Brunton's works. In 1834, noted actor and theatre manager William Charles Macready compares Brunton to Austen, to Brunton's advantage:

> [Austen] does not probe the vices; but lays bare the weaknesses of character: the blemish on the skin, and not the corruption at the heart is what she examines. Mrs. Brunton's books have a far higher aim; they try to make us better, and it is an addition to our previous faults if they do not. The necessity, the comfort and the elevating influence of piety is continually inculcated throughout her works – which never appear in Miss Austen's.[11]

In her second novel, Brunton moves away from the improbable adventures of her first, but maintains the 'elevating influence of piety'. *Discipline* found a solid readership as well, drawing praise for its representation of the Scottish Highlands and going into three editions before 1816.

Even more widely read than Brunton, Susan Edmonstone Ferrier rose to enormous popularity in Scotland in the 1810s; she was a great favourite of Sir Walter Scott's. Like Brunton, she wrote three novels, *Marriage* in 1810, though not published until 1818, *The Inheritance* in 1824, and *Destiny* in 1831; her popularity with the reading public can be seen in the rapidly rising sums she received from her publishers, from £150 for the first novel to £1,000 for the second to £1,700 for the last.[12] She was, during her lifetime and for decades afterward, acclaimed as one of the foremost didactic novelists of her day. As late as 1878, *Temple Bar* magazine praised Ferrier's works for their 'healthy moral tone' even as it noted her importance to Scotland's literary history by comparing her to Austen, saying that Ferrier

> may be said to have done for Scotland what Jane Austen and Maria Edgeworth have respectively done for England and Ireland—left portraits, painted in undying colours, of men and women that will live for ever in the hearts and minds of her readers.[13]

Both Brunton's *Discipline* and Ferrier's *Marriage* begin in England and end in Scotland, and both represent Scotland as a physical location associated with moral values and a developing sense of spiritual awareness for those who are receptive to change.[14] Brunton's and Ferrier's work in these novels illuminates these novelists' Scottishness as it affects their didactic perspective on class and national identity.

A National Bildungsroman   183

Brunton's *Discipline* tells the story of wealthy, spoiled Ellen Percy, the only daughter of a widowed West Indian merchant with an aristocratic pedigree. At sixteen she is introduced into London society; as a wealthy and beautiful heiress to £200,000 she wields enormous power in her social circle, and as the head of her father's household after her mother's death she wields enormous power at home as well. Her pride and self-importance are further inflated by the attention she receives as an heiress on the marriage market. Her two principal suitors are a study in contrasts. Lord Frederick de Burgh is a languid aristocrat who hopes that marriage to the Percy fortune will refill his family's coffers. Mr Maitland, on the other hand, loves Ellen for herself despite her coquetry and her pride, but finally renounces her and flees to the West Indies when he realizes that she is not capable of appreciating a man of virtue. In Mr Maitland's absence Ellen becomes more intimate with Lord Frederick; she does not love him, but she is driven by her own sense of self-importance until she finally finds herself on the point of eloping with him to Scotland. The elopement never takes place, however, because Lord Frederick hears that Mr Percy has lost his entire fortune in a bad investment. Ellen returns to her home, shaken by the news, and finds that her father has committed suicide. Left penniless and abandoned by her former friends, Ellen lives in poverty until her former governess, the pious and good Miss Mortimer, takes her in. Under her tutelage Ellen begins to experience a spiritual and religious awakening, but the process is interrupted by Miss Mortimer's untimely death a year later, and Ellen again finds herself alone and poor. She takes a position as a governess in Edinburgh, but her suspicious and cruel mistress has her sent to a madhouse. When she is finally released, Ellen supports herself by selling toys of her own making and is at last befriended by Charlotte Graham, the daughter of the Scottish Lord Eredine, who invites Ellen to her house in the Highlands. Imprisonment and deprivation have furthered Ellen's spiritual and religious transformation, and she is now a suitable match for the still-enamoured Mr Maitland, also known as Henry Graham, who turns out to be Charlotte's brother.

Discipline is an interesting amalgam of influences, a novel of spiritual progress that dips deeply into didacticism, combined with an episodic narrative of physical travel from urban England to regional Scotland. It is a kind of domestic *Pilgrim's Progress*, in which the protagonist's physical journey from home to home coincides with her gradual religious transformation. It is also very markedly a novel of national identity. Even from the first sentence, the novel invites the reader to consider the narrative as a product of a distinctly British union of characteristics, as the narrator, speaking retrospectively, notes:

> I have heard it remarked, that he who writes his own history ought to possess Irish humour, Scotch prudence, and English sincerity; – the first, that his work may be read; the second that it may be read without injury to himself; the third, that the perusal of it may be profitable to others.[15]

184 *Teri Doerksen*

Although the narrator then goes on to confess that she possesses only the English sincerity, the reader has already been alerted to the idea that writing itself, and particularly narrative writing, is by necessity a hybrid task, and that even levels of such common characteristics as humour and prudence may carry with them implications of national identity.

A complex interrelation of class, state religion, and socio-economic status is also introduced even before the heroine. The narrator, Ellen Percy, notes as background to the story that her father 'never mentioned his family, except to preface a philippic against all dignities in church and state. Against these he objected, as fostering "that aristocratical contumely, which flesh and blood cannot endure."' She explains her father's resentment by elaborating his history: his own father 'a cadet of an ancient family, was doomed to starve upon a curacy, in revenge for contaminating the blood of the Percys by an unequal alliance'.[16] Ellen's grandfather was born into an aristocratic family with connections to church dignitaries; her father was born into poverty as the son of an impecunious curate but rose to wealth as a successful merchant; she herself is the heiress to an immense fortune, and her journey of religious self-discovery is the ostensible subject of the book. Brunton thus establishes that a union of national characteristics in the person of the narrator/protagonist is necessary to tell a history of socioeconomic and religious transformation.

The novel's didactic impulses are enacted through the representation of a gradual progression of change in Ellen Percy contrasted with the existing moral and spiritual merit of characters like Miss Mortimer and, especially, Mr Maitland. The moral, religious, and spiritual alterations in Ellen Percy that are the principal focus of the text's didactic message are accompanied by an associated series of additional changes in physical location and national affinity (from England to Scotland, and toward the union of characteristics noted above), and eventually in her name, from Percy to Graham. Brunton modifies Maitland's characterization – though not his character – more subtly and mostly by revealing more about his extant characteristics or the inevitable reward of his merit than by illustrating changes that he undergoes. Still, his eventual repatriation to Scotland and resumption of his birth name parallel the corresponding alterations in Ellen and suggest that they are didactic counterparts. Before the characters can marry at the end, before they can create a union of both policy and affection, they must incorporate elements of the English and the Scottish.

The word 'British' is a useful touchstone here. It appears only four times in the novel, the first two specifically associated with Maitland, both illustrating his capacity to transform others positively, and the second two appearing at moments when Ellen Percy is undergoing a positive transformation while apart from Maitland. The concept of Britishness, then, seems strongly associated in the novel with the aspiration toward and achievement of moral and spiritual transformation. Throughout the novel, Maitland is associated with Britishness, and it is only as his identity is folded into Henry Graham's that his Scottishness per se becomes more than a minor element

A *National* Bildungsroman   185

of his character. Still, from the beginning he is a hybrid character, successful in England but born in Scotland, the son of an English mother and a Scottish father. Maitland is introduced early in the novel, when Ellen is just coming out in society and is chafing at the chaperonage of her mother's dear friend Miss Mortimer. In an attempt to terrify Miss Mortimer, Ellen and her school friend Julia Arnold engage in a carriage race, with all of their suitors on horseback accompanying them. Miss Mortimer tries to stop Ellen, saying calmly that the path is narrow and that such a race could endanger passers-by. Ellen checks her horses – only to see one of her suitors pass her by and knock a woman into the path of Ellen's curricle:

> From the guilt of murder I was saved by fortitude of a stranger. He boldly seized the rein; and, *with British strength of arm* turning the horses short round.... At length [the woman] opened her eyes; and so heavy a weight was lifted from my heart, that I could not refrain from bursting into tears; but unwilling to exhibit these marks of a reproving conscience, I turned proudly away.[17]

Maitland's Britishness is associated here with strength and heroism, but also with salvation and positive transformation; without Maitland's intercession Ellen would have been guilty of murder. He is a mediating force: events set in motion by Ellen's pride continue despite her own willingness to amend, and only Maitland can intercede effectively to save her.

Maitland's Britishness, and the connection between moral merit, moral improvement, and British identity are furthered in the description Ellen offers of the man who has assisted her. She contrasts his 'tolerably regular' features with 'a certain *bony* squareness of countenance, which we on the south side of the Tweed are accustomed to account a national deformity', and although she notes that '[h]is accent was certainly provincial', she believes that 'without the assistance of his name, I could not decidedly have pronounced him to be a Scotchman'. She finishes by noting his language, which marks him as 'a gentleman; [because it is] always correct, often forcible, and sometimes elegant'.[18] Here the description highlights that Maitland is Scottish while simultaneously calling his Scottish identity into question: he has the squareness of countenance and the provincial accent, yet she 'could not decidedly have pronounced him a Scotchman', and the final impression of him was of his language, which identified him as 'a gentleman', even in London. Even here, as Maitland is first introduced, the narrative appears to incorporate elements of both the English and the Scottish into his characterization, while marking him as quintessentially British. Later, the novel associates Maitland and his quintessential Britishness with the achievement of moral and spiritual transformation; the narrative describes 'the eloquence of Maitland ... before British senates', and emphasizes the strength and ardour of his anti-slavery rhetoric, which inspires 'All England, all Europe' to fight against the slave trade.

186 *Teri Doerksen*

The last series of disclosures about Maitland's character come at the end of the novel. For several chapters Charlotte Graham has regaled Ellen with tales of her larger-than-life brother, whose bravery, dedication to his people, and moral righteousness are beyond compare. He rescues cattle and sheep, and even after he moves to England sends Bibles to local schoolchildren and counsels local leaders.[19] He is repeatedly lauded as the prototypical Highlander, the ideal brother and son, the consummate landlord, and one imagines, the perfect husband. Charlotte also shares at this point that she and her brother, though Highlanders through and through, are half English, as his mother was 'a Southron herself'.[20] The narrative's biggest revelation, of course, is that Henry Graham is Maitland. For the reader, as for Ellen Percy, Maitland's qualities and Graham's now suddenly overlap – the quintessential Highlander is also the gentleman with 'British strength of arm'; the beloved son of the Scottish Laird is also the voice that swayed all England and all Britain with its eloquence, the 'upstart mercantile name' (Maitland) is owned by a man with a recognizably Scottish aristocratic title. Mr/Henry/Maitland/Graham becomes a single multivalent construction, the prodigal son returning much beloved to his home in the Highlands, but possessed of English blood and a reputation as an orator with the power to influence British law. Many aspects of the Act of Union are already embodied in him, with Scotland and England coming together to the advantage of both, except that he lacks the means to perpetuate the union. For that he needs Ellen Percy.

Ellen Percy is a hybrid character, crossing metaphorical boundaries of socio-economic and class status as well as physical boundaries, like the border between England and Scotland. Ellen's gradual moral and spiritual transformation parallels the narrative of national *Bildungsroman* also embodied in the novel. Many critics have seen the novel as being made up of dramatically different narrative modes; Ainsley McIntosh, for example, argues that 'when Ellen enters Scotland ... the focus of *Discipline* diverges from didacticism into national tale',[21] and Isabelle Bour sees the novel as 'an unstable generic mixture' that moves from the novel of manners to the Gothic to the regional novel.[22] I would argue, instead, that the novel as a national *Bildungsroman* maintains its didacticism while at the same time it reflects many of the complexities of the nation it represents. During the course of the novel, Ellen embodies a complex range of British national identities and operates in many physical and socio-economic milieus. The story of national coming-of-age resonates with Ellen's simultaneous narrative of personal moral transformation – and both are framed by the familiar didactic tale about being born again.

The narrative begins by presenting Ellen as a fixed type, a proud and immutable character embedded in an English urban environment and fixed in the rising wealthy mercantile class. As the novel progresses, she proves to be very mutable indeed. Like Maitland, she proves capable of embodying many different identities. Her socio-economic status, for example, is already

A *National* Bildungsroman   187

vexed, as she is the granddaughter of an aristocratic family and not simply the daughter of a rich merchant; after her father's financial ruin and subsequent suicide, she joins the ranks of the urban poor, then the rural poor when she is taken in by Miss Mortimer, and then the serving classes when she takes the position as a governess in Edinburgh. She is essentially outside of the socio-economic system entirely when she is imprisoned in the madhouse, but then joins the ranks of the poor trading classes as she sells her toys to buy food and lodging, then moves to the Highlands as a guest of a Scottish laird and eventually marries Henry Graham, who is his father's heir after his elder brother's death overseas. She ends the novel in the aristocracy, coming full circle from the social class to which her grandparents belonged, though in Scotland instead of England. Literal journeys and moral transformation are connected in the novel, and Ellen Percy's travels provide a loose framework through which to examine the several transformations that she undergoes. She begins in the English metropolis, then takes refuge in the English countryside with Miss Mortimer, moves across the Tweed to urban Scotland, and then, after a final transformative experience, moves to her final rural destination in the Scottish Highlands, moving ever northward as her moral and spiritual journey progresses toward greater enlightenment.

Ellen Percy's transformative progression out of 'heartless selfishness'[23] begins with a conundrum that is typical of both the domestic and the didactic novel, the choice between two suitors: Mr Maitland, who is aware that she is not yet ready to be a virtuous wife and partner, and Lord Frederick, the scion of a noble house whose interest in Ellen is purely financial. Ellen Percy's sentiments match those of her suitors. Though she rejects Maitland's proposal, as he leaves, she admits that 'never did I feel so desolately alone, as when I turned to the chamber where Maitland had been and felt that he was gone'.[24] Similarly, despite the fact that she agrees to elope with Lord Frederick, throughout their courtship she feels 'a lingering reluctance' about marrying him.[25] Daniel Defoe's commentary on the Union could have been Brunton's inspiration; the relationship with Maitland is motivated on both sides by affection without policy, while the one with Lord Frederick is motivated entirely by policy without affection.

Brunton constructs a narrative that carefully establishes parallels between Ellen's literal and spiritual journeys, and the final two mentions of use of the term 'British' punctuate the most transformative of the way-stations on the journey. Ellen's first physical removal, the attempted elopement with Lord Frederick, precipitates a cascade of others, leading inevitably toward the north, toward greater self-awareness and morality, and, ultimately, toward a union of both policy and affection. The goal of the elopement, naturally and rather ironically, is Scotland, but Ellen gets no farther than Barnet before she learns that her father is destitute and Lord Frederick has moved on to other prey. As Lord Frederick so eloquently puts it in a note to his friend who is waiting with Ellen, 'The Percys are blown to the devil. The old one has failed for nearly a million.... See what a narrow escape I have had from blowing

188 *Teri Doerksen*

out my own brains'.[26] When Ellen returns home it is to find her own father has committed suicide, and she is precipitated out into a world of 'noise and motion' – and penury – in London's East End.[27] She is rescued from this urban poverty by Miss Mortimer, who offers her refuge.

Miss Mortimer has gone to great lengths to locate her and bring her back to her simple cottage; when Ellen looks about her new abode she discovers that she has been given the gayest room in the house, in which the shelves contain 'a few volumes of history, and the best works of our British essayists',[28] along with her own mother's Bible on the bedside table. Miss Mortimer's cottage serves in the novel as a kind of spiritual halfway house, where the protagonist can begin to make moral progress. The reference to specifically British essayists is not accidental; here Brunton introduces the dissonance between national elements, both across social class divides and across national boundaries within Britain. Brunton constructs Ellen's first spiritual trial at the intersection of these competing national interests with the appearance of a poor Scottish family; their plight and their 'Caledonian accent ... and national bashfulness' pique her interest. Their story is an ideal morality tale to mitigate Ellen Percy's pride: when she was the rich and careless Miss Percy, her own selfish desire for hothouse flowers out of season had caused her gardener, the father of the Campbell family, to fall deathly ill and had precipitated the family out of the respectable working classes and into indigence. The narrative juxtaposes Ellen's spiritual progress, her dawning awareness of the fragility of socio-economic class position, and the mercantile nature of national interactions between Scotland and England, particularly the commodification of individuals – Campbell had 'been allured from his country by the demand in England for Scotchmen of his trade'.[29] In the national *Bildungsroman*, this is a scene of adolescent angst, foregrounding the dissonances and growing pains of Ellen Percy and of the Union.

The centrepiece of this *Bildungsroman* takes place in urban Scotland, when Ellen Percy is imprisoned in a madhouse. Again, the literal journey, the moral journey, and the narrative of developing nationhood overlap. The encounter with the Campbells provides the backdrop for this next step of Ellen's journey, in which the fate of the Scottish family is visited upon herself. After Miss Mortimer's death she finds herself homeless and destitute, and she travels to Edinburgh, where she is to become a governess – an English commodity in a Scottish household – and then, like a commodity, she is cast off as her father had discarded the Campbells. This commodification is all the more interesting for, as Andrew Monnickendam has recently pointed out, Ellen is in high demand as a governess because she can instruct young Scottish women in the harp, 'that most powerful symbol of resistant nationalism'.[30] The narrative here complicates Scottish nationalism by presenting Ellen as a Southron who embodies Scottish nationalism; in contrast, the text represents Edinburgh as a place of urban desolation, where Ellen finds houses empty of their owners and, eventually, employers devoid of human

A *National* Bildungsroman   189

feeling. Ellen here has the capacity to be a more powerful symbol of Scottish nationalism than the natives of Edinburgh.

In the context of the didactic *Bildungsroman*, Ellen Percy needs to undergo dramatic change before she can be fully integrated into adult life. Ultimately Ellen's jealous employer has her confined in a madhouse, which the novel configures as a place of spiritual rebirth. The single chapter about the madhouse is set apart by the narrator from the rest of the narrative; the days spent there, she says 'are a blank in my being'.[31] The chapter itself follows the conventional pattern of a moral rebirth narrative, from 'the helplessness of infancy'[32] through a progression of spiritual awakenings in which she finally appreciates the 'full value' of religion and discovers an 'inexhaustible source of enjoyment' in the Bible she is given.[33] The narrative incorporates the language of national unification into the chapter as well. The word 'British' appears here for the fourth and last time, in this case as a part of a metaphor that Ellen uses to describe her eagerness to regain freedom. As the doctor, the 'medical judge', approaches, she feels more anxiety than a 'British mother trembling with the Gazette in her hand'.[34] The modifier here is crucial – without the modifier the comparison means nothing, but the word 'British' is transformative, indicating a similarity of feeling among parents of soldiers who together fight against a common foe. 'British' here signals commonality and unified purpose – and as Ellen steps transformed into Scotland, she sees 'the native land of the exile' before her, replete with 'brethren and friends'.[35] From this point Ellen Percy perceives a common bond with the people of Scotland, and begins to establish and re-establish connections at all socio-economic levels, from her neighbour Cecil, to the Campbell family newly returned from England, to Charlotte Graham who bears her off to the Highlands.

When Ellen Percy finally meets Henry Graham, then, she is already 'reborn' and firmly entwined in an intricate web of Scottish and English affiliations. Where Maitland/Henry Graham is a literal hybrid, a child of both English and Scottish parentage, Ellen is a figurative hybrid, a character who incorporates multiple national, socio-economic, and moral identities into a single individual, and who is destined to come to the Highlands and marry Henry Graham. When Ellen first meets Cecil Graham, Cecil predicts that the man who would inherit Eredine (Mr Kenneth, before his untimely death) was destined to marry an English woman, like his father before him:

> 'Indeed, [the Southron woman] was just [Lord Eredine's] fortune, lady', said Cecil, 'and he could not go past her. And Mr Kenneth himsel' too is ordained, if he live, save him, to one from your country'.
>
> 'Have you the second-sight, Cecil, that you know so well what is ordained for Mr Kenneth?'
>
> 'No, no, lady', said Cecil, shaking her head with great solemnity, 'if you'll believe me, I never saw any thing *by* common. But we have a word that goes in our country, that "a doe will come from the strangers'

190 *Teri Doerksen*

land to couch in the best den in Glen Eredine." And the wisest man in Killifoildich, and tha's Donald MacIan, told me, that "the loveliest of the Saxon flowers would root and spread next the hall hearth of Castle Eredine".[36]

Unlike the hothouse flowers that Ellen once coveted, whose nurture caused the near-death of Campbell the gardener, Ellen herself is now 'the loveliest of the Saxon flowers' whose destiny is to take root in Scottish soil and propagate unification. The proposed union between Ellen and Maitland was initially characterized by affection without policy, but the outcome of the novel's didactic impetus is not only Ellen's moral and religious transformation, but a marriage of policy united with affection. Both Ellen and Maitland are hybridized creations, with Maitland's mercantile Englishness and hereditary Southern aristocratic sensibilities balancing Ellen's blend of English and Scottish class and moral characteristics. The outcome of this didactic *Bildungsroman* is a re-imagined Act of Union, in which both parties incorporate aspects of the other's origins without losing the variation and complexity of their identities.

Like *Discipline*, Susan Ferrier's *Marriage* presents the reader with an interpretation of the Act of Union and Great Britain's subsequent progress toward a more inherently felt unification of its component countries, but unlike *Discipline*, Ferrier's novel represents the transformation taking place over generations, rather than in the course of a single courtship. The Scotland and England represented in the earlier parts of Ferrier's *Marriage* are never united, even when English and Scottish people marry, and while England is represented as the more politically powerful of the two, it is also presented as a morally bankrupt nation. 'Marriage', here, becomes a metaphor for the unequal alliance between nations, forced together in an unhappy union. By the end of the novel, however, a very few happy marriages are modelled within the text, each of them taking place between two people of mixed Scottish and English ancestry with a strong sense of national, moral, and religious feeling connecting them. Like *Discipline*, then, *Marriage* becomes a careful allegory of the progress toward a more complete union between Scotland and England.

Marriage is a novel that explores displacement and identity. Earlier English novels, like *Mansfield Park* (1814), often explored displacement for a single character; Austen, for example, describes Fanny Price's gradual acclimatization to her aunt and uncle's home, followed by a moment of extreme dissociation with her previous home when she is thrust back to Portsmouth, and a re-identification with Mansfield Park when she returns. *Marriage*, on the other hand, is a two-generational novel, like Inchbald's *Simple Story* (1791) or Brontë's *Wuthering Heights* (1847). As in Colley's formulation, each protagonist develops a sense of her own identity in a sense of dissimilarity from those without, but the longer time period allows for a perspective on Union over the course of time, instead of in a single historical moment. *Marriage* also extends the concept of intergenerational displacement with a pattern of deaths that occur at key moments, allowing an older generation to be replaced with scions of the newer generation, and suggesting the need to displace older ideas and immovable individuals before progress can be made toward Union.

The first half of *Marriage* tells the story of Lady Juliana, the Earl of Courtland's daughter, who refuses to marry a wealthy but unattractive duke, and instead marries a young Scottish soldier for love. Her introduction in the opening chapter is, Monnickendam notes, 'one of the most dramatically effective openings in fiction', and Ferrier has packed it with her trademark motifs: 'vanity, lapdogs with daft names, wit, irony in company with indirect style'.[37] As this pithy analysis suggests, Ferrier creates a Lady Juliana who is both shallow and selfish, and who, in a sort of reverse-Pemberley moment, is brought to a new sense of the importance of ready cash when she sees the poverty of the 'estate' to which her husband takes her in Scotland. Juliana is disgusted with Scottish food, customs, people, and hospitality, and not long after the birth of her twin daughters, she returns to England and never returns to Scotland. She takes the prettier twin, Adelaide, with her; the other, Mary, she leaves to be raised by Mr and Mrs Douglas, Mary's good, moral, and religious aunt and uncle in Scotland. Later in the novel, the Scottish twin is sent to live with her mother and is repulsed by the extravagant wealth and moral heedlessness of her relations. Like Fanny Price, she finds the transition complex, difficult, and very educational. Both encounter emotional neglect where they had thought they would find kinship and affection, but Fanny also contends with physical poverty, while Mary meets with moral impoverishment amidst opulence. In Austen's novel, the differences between the Prices and the Bertrams are primarily those of class and between Fanny and the Crawfords are primarily moral. In Ferrier's novel, however, class and moral differences are both embedded within differences of national identity, and the two-generation structure suggests the shift in national identity over time.

The first half of *Marriage* suggests the complexity of developing a sense of national identity in the immediate wake of the Act of Union; marriages between English and Scottish citizens offer insight into the vexed nature of such a transition. The first of these marriages takes place between Lady Juliana, the English earl's daughter and Henry Douglas, the second son of a Scottish laird. The match is clearly doomed from the outset. Juliana, shallow and silly, is described as damaged by a flawed education:

> Educated for the sole purpose of forming a brilliant establishment, of catching the eye, and captivating the senses, the cultivation of her mind or the correction of her temper had formed no part of the system by which that aim was to be accomplished.[38]

Exterior appearance has been emphasized to the exclusion of substance, so, unsurprisingly, exterior appearance is what she privileges in making her own choice, and she marries 'her handsome but penniless lover' over an anvil in Scotland, taking with her in her exile 'two dogs, a tame squirrel, and a mackaw, [to complete] the establishment',[39] as if to emphasize that marriage had not imbued Lady Juliana with either maturity or wisdom.

The second marriage takes place between Henry's brother Archibald Douglas, heir to a small Scottish estate, and the orphaned half-Scottish Alicia Malcolm. They wed only because Alicia has found true love with her cousin, Sir Edmund, but has been forbidden to marry him by his mother, who suspects her 'of having plotted to ally her base Scotch blood to the noble blood of the Audleys'.[40] Out of duty, she marries another to keep her cousin from pursuing her. The new Mrs Douglas is posited as a near-ideal hybrid, 'blending the frankness of the Scotch with the polished reserve of the English woman, [with a] total exemption from vanity'.[41] Her marriage, however, is lacklustre and childless, and both she and her husband suffer from the barrenness of the union. The two marriages offer contrapuntal images of the union of England and Scotland: one is characterized by love with no sense, and the other by sense with no love. As Defoe might have re-characterized it, one is a union of affection without policy, and the other a union of policy without affection. As in *Discipline*, policy, here, is the privileged category: the marriage of affection dissolves rapidly in the face of hardship, while the marriage of policy manages to endure, even if it is unable to perpetuate itself. Where *Discipline* showed courtships, however, *Marriage* shows the actual unions and their outcomes.

And, the text suggests, policy alone holds the promise of a more coherent union over the course of time, but only policy together with affection holds the promise of long-term success. As the novel progresses into the present day of the Regency, a new set of marriages are introduced, holding with them the potential for a union that unites policy and affection. Mary's English cousin Lady Emily, daughter of the current Earl of Courtland, loves Mary's half-Scottish younger brother Edward, and they are promised to one another with the full approval of both families. Mary's half-Scottish sister Adelaide, grown vapid and vain under her mother's tutelage, nevertheless develops a true mutual affection for her cousin Lord Lindore, Lady Emily's brother, to whom she is attracted because of 'his inconstancy and libertine principles'.[42]

Mary herself finds true love while staying with her mother in England, and her alliance provides the template for an ideal union of Scottish and English characters into a single national identity. Like Mary, Charles Lennox is the child of a Scottish father and an English mother, and like her he has been nurtured by a woman who has a strong sense of national identity, but who values religious and moral character above blind adherence to national loyalties. For Mary's guardian, Mrs Douglas, 'To engraft into her infant soul the purest precepts of religion was ... the chief aim', and 'charity and goodwill' combined with the natural graces are the heart of wholesome education.[43] Presbyterianism is not distinguished in the text from Anglicanism; both are described simply as 'pure religion', in contrast with the wary eye the novel cast toward the Methodists.[44] Lennox is raised by a godly woman who lately has gone blind; they meet because Mary from charity nurses the blind mother through a lengthy illness. Mary is raised in Scotland but transplanted into England; Lennox is raised in England but serves in the army in the north and on the Continent; both are thorough hybrids, combining characteristics of the English and the Scottish national characters and blending them with both affection and policy. Lennox turns out, purely by chance, to be the heir to a small estate in England and also the large estate next door to the one inherited by Archibald and Alicia Douglas, uniting portions of the two countries under a single ownership, governed by shared religious precepts and mutual heritage.

As a contrast, the novel presents the match between Lindore and Adelaide as a kind of morality play, which has implications for this reading as well. Adelaide becomes jealous when Lindore has an affair with a mutual acquaintance and, partly from pique, partly from avarice, she marries the elderly and intransigent English Duke of Altamont. When his wealth turns out to be accompanied by ill humour and a profound lack of fancy dress balls, she elopes with her cousin Lindore and, like Fanny Price's cousin Maria, is relegated to the Continent in perpetuity, but married to Lindore in a match that loses its charm for both principals almost immediately. Adelaide's marriage, characterized by lack of affection and lack of policy, suggests the remaining threats to the continuance of a settled union: Adelaide first finds that 'of all yokes, the most insupportable is the yoke of an obstinate fool'. The narrator makes clear that 'good sense or good humour on either side would have gracefully yielded'[45] – but without sense and humour, policy and affection, the alliance crumbles into oppression. The two marriages formed in policy, in contrast, Mary's and Emily's, flourish, and both couples happily blend Scottish and English values in a single unified family, with Mary settling with her husband in Scotland and Lady Emily settling with her husband in England, but both maintaining close sisterly ties with one another.

Ferrier, like Brunton, is invested in constructing a developmental narrative of nationhood out of the pooled discourses of the didactic and domestic novel. Both Brunton's and Ferrier's novels, positioned at the apex of the late eighteenth-century rise in women's didactic fiction, exemplify the complexity of a subgenre at its pinnacle: they integrate elements that appeal to readers of the domestic novel, the regional novel, the didactic novel – and incorporate references that make clear their affinity with the political novels of the late century as well. Poised at the culmination of the Scottish Regency, both novelists enact a complex series of negotiations regarding Scottish, English, and British identities, and perhaps inevitably reimagine the Act of Union in the process. Although they work on different timelines – *Marriage*

194 *Teri Doerksen*

across two generations and *Discipline* in only one – they both engage in creating a kind of national *Bildungsroman* to present complementary representations of the Act of Union, and each does so while maintaining a sense of the complex regional identities within each area of Britain. Ellen Percy's literal and metaphorical journey toward a unified moral and national identity in *Discipline* parallels the Douglas family's movement toward unions that blend policy and affection; Ellen's marriage to Maitland and Mary's to Charles Lennox both combine Scottish and English elements in each member of the couple. The single unified British nation suggested at the ends of these novels is the result of a joining together of multifaceted, non-monolithic regions cross-hatched with dozens of dialects, cultural histories, and practices. In both *Marriage* and *Discipline*, the characters that metaphorically enact the union embody aspects of many regional, socio-economic, cultural, religious, moral, and class categories, suggesting that the final union of both policy and affection is possible not because it eliminates differences but because it embraces them.

Notes

1. D. Defoe, *Union and No Union. Being an Enquiry in the Grievances of the Scots. And how far they are right or wrong, who alledge that the Union is Dissolved* (London, 1713), pp. 3–4.
2. L. Colley, *Britons: Forging the Nation 1707–1837* (New Haven, CT: Yale University Press, 1992), p. 17.
3. B. Anderson, *Imagined Communities: Reflections on the Origin and Spread of Nationalism* (New York: Verso, 1991), p. 6.
4. Ibid., 44.
5. E. Gottlieb, *Feeling British: Sympathy and National Identity in Scottish and English Writings, 1707–1832* (Lewisburg, PA: Bucknell University Press, 2007), p. 21.
6. Ibid.
7. M. M. Martin, *The Mighty Scot: Nation, Gender, and the Nineteenth-Century Mystique of Scottish Masculinity* (Albany, NY: State University of New York Press, 2009), p. 12.
8. K. Kirkpatrick, Introduction to *Marriage* by Susan Ferrier (Oxford: Oxford University Press, 2001), p. vii.
9. M. McKerrow, *Mary Brunton, The Forgotten Scottish Novelist* (Orkney: The Orcadian Limited, 2001).
10. D. Le Faye (ed.), *Jane Austen's Letters* (Oxford: Oxford University Press, 1995), p. 234.
11. W. C. Macready, *The Diaries of William Charles Macready, 1833–1851 with 49 Portraits,* vol. 1, ed. William Toynbee (New York: G. P. Putnam and Sons, 1912), p. 107.
12. Anonymous, 'Miss Ferrier's Novels', *Temple Bar: A London Magazine for Town and Country Readers,* 54:216 (1878), pp. 315 and 319.
13. Ibid., p. 308.
14. See also C. Grogan, Chapter 9 of this volume, p. 167.
15. M. Brunton, *Discipline* (New York: Pandora Press, 1986), p. 1.

16. Ibid., p. 3.
17. Ibid., p. 22, italics mine.
18. Ibid., p. 23.
19. Ibid., pp. 338–39.
20. Ibid., p. 250. The term 'Southron', meaning 'person from the south', was used by the Scots to refer to the English, and suggests the Scottishness of the Grahams while simultaneously reaffirming that they are descended from an English mother.
21. A. McIntosh, 'Domestic Fiction', in G. Norquay (ed.), *The Edinburgh Companion to Scottish Women's Writing* (Edinburgh: Edinburgh University Press, 2012), p. 55.
22. I. Bour, 'Mary Brunton's Novels, or, the Twilight of Sensibility', *Scottish Literary Journal*, 24:2 (1997), pp. 24–35, on p. 30.
23. Brunton, *Discipline*, p. 86.
24. Ibid., p. 142.
25. Ibid., p. 152.
26. Ibid., p. 161.
27. Ibid., p. 170.
28. Ibid., p. 179.
29. Ibid., p. 186.
30. A. Monnickendam, *The Novels of Sir Walter Scott and His Literary Relations: Mary Brunton, Susan Ferrier and Christian Johnstone* (New York: Palgrave Macmillan, 2013), p. 49. Monnickendam, of course, is referencing Katie Trumpener's arguments in *Bardic Nationalism: The Romantic Novel and the British Empire* (Princeton, NJ: Princeton University Press, 1997), pp. 128–61.
31. Brunton, *Discipline*, p. 285.
32. Ibid., p. 295.
33. Ibid., p. 298.
34. Ibid., p. 299.
35. Ibid., p. 300.
36. Ibid., p. 247.
37. Monnickendam, *Novels of Sir Walter Scott*, p. 73.
38. S. E. Ferrier, *Marriage* (Oxford: Oxford University Press, 2001), p. 4.
39. Ibid., p. 7.
40. Ibid., p. 78.
41. Ibid., p. 75.
42. Ibid., p. 280.
43. Ibid., pp. 158–59.
44. Ibid., p. 251.
45. Ibid., p. 396.

Afterword
Lessons Learned

Shelley King

In bringing together ten essays on ten women writers who published didactic novels between 1790 and 1820, Hilary Havens has, in fact, embarked on a didactic mission of her own, showing what lessons might be learned by reconsidering novels by female authors of note, including Maria Edgeworth, Elizabeth Hamilton, Mary Hays, Hannah More, and Charlotte Smith. The choice of the didactic novel as a field of study is challenging – the characteristics of didactic literature can seem amorphous or potentially all-encompassing, as recent collections focused on the genre indicate. In setting the parameters for *What Nature Does Not Teach: Didactic Literature in the Medieval and Early-Modern Periods*, editor Juanita Ruys establishes that 'a text can be considered didactic if it was created, transmitted, or received as a text designed to teach, instruct, advise, edify, inculcate morals, or modify and regulate behaviour'.[1] Encompassing texts as diverse as how-to manuals, spiritual autobiographies, and encyclopaedia entries, the study of didactic literature offers a potentially infinite scope. In *Didactic Novels and British Women's Writing, 1790–1820*, Havens adopts the pragmatic strategy of carefully delimiting the field: her collection constitutes an important juncture in the study of Romantic women writers by offering a deliberately narrow focus on a specific type of didactic fiction – novels by women whose works explore of the relationship between the private sphere of women's lives and the public sphere of political and social debate. Studies of didactic fiction usually emphasize works designed either for children or for socially disadvantaged audiences. That is not the case in this volume, where Hannah More's authorship of the *Cheap Repository Tracts* (1795–97) earns less notice than her role as the creative mind behind *Cœlebs in Search of a Wife* (1808). Similarly, Maria Edgeworth is examined not primarily as the author of *Practical Education* (1798) and *Early Lessons* (1801), but instead as a novelist whose works address a young adult rather than a juvenile audience in *Moral Tales* (1802) and an adult audience in *Patronage* (1814); Charlotte Smith features not as the author of multiple children's books including *Rural Walks* (1795), *Rambles Further* (1796), and *Minor Morals* (1798), but as a writer developing her understanding of the implications of the French Revolution through a series of novels for adult readers. In shifting the focus of interest away from the power imbalance normally associated with negative responses to the didactic – teacher/pupil, adult child, upper class/lower class – Havens enables her readers to take a more nuanced and positive look at what the didactic novel as a distinct genre might offer women writers in this period. As Havens points out in her Introduction, this collection seeks 'to demonstrate the reforming potential of this feminine and ostensibly constricting genre, which enabled women to engage with concurrent ideologies despite their invisibility in more public forums'.[2] I would argue her collection does this and more: it engages in the recuperation of 'didactic' as a term of respect if not approbation in the literary history of the novel.

Didactic literature has not in general been well received by contemporary critics, who have resisted finding literary merit in its pages. The reception of Maria Edgeworth's work is a case in point. In 'Maria Edgeworth and the Romance of Real Life', Michael Gamer points out that she is 'an author whose didacticism often has struck modern readers as either gendered liability, technical regression, or familial obligation'.[3] Gamer's comment reflects the degree to which didactic fiction has frequently been understood as the prerogative of women writers (often associated with works for children and by implication less important to literary history) or as a technically unsophisticated subgenre in the history of the novel, but seldom as a conscious or astute choice of genre. Nor is Edgeworth's case unusual – more often than not critics of women writers of the Romantic period have been somewhat apologetic regarding the didactic leanings of their authors, suggesting that they succeed in spite of rather than because of the lessons their fictions might teach. Havens's collection reverses this tendency, locating the success of Romantic women writers in terms of both the marketplace and literary history precisely in their choice of the didactic novel as a medium.

There can be no doubt that by the standards of the time, didactic fiction by women was often highly successful in the marketplace. As Patricia Demers points out in her essay on Hannah More's *Cœlebs In Search of a Wife*,

> It is not only a synthesis of her talents; it remains a gauge of her popular appeal. Garnering mixed reviews, her religious novel was a curious bestseller that went through twelve London editions in its first year and was subsequently translated into French and German. In fact, *Cœlebs* 'brought more profits even than [Sir Walter Scott's] *Waverley*'.[4]

Elizabeth Hamilton's *Cottagers of Glenburnie* (1808), if not so profitable as More's novel, nevertheless enjoyed wide distribution and influence, as Claire Grogan notes.[5] Didactic fiction in this period was also widely reviewed, with varying degrees of praise for the lessons offered in its pages. Amelia Opie's *Simple Tales* (1806), for example, were celebrated as being 'of that unexceptionable nature in point of morality, that they may be with perfect safety put into the hands of persons of any age or sex'.[6] What critics valued in Opie's

198 *Shelley King*

work was the balance she struck between instruction and entertainment. As the reviewer of her *Tales of Real Life* (1813) notes in *The Monthly Review*,

> While some authors are satisfied with merely amusing, and others almost affront their readers by the pertinacity of their admonitions, Mrs Opie appears to take a happy medium; generally proposing to herself to shew the effects of some virtue or the consequences of some error, and seldom losing sight of this object, though she courteously allows her readers to draw their own conclusions from her tales.[7]

In short, the modern critical revulsion normally expressed toward any work with even a hint of didacticism is both anachronistic and misleading: Romantic readers valued entertaining didactic fiction, and Romantic women writers found in the genre a means of enabling their participation in the most important social and political debates of the day.

The chronological structure of *Didactic Novels and British Women's Writing, 1790–1820* is designed to enable readers to observe the development of didactic content and style as the women's novels represented engage first with the political issues associated with the French Revolution and subsequently focus on the British nationalisms that emerged in its wake. Readers of essay collections, however, need not be bound by chronology and printed sequence. Assembled in another configuration, the essays in this collection offer a narrative complementary to the chronological survey. Readers taking an alternative path of engaging with the chapters might develop a different focus by considering them in groupings that emphasize thematic connections. Such groupings would include the chapters by Ada Sharpe and Eleanor Ty, Jonathan Sadow, Andrew O'Malley, and Grogan that work to define the complexity of the didactic novel as a genre as developed by Hays and Fenwick. A second grouping would bring together the chapters by Megan Woodworth and Havens that invite readers to rethink critical responses to the didactic approach adopted by West and Edgeworth. Finally, chapters by Morgan Rooney, Teri Doerksen, Sharon M. Setzer, and Demers encourage readers to consider the necessity of understanding the role played by the historical moment, whether in examining writers like Smith and More whose work reflects an evolving commitment to the genre across time, or the importance of a clearly defined cultural moment in evaluating the didactic impact of work by Brunton, Ferrier, and Robinson. Approaching the collection in this way complicates our understanding of didactic fiction as practised by women writers in this period by creating new comparisons and conversations.

Sharpe and Ty's chapter 'Mary Hays and the Didactic Novel in the 1790s' provides an excellent starting place, not only for the clarity with which it outlines the conscious experimentation with genre Hays brought to her work, but also for the way in which it articulates the connections between what has been identified as radical and conservative didacticism. An accomplished theorist of genre, Mary Hays was forthright in asserting the role fiction such as hers might play in the evolution of the novel. In her 1797 essay 'On Novel Writing', Hays describes the social value of the novel as a literary form:

> The business of familiar narrative should be to describe life and manners in real or probable situations, to delineate the human mind in its endless varieties, to develope [*sic*] the heart, to paint the passions, to trace the springs of action, to interest the imagination, exercise the affections, and awaken the powers of the mind. A good novel ought to be subservient to the purposes of truth and philosophy.... The excellence of a novel is of a distinct nature, and must be the result of an attentive observance of mankind, acute discernment, exquisite moral sensibility, and an intimate acquaintance with human passions and powers.[8]

In particular, she argues that the moral – hence didactic – value of the modern novel resides less in providing ideal models for the reader to follow than in offering insights into the social sources and personal consequences of real human behaviour:

> A more effectual lesson might perhaps be deduced from tracing the pernicious consequences of an erroneous judgment, a wrong step, an imprudent action, an indulged and intemperate affection, a bad habit, in a character in other respects amiable and virtuous, than in painting chimerical perfection and visionary excellence, which rarely, if ever, existed.[9]

As Sharpe and Ty note, in her discussion of the 'business of familiar narrative' Hays 'outlines an alternate theory of didactic fiction that focuses on the function of narrative in exercising and developing critical thinking in the (female) reader by tracing human trial and error "in real and probable situations"'.[10] Challenging critics such as Lisa Wood, who 'equates didacticism with antirevolutionary ideology in women's writing of this period, and describes the popular didactic novel as "concerned less with literary effect than with conveying and enforcing a conformist moral message"', Sharpe and Ty assert that the didactic function of narrative articulated by Hays suggests that didactic fiction as a genre embraces a wider range of political positions than has heretofore been recognized.[11] They also identify two distinct modes of instruction in didactic fiction by women in this period: that of Hays, which proceeds through reflection on immediate experience and on the recasting of familiar narrative tropes to elicit further reflection on social and political challenges faced by women, and that of writers such as Brunton and Edgeworth, who are 'first and foremost concerned with modelling "correct" ways of seeing as the basis for the cultivation of rational self-control' and who 'set out to correct female characters' modes of perception in order to induct them into disciplined subject positions'.[12]

200 *Shelley King*

Sharpe and Ty's argument for the importance of recognizing genre experiments in approaching didactic fiction in this period is also taken up by Sadow in his chapter 'Moral and Generic Corruption in Eliza Fenwick's *Secresy*'. He asserts that although 'Women's didactic fiction of the late eighteenth century largely acted as a form of political dialogue', an essential 'part of that political and gendered discussion was a self-conscious inquiry into the nature, use, and value of fictional modes'. Noting that 'the self-conscious understanding of genre exhibited by these works – *Secresy* (1795) in particular – suggests, if not transcendence, a generic complexity that is often ignored in studies of didactic fiction',[13] Sadow demonstrates the ways in which Fenwick wrestles as a writer with the constraints of the dominant plot structures governing the novel in this period. Together these chapters establish the need for recognition of the narrative sophistication deployed in didactic novels by authors such as Hays and Fenwick.

From this beginning readers might turn next to chapters by O'Malley and Grogan who complicate our understanding of the didactic novel by shifting focus from the peer-to-peer stance adopted by Hays and Fenwick to examine writers who play with questions of authority and audience. O'Malley looks at the emergence of a new young adult target, examining Edgeworth's *Moral Tales* and a political education. In 'Maria Edgeworth's *Moral Tales* and the Problem of Youth Rebellion in a Revolutionary Age', he draws attention to the contribution made by Edgeworth to the creation of a new category of literature – what is now referred to as Young Adult fiction. As a writer who had already established a reputation as a novelist with *Castle Rackrent* (1800) and as an educator with *Practical Education* (1800) and *Early Lessons*, Edgeworth was well positioned to recognize both the romance of revolution that appealed to young people and the need for sensitive guidance. As O'Malley writes,

> Despite an apparent unwillingness to make direct connections between youthful rebellion and the revolutionary climate, Edgeworth clearly felt that this particular historical juncture demanded a literary response geared to a category of young people – no longer strictly children, nor properly matured into adulthood – whose passions had taken on a new and dangerous aspect in the period.[14]

Drawing on Perry Nodelman's work establishing the 'hidden adult' in books for children, O'Malley's chapter also contributes a means of thinking about the role played by figures of moral authority in a range of didactic novels, who are often older and almost exclusively wiser than the readers or young characters in the narrative.

Grogan's chapter 'Didacticism after Hannah More: Elizabeth Hamilton's *Cottagers of Glenburnie*' also productively directs attention to the power dynamic associated with the audience for didactic novels. By placing Hamilton's novel in the context of More's *Cheap Repository Tracts*, Grogan

Afterword   201

highlights the complexity of its didactic stance. Quoting astutely from More's comments denigrating her audience, Grogan establishes the power imbalance that marks the didacticism of the *Tracts*, in which social superiors set moral lessons for lower-class readers, in order to argue that Hamilton addresses multiple audiences in her novel:

> Somewhere during composition, her narrative became more complicated – what began as a tract ended up as a novel. More's work might have been the starting point, but Hamilton's finishing point offers a more complex and nuanced tale. Her concern that middle-class readers (whom she implies would not be critical of a simple tract) might not respond as favourably to *The Cottagers of Glenburnie* suggests that the poor are not the only intended readers of the work. Thus, while More implicated middle-class readers in her tracts through their roles as purchasers and distributors, Hamilton's work actually provides a series of plot lines that follow different social classes.[15]

Together the chapters by O'Malley and Grogan point to the range of audiences imagined by didactic novelists and the reach of their influence across age groups and social classes.

Having established the scope of didactic fiction as a genre as practised by women novelists in the period, readers of this collection may then turn to specific instances in which close-reading from the perspective of genre enables new insights into familiar texts. Woodworth's chapter '"Vehicles for Words of Sound Doctrine": Jane West's Didactic Fiction' and Havens's 'Maria Edgeworth's Revisions to Nationalism and Didacticism in *Patronage*' offer new readings of novels that have been dismissed as merely didactic by contemporary critics. Taking Miriam Wallace's exhortation 'calling for novels of the 1790s to be "read attentively" for how they use "political romance and parody, how they engage larger political and social debates, and how they render both parodic and stock figures"'[16] as a model, Woodworth challenges readers to re-examine the role of West's authoritative narratorial character Prudentia Homespun. Wallace argues that by looking beyond the simplistic critical move of separating didactic fiction into Jacobin and anti-Jacobin camps, 'we stand to develop a richer sense of how narrative fiction contributed to constructing an engaged and engaging public sphere of ideological debate'.[17] Woodworth makes the case for recognizing West as an author who possesses the narrative sophistication to deploy Homespun, the putative moral authority in the text, as a figure who might also be regarded as an object of satire.

If Woodworth illustrates how rethinking the implications of didactic literary tropes might lead to a re-evaluation of the textual complexity of a novel heretofore dismissed as simplistically adumbrating moral and political conservativism, Havens, in 'Maria Edgeworth's Revisions to Nationalism and Didacticism in *Patronage*', reminds scholars that close attention to textual revision can reveal subtle nuances of didactic intent even within a novel that was severely critiqued for its didactic approach at the time of its initial publication. Reviews of *Patronage* might celebrate its moral purpose yet still find that the novel 'tires us by constant repetition, and diffuses an air of uniformity, approaching to dulness, over the whole work'. Edgeworth's response to such criticism is the subject of Havens's inquiry, which shows the conscious steps the author took to soften and reshape the didactic language in multiple revisions to subsequent editions of the novel. Havens argues that 'while her revisions to the 1825 edition of *Patronage* address and dismantle the cloying didacticism that annoyed her reviewers, they also silenced the novel's most strident depictions of nationalism ... and altered the novel's generic identity'.[18] Engaging with editorial revision in *Patronage* thus draws attention to the need for close scrutiny of specific dates and editions when engaging with the didactic novel in this period.

One final set of chapters completes the study by demonstrating the tension between rigorous engagement with the specific historical moment and recognition that didactic strategies and content sometimes remain constant across a career and sometimes change and evolve radically. Rooney in 'Charlotte Smith and the Persistence of the Past', analyses the author's sustained response to Edmund Burke's *Reflections* across three novels and half a decade, mapping her strategies of critique and diminishing faith in the success of revolutionary ideologies. Rooney's precise anatomy of the development of Smith's thought is balanced by Doerksen's 'A National *Bildungsroman*: Didacticism and National Identity in Mary Brunton's *Discipline* and Susan Edmonstone Ferrier's *Marriage*', which compares the representation of English and Scottish identity in almost contemporaneous novels addressing the same political issues. Doerksen argues:

> The novels' inherent didacticism becomes a platform to reinterpret the Act of Union – the uniting of Scotland and England in these novels is a process under constant negotiation. *Discipline* and *Marriage* use and modify the familiar discourses of domestic and didactic fiction to illustrate the internal changes that must take place before Scotland and England can achieve a union of affection, and not merely of policy.[19]

Smith, Ferrier, and Brunton each address the key national political issues of their day, using familiar didactic tropes including marriage and inheritance to develop parallels between the domestic experiences of young people, especially women, and contemporary public-sphere political events.

If Rooney insists on close attention to fine degrees of change in Smith's ideas over a six-year span of time, Demers, in 'Lessons of Courtship: Hannah More's *Cœlebs in Search of a Wife*', demonstrates that this exercise in Evangelical didacticism in the guise of a courtship novel reveals the consistency of More's political vision. As Demers asserts, her essay 'explores some possible answers [to questions of character construction and narrative skill] by attending to and assessing the stability of More's moral compass throughout her career'.[20] By contrast, Sharon Setzer, in 'Epistolary Exposés: The Marriage Market, the Slave Trade and the "Cruel Business" of War in Mary Robinson's *Angelina*', demonstrates the power of didactic fiction to model change in the public perception of an author's character. Unlike Hannah More, Mary Robinson might seem the least likely candidate to stand as a proponent of moral didacticism, given her early career on the stage and subsequent fame as a royal mistress. Nevertheless, in *Angelina* Robinson astutely deploys public-sphere debates regarding slavery and the war with France to illuminate the condition of women in Britain in the 1790s while creating a didactic authority in the character of the Marchioness. As Setzer argues, the Marchioness is 'Characterized as an "affectionate monitress" and an "excellent preceptress",... [who] figures Robinson's reinvention of herself as a moralist, one who would ultimately claim affiliation with the radical school of Mary Wollstonecraft rather than with the conservative camp of Hannah More'.[21]

* * *

The essays in *Didactic Novels and British Women's Writing, 1790–1820* thus constitute an intensive course in the contribution made by didactic fiction to the history of the novel and to the history of women's writing between 1790 and 1820. Taken together they reveal the sophisticated and nuanced literary history belonging to a genre that has long been dismissed or treated apologetically as somehow necessarily falling short of literary excellence. Perhaps its most important contribution, however, is to invite readers to reconsider their own critical prejudices regarding didacticism – to remember a moment in literary history where having one's work denominated as 'didactic' might be regarded as a mark of approbation, and when the emerging genre of the didactic novel provided a means of empowering women writers to participate in public-sphere debates regarding social and political change.

Notes

1. J. F. Ruys, 'Introduction: Approaches to Didactic Literature – Meaning, Intent, Audience, Social Effect', in J. F. Ruys (ed.), *What Nature Does Not Teach: Didactic Literature in the Medieval and Early-Modern Periods* (Turnhout: Brepols, 2008), pp. 1–38, on p. 5.
2. H. Havens, Introduction of this volume, p. 2.
3. M. Gamer, 'Maria Edgeworth and the Romance of Real Life', *NOVEL: A Forum on Fiction*, 34:2 (2001), pp. 232–66, on p. 233.
4. P. Demers, Chapter 6 of this volume, p. 107.
5. C. Grogan, Chapter 9 of this volume, p. 167.
6. *Literary Journal, a Review*, 2, n.s. (1806), p. 167.
7. *Monthly Review*, 72 (1813), p. 326.

8. M. Hays, 'On Novel Writing', *Monthly Magazine*, 4 (1797), pp. 180–81, on p. 181.
9. Ibid.
10. A. Sharpe and E. Ty, Chapter 5 of this volume, p. 93.
11. Ibid., p. 92.
12. Ibid., pp. 98–99.
13. J. Sadow, Chapter 4 of this volume, pp. 74–75.
14. A. O'Malley, Chapter 7 of this volume, p. 123.
15. Grogan, Chapter 9 of this volume, p. 165.
16. M. Woodworth, Chapter 2 of this volume, p. 38.
17. M. L. Wallace, 'Crossing from "Jacobin" to "Anti-Jacobin": Rethinking the Terms of English Jacobinism', in P. Cass and L. H. Peer (eds), *Romantic Border Crossings* (Aldershot, UK and Burlington, VT: Ashgate, 2008), pp. 99–112, on p. 100. Quoted in Woodworth, Chapter 2 of this volume, pp. 38–39.
18. H. Havens, Chapter 8 of this volume, pp. 142, 144.
19. T. Doerksen, Chapter 10 of this volume, p. 181.
20. Demers, Chapter 6 of this volume, p. 108.
21. S. Setzer, Chapter 3 of this volume, p. 56.

List of Contributors

Patricia Demers is Distinguished University Professor of English and Comparative Literature at the University of Alberta. Her recent publications include an edition of Hannah More's *Cœlebs in Search of a Wife* (Broadview Press, 2007) and an edited collection, *From Instruction to Delight: Children's Literature to 1850* (Oxford, 2015, 4th edition). She also has an essay on More in *Teaching British Women Playwrights of the Restoration and Eighteenth Century*, ed. B. Nelson and C. Burroughs (MLA, 2010) and on More and Grace Irwin in *Bluestockings Now! The Evolution of a Social Role*, ed. D. Heller (Ashgate, 2015). She has edited Lady Anne Bacon's translation (1564) of *Apologia Ecclesiae Anglicanae* for the Modern Humanities Research Association (2016).

Teri Doerksen is Professor of English in the Department of English and Modern Languages at Mansfield University of Pennsylvania. She has recently published articles on illustrations in Frances Burney and Ann Radcliffe, and on representations of Catholicism in Samuel Richardson. She is currently finishing an article about Richardson's complex mentoring relationship with Anna Meades entitled 'Mediating "Cleomira": Richardson, Celebrity, and Editorial Mediation in Anna Meades' *Sir William Harrington*', and is working on an edition of Meades's novel with annotations of Richardson's editorial intervention. Her current book project, *The Catholic Remains: Gender, National Religious Identity and Appropriated Catholicism in the English Novel, 1748–1860*, argues for a connection between eighteenth-century political tensions, changing representations of the Catholic, and the construction of English national religious identity in the late eighteenth and early nineteenth century.

Claire Grogan is Professor and Department Chair of English at Bishop's University in Sherbrooke, Quebec. She has published *Politics and Genre in the Works of Elizabeth Hamilton 1756–1816* (Ashgate, 2012). She is also the editor of Thomas Paine's *Rights of Man*, Elizabeth Hamilton's *Memoirs of Modern Philosophers*, and Jane Austen's *Northanger Abbey* for Broadview Press. Her chapter on Jane Austen and film adaptation appeared in *Women, Popular Culture and the Eighteenth Century* with University of Toronto Press (2012). Her current research considers the role of political caricature in England during the 1790s.

206 *List of Contributors*

Hilary Havens is Assistant Professor of English at the University of Tennessee. Her most recent work has appeared in *Digital Humanities Quarterly*, *Journal for Eighteenth-Century Studies*, and *SEL: Studies in English Literature, 1500–1900*. Her current project focuses on revision and print culture in the long-eighteenth-century novel. With Peter Sabor, she is the author of the *Oxford Bibliographies Online* entry for Frances Burney, and she has published articles on Burney in *The Age of Johnson* and *XVII–XVIII: Revue de la Société d'Études Anglo-Américaines des XVIIe et XVIIIe Siècles*. Her work has been supported by fellowships from the National Endowment for the Humanities, the New York Public Library, and the Huntington Library.

Shelley King is Professor and Head of the Department of English at Queen's University. She and co-editor John B. Pierce have published *The Collected Poems of Amelia Alderson Opie* (Oxford University Press, 2009), as well as Opie's *The Father and Daughter* with *Dangers of Coquetry* (Broadview Press, 2003) and *Adeline Mowbray* (Oxford World's Classics, 1999). Most recently she is the author of '"To delineate the human mind in its endless varieties": Integral Lyric and Characterization in the Tales of Amelia Opie' in Courtney Weiss and Kate Parker's *Eighteenth-Century Poetry and the Rise of the Novel Reconsidered* (Bucknell University Press, December 2013) and co-author of 'The Rediscovery of Amelia Opie's Cromer Notebook', *Notes and Queries*, 61:4 (2014).

Andrew O'Malley is Associate Professor of English at Ryerson University. He is the author of *The Making of the Modern Child: Children's Literature and Childhood in the Late Eighteenth Century* (Routledge, 2003) and *Children's Literature, Popular Culture, and Robinson Crusoe* (Palgrave, 2012). His other recent publications include articles in *Eighteenth-Century Life*, *The Lion and the Unicorn*, *English Studies in Canada*, and *The Journal for Eighteenth-Century Studies*, as well as book chapters on eighteenth-century chapbooks, the figure of the child in eighteenth-century fiction, and children's robinsonades. He is currently working on a digital humanities project investigating how the idea of 'innocence' shaped discourses around childhood and fuelled controversies over children's consumption of popular culture (especially comic books) in the mid-twentieth century.

Morgan Rooney is an Adjunct Research Professor and educational developer at Carleton University in Ottawa, Ontario, as well as a part-time instructor for the University of Ottawa. He is the author of *The French Revolution Debate and the British Novel, 1790–1814: The Struggle for History's Authority* (Bucknell University Press, 2013) and has published articles on the French Revolution debate, women novelists in the Romantic period, and the anti-Jacobin novel in journals such as *Eighteenth-Century Studies* and *Eighteenth-Century Fiction*. His teaching ranges from first-year introductory courses and upper-year courses

List of Contributors 207

on eighteenth-century and Romantic literature to a 'Preparing to Teach' certificate course for PhD candidates at Carleton who are preparing for careers in academia. His current research project focuses on canon formation in the late eighteenth and early nineteenth centuries.

Jonathan Sadow is Associate Professor of English at the State University of New York, Oneonta, NY and is also a member of the Department of Women's and Gender Studies. His work on genre has appeared in *Theory and Practice in the Eighteenth Century* edited by Alexander Dick and Christina Lupton (Routledge, 2008), *The New York Journal of Folklore*, *Lumen: The Journal of the Canadian Society for Eighteenth-Century Studies*, and *Digital Defoe*. His work addresses intersections of genre with both philosophy and gender, particularly in the works of Eliza Haywood, Frances Sheridan, and Charlotte Smith.

Sharon M. Setzer is Professor of English at North Carolina State University. She had edited Mary Robinson's *Memoirs*, James Boaden's *Life of Mrs. Jordan*, and Thomas Campbell's *Life of Mrs. Siddons* (Volumes 1–5 of *Women's Theatrical Memoirs*, Pickering & Chatto, 2007) as well as Robinson's *Letter to the Women of England* and *The Natural Daughter* (Broadview Press, 2003), and *Angelina* (Volume 3 of *The Works of Mary Robinson*, Pickering & Chatto, 2009). Her other recent publications include a co-edited volume of Robinson's non-fiction prose (Volume 8 of *The Works of Mary Robinson*, Pickering & Chatto, 2010), a chapter on her *Memoirs* in *Romantic Autobiography in England*, edited by Eugene Stelzig (Ashgate, 2009), and essays on Robinson in *Criticism*, *Nineteenth-Century Contexts*, and *Philological Quarterly*. She is currently working on a Broadview Press edition of Robinson's *Memoirs*.

Ada Sharpe is a postdoctoral fellow at the Department of English at Harvard University. Her research engages with issues surrounding gender, art, and work in British women's writing of the late eighteenth and early nineteenth centuries as well as representations of amateur art-making and artistic labour in British women's writing of the same period, particularly in the novel. Currently, she is working on completing a book project on the professionalization of accomplishment and amateur art-making in British fiction written by women in the period 1790–1820. She has published in *European Romantic Review* (2012), *Literature/Film Quarterly* (2013), and *Victorian Review: An Interdisciplinary Journal of Victorian Studies* (2014), as well as reviewed monographs for *Papers of the Bibliographical Society of Canada/Papiers de la Société bibliographique du Canada* (2012), and *Tulsa Studies in Women's Literature* (2010).

Eleanor Ty is Professor of English at Wilfrid Laurier University, Waterloo, Ontario. She has published on Asian North American literature and eighteenth-century British literature. She is the author of *Empowering the Feminine: The Narratives of Mary Robinson, Jane West, and Amelia Opie,*

208 *List of Contributors*

1796–1812 (University of Toronto Press, 1998) and *Unsex'd Revolutionaries: Five Women Novelists of the 1790s* (University of Toronto Press, 1993), and has edited two novels by Mary Hays. Her recent works include: *Canadian Literature and Cultural Memory*, co-edited with Cynthia Sugars (Oxford University Press, 2014), *The Memory Effect: The Remediation of Memory in Literature and Film*, co-edited with Russell J. A. Kilbourn (Wilfrid Laurier University Press, 2013), *Unfastened: Globality and Asian North American Narratives* (University of Minnesota Press, 2010) and *Asian Canadian Writing Beyond Autoethnography*, co-edited with Christl Verduyn (Wilfrid Laurier University Press, 2008).

Megan Woodworth is an instructor in the English Department at St. Thomas University, Fredericton, New Brunswick and in the Faculty of Arts at the University of New Brunswick, Fredericton, where she is also an Honorary Research Associate in English. Her research explores gender, politics, and war in eighteenth-century English literature; her current project considers the connections between discourses of liberty and independence connected to the American Revolution and themes of filial disobedience in British novels published between 1760 and 1790. She has written articles and book reviews on Jane Austen, Frances Burney, and the eighteenth-century novel for *Persuasions Online*, *Eighteenth-Century Fiction*, the *Journal for Eighteenth-Century Studies* and *The Encyclopedia of British Literature 1660–1789* (Blackwell, 2015). Her first book, *Eighteenth-Century Women Writers and the Gentlemen's Liberation Movement*, was published by Ashgate in 2011.

Index

Abingdon, Willoughby Bertie,
  4th Earl 58
Abolitionist movement 58, 63; *see also*
  slave trade
Akenside, Mark 119
America 22, 29, 33
Analytical Review, The 40, 59–60, 78
Anderson, Benedict 180
Anti-Jacobin 12, 14, 38, 124, 125, 128,
  129; fiction 126, 163; interpretation
  of texts 48, 49; versus Jacobin 14,
  38, 52, 92, 103–4 n. 16, 124, 163,
  201; *see also* Jacobin
*Anti-Jacobin, The, or, Weekly
  Examiner* 38
Anti-Jacobin Review, The 38, 128
Armstrong, Nancy 7
Astell, Mary; *A Serious Proposal to the
  Ladies* (1694) 3–4
Aubin, Penelope 5
Austen, Jane 182; *Mansfield Park*
  (1814) 71 n. 42, 190, 191, 193;
  Northanger Abbey (1817) 68

Bannet, Eve Tavor 2
Barrow, William; *An Essay on
  Education* (1802) 124
Beckford, William 77
Behn, Aphra; *Oroonoko* (1688) 5
Benger, Elizabeth 163, 171, 174
Bildungsroman 6, 181, 186, 188–90, 193
Blanchot, Maurice 76
Bolingbroke, Henry St John, 1st
  Viscount 49, 50
Bour, Isabelle 186
Bourdieu, Pierre 76
Britain; response to radical threat
  9, 22, 27; *see also* Nationalism, British
British Critic, The 69, 79, 107
Brontë, Emily; *Wuthering Heights*
  (1847) 190

Brooke, Frances; *The History of Lady
  Julia Mandeville* (1763) 8
Brunton, Mary 16, 91, 92, 180, 198,
  199; *Discipline* (1814) 95, 181–90,
  192, 193–94; *Emmeline* (1819) 95,
  181; *Self-Control* (1811) 94, 95,
  98–99, 181–82
Bundock, Christopher 76
Bunyan, John; *The Pilgrim's Progress*
  (1678) 183
Burke, Edmund 23, 26–27, 28, 30,
  31, 32, 85, 126; *Reflections on the
  Revolution in France* (1790) 9–10,
  21, 24, 25, 27, 67, 202
Burke, Peter 106
Burney, Frances; *Evelina* (1778) 8
Burns, Robert 167–68, 172
Butler, Marilyn 54 n. 67, 75, 143, 153,
  159 n. 75

Canuel, Mark 108
Carroll, Lewis; *Alice's Adventures in
  Wonderland* (1865) 133
Castle, Terry 76, 82
Cervantes, Miguel de; *Don Quixote*
  (1605, 1615) 5
Chandler, Anne 78
Chesterfield, Philip Stanhope,
  4th Earl 50
Children 15, 42, 51, 115, 124–25, 131,
  136, 169; as readers 117, 132–34;
  education of 1, 4, 59, 85, 113,
  117, 124, 130–31, 143; writing for
  124–25, 132
Children's literature 124, 132,
  141 n. 67
Christian Observer, The 107, 108, 110
Class; critique of aristocracy 47–48,
  136; middle- 3, 46, 92, 99, 102, 106,
  128, 165, 169, 172; preservation
  of distinctions 9–10, 30, 100, 128,

160–62, 165, 168, 173, 184, 186–87, 189, 191; privilege 75; professional- 45; reform 107, 167; upper- 50, 62, 128, 129, 183; working- 16, 100–1, 106, 134, 160, 163

Clewberg-Edelcrantz, Abraham Niclas 146

Coleridge, Samuel Taylor 39, 66

Colley, Linda 179, 190

Colquhoun, Patrick; *A Treatise on Indigence* (1806) 160, 163

Conduct books 2–5; by women 3–4; on education 3–4; on the novel 4–5

Connolly, Claire 153, 157 n. 18

Conway, Alison 23

Cowper, William 110, 119

Craciun, Adriana 57

Critical Review, The 98, 101–2, 142, 143, 146

Cruikshank, Isaac; 'A Republican Belle' (1794) 127

Davidson, Jenny 156 n. 14

Davies, Rebecca 1

Defoe, Daniel; *Robinson Crusoe* (1719) 5, 130; *Union and No Union* (1713) 179, 187, 192

Demers, Patricia 197, 198

Didactic 107, 118, 170; anti- revolutionary versus reformist 91, 92; heavy-handed 142–44, 150, 152–54, 156 n. 2; limitations of 83; novel 5–9; 75, 76–77, 79, 86; political uses of 1–2, 11–13, 21, 41, 46, 56, 64, 67–68, 74, 76, 90–93, 108, 123–25, 132, 144, 147, 160, 164, 166, 181, 193, 196, 198, 202

Doerksen, Teri 198, 202

Domestic economy 116–18, 169

Douthwaite, Julia 76, 79

Duncan, Ian 170

Edgeworth, Maria 91, 92, 167, 174, 182, 196, 198, 199; 'Angelina' (1802) 123–28, 130–33, 135–36; *Belinda* (1801) 94, 98–99, 115, 150, 156 n. 1; *Castle Rackrent* (1800) 200; *Early Lessons* (1801) 196, 200; 'Forester' (1802) 123–26, 128, 130, 132–36; *Letters for Literary Ladies* (1795) 126; *Moral Tales* (1802) 123–26, 128, 131–32, 136–37, 196, 200; *Patronage* (1814, rev. edn 1825) 142, 144–50, 150–55; 196; *Practical*

Education (1798), with Richard Lovell Edgeworth 130, 143, 196, 200; *Professional Education* (1809), with Richard Lovell Edgeworth 143, 144, 147; 'The Purple Jar' (1796) 131, 136

Edgeworth, Richard Lovell 125

Edinburgh Review 107, 142, 173, 174–75

Education; by example 130–31; of women *see* women, education of

Egenolf, Susan 168, 171

Emotion 78, 84, 85, 96–98

Enlightenment 49, 91, 102, 108, 126, 128, 138 n. 21, 146

Epistolary form 78, 95, 145

Favret, Mary 66

Female Spectator, The (1744–46) 3

Female Tatler, The (1709–10) 3

Fenwick, Eliza 14, 198; *Secresy: or The Ruin on the Rock* (1795) 75–77, 79–87, 87 n. 10, 89 n. 48, 200; versus Jean-Jacques Rousseau 75, 80; versus Mary Wollstonecraft 74–75, 76, 79, 85–86, 87 n. 4, 88 n. 20

Ferrier, Susan Edmonstone 16, 180, 198; *Destiny* (1831) 182; *The Inheritance* (1824) 182; *Marriage* (1818) 181–82, 190–94

Ferris, Ina 29

Fiction; libertine 80, 84, 86; nationalist 144, 172; reformist 23, 46, 75, 90, 91, 92, 107, 128, 136, 142, 169, 172; sentimental 76–77, 78, 79, 86–87, 128, 139 n. 34; young adult 123, 124, 131, 137 n. 5, 200

Fielding, Henry 7

Fielding, Sarah; *The Adventures of David Simple* (1744) 7; *The Governess; Or, the Little Female Academy* (1749) 7–8; *The History of Ophelia* (1761) 7

Fletcher, Loraine 26

Ford, Susan Allen 39, 51, 54 n. 67

Fordyce, James; *Sermons to Young Women* (1765) 3, 5, 7

Fraiman, Susan 63

France; British prejudice against 143–46, 154; British (literary) war with 10–11, 14, 57–58, 60, 125; Waterloo and Treaty of Paris (1815) 155; *see also* French Revolution

Index 211

French Revolution 9, 19 n. 48, 69, 92, 123–24, 131–32, 144, 164, 196, 198; 'Declaration of the Rights of Man' (1789) 132; Reign of Terror 144, 162, 164

Gamer, Michael 143–44, 197
Garrick, David 106
Gay, John; *The What D'Ye Call It* (1715) 156 n. 1
Genre; didactic 1, 16–17 n. 4, 90–91, 196, 198–99, 201–2; distinctions 81–82, 200; subversions 93
Gentleman's Magazine, The 142, 146
Gilmartin, Kevin 11, 161, 162, 163, 166, 175 n. 3
Gisborne, Thomas; *Enquiry into the Duties of the Female Sex* (1797) 5
Glorious Revolution (1688) 25–26, 67, 68
Godwin, William 21, 39, 49, 56, 79, 90, 94, 96; *Caleb Williams* (1794) 57; *An Enquiry Concerning Political Justice* (1793) 49, 126, 128
Golightly, Jennifer 75
Gothic 76–77, 78, 79, 90
Gottlieb, Evan 180
Gouges, Olympe de; 'Declaration of the Rights of Woman' (1791) 10
Gray, Thomas; 'Elegy Written in a Country Churchyard' (1751) 167–68
Gregory, John; *A Father's Legacy to His Daughters* (1774) 3, 5
Grenby, M. O. 11, 12, 117, 123, 124
Grogan, Claire 38, 197, 198, 200–1
Grundy, Isobel 74, 76
Guest, Harriet 144

Halsey, Katie 39
Hamilton, Elizabeth 16, 196; *The Cottagers of Glenburnie* (1808) 162–63, 164–73, 174–75, 197; *Letters on the Elementary Principles of Education* (1801) 4, 5; *Memoirs of Modern Philosophers* (1800) 5, 94, 126, 127, 129, 130, 168; versus Hannah More 160, 162–65, 172, 173, 175, 200
Handwerk, Gary 94
Havens, Hilary 74, 196–97, 198, 201–2
Hays, Mary 14, 56, 127, 196, 198–99, 200; gradation 97–98; 'Improvements Suggested in Female Education' (1797) 99; *Memoirs*

of Emma Courtney (1796) 63–64, 90–91, 94, 95–100; 'On Novel Writing' (1797) 93–94, 97, 199; relationship with William Frend 96; versus Mary Wollstonecraft 90; *The Victim of Prejudice* (1799) 90–91, 94, 100–102
Haywood, Eliza 5–6
Heidegger, Martin 76
Heisel, Andrew 108, 119
'Hidden adult' 125, 132, 136, 200; *see also* Nodelman, Perry
History-as-inheritance 14, 21–22
Holcroft, Thomas; *Anna St. Ives* (1792) 94
Holland, Henry 142
Hornbuckle, Calley 76, 84–85

Inchbald, Elizabeth 57; *Nature and Art* (1796) 101; *A Simple Story* (1791) 190
Independence 16, 40, 45, 53 n. 19, 59, 61, 64, 68, 100–2, 115, 129–30, 142
India 149–50
Irish Rebellion (1798) 9, 123, 131

Jacobin 11, 58, 79–80, 90, 95, 99, 123, 129, 161, 164; *see also* Anti-Jacobin
John I 66
Johnson, Claudia 41, 54 n. 67
Johnson, Samuel 78, 106
Jones, Vivien 98
Joy, Louise 95

Keats, John 21
Kelly, Gary 11–12, 90, 126, 144, 172
Kirkpatrick, Kathryn 181

Laclos, Pierre Choderlos de 79, 83; *Les Liaisons Dangereuses* (1782) 80, 86
Leadbeater, Mary; *Cottage Dialogues* (1811) 174
Ledoux, Ellen Malenas 75
Lennox, Charlotte 8
Lloyd, Charles; *Edmund Oliver* (1798) 94
Lloyd, Pamela 40
Locke, John; *Some Thoughts Concerning Education* (1693) 131, 136
London, April 39
London Review, The 107
Luzzatto, Sergio 132

212 Index

MacNeill, Hector 172
Macready, William Charles 182
Madness 59, 94, 135
Malthus, Thomas Robert; *An Essay on the Principle of Population* (1798) 160, 163
Mandal, Anthony 91
Mandeville, Bernard; *The Grumbling Hive* (1705) 50
Marriage 23–26, 29, 41, 43–46, 48–49, 75, 79, 100, 105 n. 64, 191, 193; between nations 16, 182, 184, 186, 190, 192–94; divorce 142; market 60–61, 63, 64, 111–12; negative examples of 112–13
Martin, Maureen M. 180, 181
Mason, William 110
Mathias, Thomas James; *The Pursuits of Literature* (1794–97) 56–57
McCormack, W. J. 157 n. 22
McGann, Jerome 21
McGavran, Jr, James Holt 33–34
McIntosh, Ainsley 186
McKerrow, Mary 181
Mee, Jon 108
Military and/or navy 29, 147, 148, 149, 154; impressment 147
Milton, John 119; *Paradise Lost* (1667) 49, 110–11
Monnickendam, Andrew 188, 191
Monthly Magazine, The 99
Monthly Review, The 107, 151, 198
More, Hannah 1, 8, 14–15, 16, 39, 100, 196, 198; 'The Bas Bleu' (1787) 109, 110; *Cheap Repository Tracts* (1795–97) 15–16, 160, 161–63, 164, 166, 167, 176 n. 22, 196; *Cœlebs in Search of a Wife* (1808) 11, 14–15, 107–19, 196, 197; Evangelical reform 106; *The Fatal Falsehood* (1779) 111; 'Hints towards Framing a Bill...' (1792) 60–61; *The Inflexible Captive* (1774) 111; *Percy* (1777) 111; 'Preface to the Tragedies' (1801) 114; *Sacred Dramas* (1782) 114; 'Sensibility' (1782) 109, 110; 'Sir Eldred of the Bower' (1776) 109–10; *Strictures on the Modern System of Female Education* (1799) 4, 5, 68, 113–14, 119; *Village Politics* (1793) 160–61, 164; *see also* Hamilton, Elizabeth, versus Hannah More *and* Wollstonecraft, Mary, versus Hannah More

Morning Chronicle, The 67
Morning Post, The 64, 65, 67
Multi-national 145–46; *see also* nationalism
Myers, Mitzi 92, 99, 100, 113, 123, 126

Nancy, Jean-Luc 76
Napoleon 155, 164
Nationalism 106, 144, 147–50, 154–55, 179, 193; British 13, 143, 145, 198; Scottish 13, 15–16, 172, 180–81
Navy *see* military and/or navy
'New Philosophy' 125, 128, 129, 133, 137
Newman, Gerald 40
Newton, John 171
Nodelman, Perry 125, 132–33, 136, 137, 200
Novel; as a means to form subjectivity 92, 93, 95, 97; form 41, 74, 75, 78, 86, 107; link to conduct books 2, 7–9, 38, 41, 74, 108; of sensibility 90, 135, 137; tendency 1, 39, 40–41, 68, 93–94, 165; versus sermon 109–10, 118–19
Nowka, Scott A. 90
Nussbaum, Felicity 95

Ó Gallchoir, Cliona 123, 126, 131, 146, 158 n. 33
O'Malley, Andrew 198, 200–1
Opie, Amelia 91, 92; *Adeline Mowbray* (1804) 94; *The Father and Daughter* (1801) 94, 101; *Simple Tales* (1806) 197–98; *Tales of Real Life* (1813) 198
Orphan 3, 44, 129

Paine, Thomas; *The Age of Reason* (1794–95) 161; *Common Sense* (1776) 47; *Rights of Man* (1791–92) 25, 58, 61, 160–61, 162, 164
Parkes, Simon 29
Parody 75, 82
Patronage 142, 143
Pearson, Jacqueline 147–48
Pennington, Lady Sarah; *An Unfortunate Mother's Advice to her Absent Daughters* (1761) 3, 4
Periodical 2–3, 6
Perkins, Pamela 174
Pitt, William, the younger 57, 58, 65, 160
Plantagenet, Eleanor 66

Index 213

Polwhele, Richard; *The Unsex'd Females* (1798) 57, 90
Poovey, Mary 8
Price, Fiona 97
Price, Richard; *A Discourse on the Love of Our Country* (1789) 67, 68
Primogeniture 24–25, 30, 31
Prison 149, 152–54, 159 n. 75

Quarterly Review 142, 143

Radcliffe, Ann 77, 98; *The Italian* (1797) 78, 97; *The Mysteries of Udolpho* (1794) 97; *The Romance of the Forest* (1791) 79, 85
Ramsay, Allan 172
Raven, James 8–9
Religion 5, 118–19, 189; Anglicanism 107, 192–93; connection to reform 107, 113; Christianity 110, 118–19, 130, 170–72; Dissenting 91, 102; Evangelicalism 108, 110, 171, 202; in the novel 107–10, 119, 183–84; Methodism 112, 193; Presbyterianism 192–93
Religious writings 5, 107
Republic of Letters 106
Revolutionary; feminism 91–92; ideals 80; language 127–128; post- 123, 126; sentiment 125; *see also* French Revolution
Richardson, Samuel 77, 83; *A Collection of the Moral and Instructive Sentiments* (1755) 6–7; *Clarissa* (1747–48) 6, 86, 93, 102; *The History of Sir Charles Grandison* (1753–54) 6, 146; Lovelace (character from *Clarissa*) 49, 84; *Pamela* (1740) 6, 95
Robinson, Mary 14, 71 n. 41, 198; affair with George IV 56, 69 n. 2, 203; *Angelina* (1796) 59–69; *The Natural Daughter* (1799) 68–69; *Vancenza; Or, the Dangers of Credulity* (1792) 56, 69 n. 1
Roman à clef 108
Romance form 75, 77, 79, 82, 83, 87, 90, 128, 135, 144
Rooney, Morgan 54 n. 67, 74, 198, 202
Rose, Jacqueline 125
Rousseau, Jean-Jacques 76, 82; *Émile, or on Education* (1762) 9, 10, 59, 80, 84, 124, 131, 139 n. 26; *La Nouvelle Héloïse* (1761) 74, 77, 80; *see also*

Fenwick, Eliza, versus Jean-Jacques Rousseau *and* Wollstonecraft, Mary, versus Jean-Jacques Rousseau
Ruys, Juanita 196

Sadow, Jonathan 198, 200
Sánchez-Eppler, Karen 63
Savile, George, 1st Marquess of Halifax; *The Lady's New-Year's-Gift* (1688) 2
Schierenbeck, Daniel 41, 44
Scotland 164, 166–67, 168–71, 172, 175, 187–89, 191; Acts of Union (1707) 179, 181, 190, 193–94
Scots Magazine 173
Scott, Sarah; *Millenium Hall* (1762) 7
Scott, Sir Walter 182; *Redgauntlet* (1824) 180; *Waverley* (1814) 107
Sensibility *see* novel, of sensibility
Sentimental fiction *see* fiction, sentimental
Setzer, Sharon M. 198, 203
'Shadow text' 125, 127
Shaftesbury, Anthony Ashley-Cooper, 3rd Earl 49
Shakespeare, William 119; *Othello* (1604) 49; *The Winter's Tale* (1611) 56
Sharpe, Ada 198–99
Shelley, Percy Bysshe; *A Defense of Poetry* (1821) 21
Sheridan, Frances; *The Memoirs of Miss Sidney Bidulph* (1761) 8, 76–77, 79
Sinanan, Kerry 108
Slave trade 58, 60, 62–65, 147, 185
Smith, Charlotte 14, 57, 79, 196, 198; *Desmond* (1792) 22–26; *Emmeline* (1778) 78; *Minor Morals* (1798) 196; *The Old Manor House* (1793) 22, 26–29; *Rambles Further* (1796) 196; *Rural Walks* (1795) 196; *The Young Philosopher* (1798) 22, 30–33
Smith, Olivia 173
Smith, Sydney 107, 114, 142
Social; bonds 128–29; change (through novels) 14, 40–41, 75, 86, 91, 95, 100, 102; contract 10, 25–26, 33, 67; norms 6, 8, 11, 152; programmes 166; *see also* class
Spectator, The (1711–14) 2
Spence, Elizabeth Isabella 174
St Clair, William 10
Stafford, William 94
Staves, Susan 101

214 *Index*

Stone, Lawrence 100
Stott, Anne 108, 119, 162
Sturm und Drang 131
Sublime 83–86

Tarleton, Banastre 64
Tarling, Barbara 21
Tatler, The (1709–11) 2
Tendency *see* novel, tendency
Thame, David 38, 39, 40, 94–95
Todd, Janet 74, 128
Tract 10, 15, 106, 109, 143, 160, 165, 172, 174, 175 n. 3
Trumpener, Katie 64
Trimmer, Sarah 124; *The Oeconomy of Charity* (1787) 160
Ty, Eleanor 11, 12, 38, 49, 50–51, 54 n. 67, 198–99
Tytler, William 167

Union *see* marriage, between nations
Utilitarianism 148

Vesey, Elizabeth 110
Voltaire; *Zadig* (1747) 151; *Zaïre* (1732) 149

Wales 6, 59, 60, 64, 129, 135
Wallace, Miriam L. 38–39, 65, 66, 92–93, 99, 163, 201
Walpole, Horace 77
Watson, Nicola J. 74, 75, 80, 95, 98
Watson-Taylor, George; *England Preserved* (1795) 67
War 9, 14, 29, 60, 64–66, 144, 154–55; *see also* France, British (literary) war with
Ward, John 142, 145, 146–47, 153
West, Gilbert 43
West, Jane 14, 198; *The Advantages of Education* (1793) 39–46; *A Gossip's Story* (1796) 39; *The Infidel Father* (1802) 49, 55 n. 76; *Miscellaneous Poems, and a Tragedy* (1791) 40; Prudentia Homespun (narrator in various novels) 38, 40, 43, 51–52,

94, 201; *A Tale of the Times* (1799) 39–40, 46–51, 54 n. 67
Wilberforce, William 58
Williams, David; *Lectures on Education* (1789) 80
Williams, Helen Maria; *Julia* (1790) 78
Wollstonecraft, Mary 1, 8, 11, 14, 21, 39, 56; *Maria: Or the Wrongs of Woman* (1798) 74, 75, 77–78, 79, 80, 83, 86–87; *Mary: A Fiction* (1788) 81; reviews by 53 n. 31, 59, 78, 80; *Thoughts on the Education of Daughters* (1787) 4, 5, 10; *A Vindication of the Rights of Men* (1790) 62; *A Vindication of the Rights of Woman* (1792) 10, 57, 60, 62, 67–68, 81, 99; versus Hannah More 1, 11, 13, 56, 61, 99, 115, 118; versus Jean-Jacques Rousseau 10, 59, 74, 75, 80–81, 86; *see also* Fenwick, Eliza, versus Mary Wollstonecraft *and* Hays, Mary, versus Mary Wollstonecraft
Woman Not Inferior to Man (1739) 4
Women; as artists 114, 118; as educators 1, 13; as mothers 1, 11, 13; as readers 91, 93, 116; education of 40–41, 45, 46, 51, 59, 75, 80, 84, 85–86, 90, 114, 169–70; employment of 99–100; 'fallen' 14, 45, 50, 91, 99, 100–2, 130; gaze of 98–99; masculine (education of) 4, 41, 44–45, 115–17, 127; novelists outperforming their male counterparts 8–9, 15, 20 n. 75; seduction of 23, 40, 44, 45, 50, 101–2; subjectivity of 92, 101; suffering of and injustice against 90–91, 93, 101, 102
Wood, Lisa 11, 12–13, 39, 40, 92, 108, 199
Woodworth, Megan 54 n. 67, 198, 201
Wright, Julia 76, 79, 80, 81–82, 86

Young adult fiction *see* fiction, young adult
Youth rebellion 123, 129, 131